Contentious Memories

German Life and Civilization

Jost Hermand
General Editor

Advisory Board

Helen Fehervary
Ohio State University

Peter Uwe Hohendahl
Cornell University

Robert Holub
University of California at Berkeley

Klaus Scherpe
Humboldt University, Berlin

Frank Trommler
University of Pennsylvania

Vol. 24

PETER LANG
New York • Washington, D.C./Baltimore • Boston
Bern • Frankfurt am Main • Berlin • Vienna • Paris

Contentious Memories

Looking Back at the GDR

WITHDRAWN

Edited by
Jost Hermand
& Marc Silberman

PETER LANG
New York • Washington, D.C./Baltimore • Boston
Bern • Frankfurt am Main • Berlin • Vienna • Paris

Library of Congress Cataloging-in-Publication Data

Contentious memories: looking back at the GDR /
Jost Hermand and Marc Silberman [editors].
p. cm. — (German life and civilization; vol. 24)
Revised and expanded papers from the 28th Wisconsin Workshop,
held in Madison, Wis., November 14–16, 1996.
Includes bibliographical references.
1. Germany (East)—Intellectual life. 2. Germany (East)—Historiography.
3. Germany (East)—Cultural policy. 4. Intellectuals—Germany (East).
5. Socialism and culture—Germany (East).
I. Hermand, Jost. II. Silberman, Marc. III. Series.
DD287.3.C66   943'.1087—dc21   97-17587
ISBN 0-8204-3843-X
ISSN 0899-9899

Die Deutsche Bibliothek-CIP-Einheitsaufnahme

Contentious memories: looking back at the GDR /
Jost Hermand and Marc Silberman, (ed.). –New York;
Washington, D.C./Baltimore; Boston; Bern;
Frankfurt am Main; Berlin; Vienna; Paris: Lang.
(German life and civilization; Vol. 24)
ISBN 0-8204-3843-X

The paper in this book meets the guidelines for permanence and durability
of the Committee on Production Guidelines for Book Longevity
of the Council of Library Resources.

Contents

Preface

When we decided to focus the 28th Wisconsin Workshop on the German Democratic Republic, we chose the title "Contentious Memories" as an explicit challenge. The speakers we invited immediately understood that we had two things in mind: first, we were aiming to engage in a scholarly dispute about a part of modern German culture that some former Cold Warriors had prematurely thrown on the junk heap of history after 1989; second, we were hoping to examine our own investments in the memory of that culture. Our expectation was that already with a distance of seven years to the collapse of the GDR the process of looking back would elicit not only more historically precise accounts but also new, changed perspectives.

For self-reflection about one's own memories is as important as more generalized forms of historical knowledge. It gives coherence to our reasoning, our feelings, and our actions. Without memory we would lose both our consciousness of history and the personal identity bound to it, and without self-reflection about our memories history and identity become rigid, paralyzed. With this understanding in mind we envisioned three aspects of memory to be disputed at the conference: the local, the utopian, and the political.

The local aspect has to do with Madison, of course. In the 1970s and 1980s the University of Wisconsin was an important center for Brecht and GDR research. Editors of journals and yearbooks such as *Brecht-Jahrbuch*, *Brecht heute - Brecht Today*, *Basis: Jahrbuch für deutsche Gegenwartsliteratur*, *Monatshefte*, and *New German Critique* were all teaching in the Department of German. What they have contributed to the interest in Brecht and GDR literature will only be fully revealed by future students of the history of German Studies in this country. In any case there were not only "liberators" and "crusaders" at work in Madison, but also those who were—sympathetic to Willy Brandt's constructive Ostpolitik—opposed to fantasies of German unification that could lead to a strengthening of nationalism. There were those as well who hoped that encouraging the democratic forces inside the GDR would lead to a socialism with a more human face. With curiosity, passion, and polemics these teachers presented their students a picture of GDR literature that was trying to be fair in the best sense of the word. One could even venture to say that without these activities—along with the translations, interviews, and interpretations in *New German Critique*—GDR authors such as Christa Wolf and Heiner Müller, Volker Braun and Irmtraud Morgner would not have become so well known in North America as they were and still are. One goal of the Workshop, then, was to bring together on the podium and in the audience some of these players to review this local history.

The utopian aspect of memory is much more complex. What was it that attracted teachers and students alike to that "other" German literature? Was it Brecht's model of negotiating negation? Was it the feminist vision expressed in the works of women writers from the GDR? Was it the fascination with the aesthetic power of Heiner Müller's plays? Was it the rare possibility to compare two different types of German literature? Was it the hopeful glimmer of a concrete utopia? Certainly it was a combination of at least two, if not all of these factors. But hope can be disappointed, as we learned from Ernst Bloch, and the simple truth is not always the best truth, as Volker Braun said. The forty-year history of the GDR is full of these hopes and disappointments, of simplistic and more complex truths. Looking back at past utopias immediately brings to mind a string of images dominated by rubble and violence stretching from Benjamin's Angelus Novus to Müller's Engel der Geschichte, but if looking history in the eye is a harsh practice, it is also one of the most effective remedies against collective amnesia. This too was a goal of the Workshop.

The political or ideological aspect of memory is equally disturbing. Why was the GDR so appealing to many liberal or left-liberal intellectuals in West Germany and North America during the 1970s despite the string of repressive measures exercised against critical writers and intellectuals in the GDR? The most obvious answer to this question must be: its antifascist commitment and its promise of a more egalitarian, humanistic society. For those who grew up in the 1950s under McCarthy or in the shadow of the Hallstein doctrine and who came of age in the 1960s during the the Vietnam War or the Eichmann and Auschwitz trials, the GDR was the other Germany, better equipped to deal with the problem of coming to terms with the past. After all, had not most of the better known anti-fascist writers returned from exile to East Germany after the war, instead of choosing the "free" West? For them, as for many others, socialism seemed to be the best bulwark against the revival of fascism. At some point, however, the balance shifted. A younger generation in the GDR could no longer identify with the heroism of the past, and the rhetoric of antifascism became an excuse to silence calls for more internal democracy. The third goal of the conference therefore was to examine the blindspots and self-deceptions of the past as well as those now forming all too quickly in the present.

Many, if not all of these questions were raised during the 28th Wisconsin Workshop held in Madison on November 14-16, 1996, leading to lively, at times even to dramatic, but always fruitful discussions. We, the organizers, especially appreciated the many out-of-town guests who made their way to Madison in order to participate in the public and in the more informal, private exchanges during the Workshop, an important sign that the strong tradition of American GDR studies will continue. The Workshop's special guest was the author Gert Neumann (Berlin) whose writing in the GDR since the early 1970s revolved around the possibility of speaking and being understood. Other presenters and respondents addressing the issues raised by the conference title were Marc Silberman (University of Wisconsin, Madison), Jay Rosellini (Purdue University, West Lafayette, Indiana), Julia Hell (Duke University, Durham, North Carolina), Nancy Kaiser (University of Wisconsin, Madison), William Maltarich, Alan Ng, and Nancy Thuleen (University of Wisconsin, Madison), Jost Hermand (University of Wisconsin, Madison), Helen Fehervary (Ohio State University, Columbus, Ohio), David Bathrick (Cornell University, Ithaca, New York), Sabine Gross (University of Wisconsin,

Madison), Frank Hörnigk (Humboldt University, Berlin), Hans Adler (University of Wisconsin, Madison), Frauke Meyer-Gosau (Berlin), and Carol Poore (Brown University, Providence, Rhode Island). Their papers and responses appear in this volume in a revised and at times expanded form.

The editors are above all indebted to the Anonymous Fund of the University of Wisconsin, which generously contributed funds to cover the travel and expenses of the Department's guests, and to the Vilas Trust, which made possible the publication of this volume.

Madison, February 1997   The Editors

Frank Hörnigk

My friend Gert Neumann

Bearing in mind the theme that you have given to this conference, the memory of literature from the GDR necessarily includes the memory of a challenge that is linked to the name Gert Neumann. It is a challenge that possibly only a few of you are aware of, because the works and biography of Gert Neumann have been recorded rather more on the margins of the fashionable discourse among the factions within GDR literature since the *Wende*. Relatively few people know of him, but many important people in the literature of this country value him.

When Gert Neumann joined the "new society" of the Federal Republic in 1989, together with us, with me and with others, he had already experienced the actual turning point in his biography twenty years earlier in Leipzig. He had studied there at the end of the 1960s, at the "Johannes R. Becher" Institute of Literature; in 1969 he was forced to leave the university and at the same time was expelled from the Socialist Unity Party (SED). It is perhaps of interest that the subject and center of the conflict then did not actually have an obvious political meaning. It was first and foremost about grammar, about semantics, about words; not so much about the ideologies of texts, but rather about the texts themselves. That is, it was about text semantics, which he saw wounded and violated in the language of the GDR. This was disputed, yet Neumann held firmly to his position—and that was exactly what could not be tolerated. One of the results, for Gert not the worst: the years until the end of the 1970s became for him years in production. At that time it was called "probation in production." The ideological term deserves for a moment a more nuanced consideration. This precept of nuance in using words was then, and remains still, essential for Gert Neumann. Practical work, working with his hands, became an essential element of his writing—writing as a craft.

He was a metalworker, and survived for years in Leipzig as a metalworker. Perhaps even "survived" in the proverbial sense, in order to be able to write through this work. But after 1989, he did not fulfill the expectations of those who thought his hour had finally come and wanted to make the most of the triumph. He continued to work, and still works, again with his hands. Recently as a bookseller, but before that, as a metalworker still. I saw him a few years ago in a shed, where he was selling display shelves for modern boutiques. It was rather cold, and the people who were interested in these items knew nothing of the man who was showing them these expensive designer shelves. And also those who could not afford them did not know him. At most, they would have been surprised by a "salesman" who led them into a back room of the store and offered old, discarded GDR furniture that he himself had refurbished, for sale at a merely symbolic price. He was against throwing away what could still be used. He called the project GULIVER. For him it was a craft, work on an object for the benefit of others. That made a lasting impression on me. And then he sat there and wrote.

Die Schuld der Worte (The Guilt of Words) is the first volume that appeared, at the end of the 1970s, specifically in 1979. Like all the other texts of Gert Neumann that followed, these early stories could not appear in the GDR. When a few of his works later actually were published in the GDR, they appeared in alternative, unofficial magazines, and were therefore scattered and not accessible to a large public. Neumann's attempt to make an entrance into GDR literature, undertaken with his decision to study in Leipzig, instead soon became a radical exit, not just from the institute, but rather a consistent withdrawal from this literature as a whole. He was not taken in, not admitted, and so in the end he did not want to belong anymore. It was a rejection that for many decades remained irrevocable for Gert Neumann. Nor could he overcome this conflict in an oppositional role, for the language could then no longer have contained that which he was seeking in it. The reason: his truth was—and is—a truth that is not between the lines but rather between the words.

His first novel, *Elf Uhr* (Eleven o'clock), written as a diary, appeared in 1981. It is a report of his observations during a year working as a metal worker in a department store in Leipzig. In 1989, the next novel appeared, *Die Klandestinität der Kessel-reiniger: Ein Versuch des Sprechens* (The Clandestine Nature of the Boiler Cleaners: An Attempt at Speaking). He was on his way to discovering the language he needed to find what he sought, and he hoped to help establish the means necessary to have a meaningful conversation with others. Two years ago, I invited Gert Neumann to read for students at the Humboldt University. He replied that he would be glad to come and that he hoped the long-postponed conversation would now be possible. Then, a few weeks later, he read, began to speak, and went on to enchant a few hundred students. Immediately thereafter some students even wrote papers about his work. But that is not important, because in one respect he is right, when he says his texts could wait. He resembles Heiner Müller in this aspect, by the way, who also always said that solitary texts should wait for history. I also think that the history for Gert Neumann and his texts is still to come.

Translated by Sara B. Young

Gert Neumann

Blackout

In the jarring world where someone always presumes to have done nothing at all..., I am now experiencing what happens when I will likewise finally give form to a pluralistically suspended declaration about the unavoidability of my position in the world, although at the moment I have plenty to say about the kind of responsibility of which I will have silently acquitted myself with this knowledge. The circumstances that make possible for me this silent change in my expression exist under a name that definitely eliminates all doubt as to whether they necessarily count as innocent. The large apartment house in which we live in Berlin-Pankow—a house that ultimately survived the familiar and then finally lost time of real socialism in the most melancholy rapture and, sufficiently leased out, entered modern times as an admired rental property and was deemed worthy as a shell for accommodating the new standards—is being modernized, enlarged, and renovated. I use all three currently appropriate linguistic concepts for describing our house because in my opinion only together do they produce the precision that linguistic resistance, thematically expressing itself in this matter with dread, demands when it happens that a Someone in this context uses the feverishly feared word felicitously surviving in grammar: "reconstructed," possibly without considering the consequences, or perhaps in defense of an accompanying, not yet entirely familiar arrogance. When in fact the GDR lost its generally unquestioned claim to reality, which had been raised in Germany to the possible from the still astonishingly unrecognized mechanism of recent history..., I too stood once on the long since collapse-prone balcony of my workroom: without a second thought I had been able to appropriate it for myself in the otherwise empty tower of our apartment as a fitting luxury that typically was overlooked in the generally decaying condition of socialism. I was enticed onto the balcony by the undoubtedly always complex desire to see with my own eyes what—as I had learned from the most varied sources— happens or would happen. In justified fear of losing my balance I remained near the double-paneled balcony door opening onto the large interior of the workroom; and I looked with multiple care from high in the tower over the balcony's unstable balustrade down to the street: from which indeed quick looks were immediately directed up out of deepest curiosity in order to visit and ask me why I had appeared there. The looks came from the passing tram down below where in reality the most valuable attention passed by and about which I had actually only known through writing; where objects expand into presences that—touching the air again—expose connections for which there was no hope in language. When, standing on the balcony, I was allowed to meet these looks, which in my experience seldom were given freely to phenomena in Germany, looks accompanied by a smile, which, owing to its short duration, come, or might come, through the collision with the gravity of usual meanings to no attribute in the German language..., it seemed unfortunate to respond in my body language to this upward look from the passing tram at a man bowed over the loose balustrade of his tower balcony in Pankow with the words "super" or "crazy": although in the encounter during these days such an answer had become a comprehensible one through the kind of attention in the German media accompanying the current circumstances. The event I believed to be watching from the balcony, which I perceived to be almost too heavy because the looks from the tram reached me, began with the adventure of telling about enjoying the cheap trip with the tram that was no longer familiar in West Berlin, and it was of no importance for understanding this adventure to know whether the riders came from the West or the East; because the long-held perception of the world in Germany and especially in Berlin suddenly was moved in the same way under the impression of the most wonderful mirroring of a value that in the usually valid condensation of the moment is able to appear only in the form of a complaint about absence. The adventure I believed to see and through which in my opinion I was recognized offered, however, as well the danger of a touristic experience of the things developed there in the sense of the construction of socialism, as they now became visible. This experience, permitted by the judgment of history and looking up from the passing tram into my premonition, wanted to communicate about something that might have been related to the possible astonishment in the experience of the unfamiliar expansion of unfreedom in one's own seeing—, and it needed an answer that did not simply transform its opportunity into a triumph over its potential. For example, the word crazy denied that the power of the request for this solidarity had indeed become the measure of the moment in the German re-encounter. It was as if the shining moments of the adventure, which in my view we wanted to speak about for the duration of the encounter of looking up and looking down, had achieved their appointed sense through a generally recognized delusion, which obviously could not, or should not, have been called a dependable stronghold for what emerged out of the moment of encounter. I believed I was watching an experience emerge with the look that attempted to ask me whether it had indeed been necessary and therefore possible after the experience of a reality named dictatorship to release the discerning conscience, believed to have been defined by the realities, into a place where - beyond the apparently unavoidable duty to discuss, maintained and now bequeathed by the conditions—there still remained something to discuss about which one could speak? In my experience with the experience of the looks from the tram it seemed to me that it was important for the density of the moment in Germany to give a sign from the gray mass of our house that validated—or tried to validate—the question I assumed in the looks to be the question that was posed. Certainly as if I knew that at least in part the experience in the tram was uncomfortable with letting the gradually but forcefully unfolding exhibition on both sides of the tracks between the "Rosenthal" and "Kupfergraben" tram stops on the theme of expired and decayed real-socialist declarations about the presumably dialectical attention to things congeal solely into an argument for the compellingly

validated truth of democratically or market-based activity. Standing
on the balcony of our house in Pankow that still told of World War
II street fights and had solidified into a monument through the self-
abandonment of ideology, I was of the opinion that the
event—seldom enough befalling us Germans—of the experience of
the disappearance of declared reality into the possibility and grace
of memory... would provide the occasion, along with the newly
found and validated view about the unity of humanity with the
surrounding conditions, to establish the speech that begins to talk,
or attempts to talk, about the experience that for the reasons already
mentioned has been impossible to bring into language in twentieth-
century Germany together with the catastrophe that we know is
necessarily connected to the respective phenomenon. Standing on
the balcony in Pankow, I had no doubt that it was a crime against
the encounter of the Germans to allow the experience in the tram to
end in the misery of the admittedly unavoidable claim about the
truth of coming conditions through an ambush out of the darkness
of the phenomenon of expired and decayed real-socialist conditions.

Today I think that my assumption on the balcony was right
concerning the object of the possible speech suspended in the
encounter of the looks. At the time I formulated an answer with a
gesture described by my distinctly extended hand waving above my
head. Although I sensed a certain lack in the generation of this
gesture, I accepted it, because I was pleased not to have fallen prey
to another possible expression: with which I would have looked
down broodingly from the crumbling balcony in order to signify an
answer in the context of the current circumstances. Later I learned
that the gesture "super" consists of the fingers spread out as if
around a tea cup; where the thumb and forefinger meet in an exact
circle. In a metaphorical sense the recipient of the gesture looks
through this circle, while the hand of the person gesturing quickly
moves away from his face. I learned of this gesture from a man
falling from a great height who said in this way "super" to his
relatives standing on the ground when he felt his adventuresome fall
fade away in the elastic band of the "bungy-jumping"; and the

unutterableness of his experience threatened to disappear in the embarrassment of the waning motion of the swing crane. Later I never encountered the gesture "crazy." When I did encounter it on television it consisted of an absentminded rocking of the upper body with both hands raised and spread out as far as possible. My own gesture, which was unfamiliar to me, I entrusted to my hope for freedom; about which I have the idea that in it an expression is expected in which the answer has an opportunity to complete that about which one might speak. The speech.... with which I am concerned today involves the renewal of the phenomenon of our house. Because the house entered modern times approximately half vacant, we renters can now move into already finished apartments so that the work in our apartments is possible. Suddenly I am living with my family for several months at the height of the tower in a completed apartment on the other side of the building's long roof. A counterpart to the workroom I once used in the tower has been built here. When I return now in the evening from some errands in Pankow, I look up at a shining disturbance: that tries to convince me, like an atelier or winter garden illuminated by my family's activities, which decision we should have made about the issue of our expression for the reality of the united Germany. Fortunately it is not difficult for us to reflect on the role provided to us in the publicity of the newest society; and to come to an understanding about it. The evening illumination for which we are responsible in Pankow—inside we speak this way—urgently needs our explanation. The condensation theory ... for the publicity of the phenomenon, which belongs to the conditions we must reach, offers gradually the opportunity to venture our attempt at such an explanation. Something like the impression of having to speak indistinctly for the duration of the speech generated in this way, so that we don't become confused by shame in the face of speech deemed necessary (Socrates), makes us hesitate still to engage the occasions offered for a speech begun for our explanation. We are in doubt about the content of the silence that—as far as the new phenomenon of our house is concerned—has very extensive circumstances in its placid responsibility. We ask whether a speech begun in this way can succeed in making contact with the meaning of the silence in the phenomenon without simply causing disappointment about the interpretation of the silence it touches on. One of the possible speeches is the following:

In the cellar of our house, which the construction liberated from every obscurity in it, there remains after the work was completed one room of unexplored meaning. The construction workers noticed it when they realized that there was no access to it. No one probably would have known about it, if it hadn't happened that my family was assigned for a certain amount of time a cellar room in which I made an unusual discovery. Although it was declared vacant, there were chemicals and equipment and results of chemical experiments in it; among which there were four books with what appeared to me to be weird contents. The books were concerned with chemical weapons; and while leafing through them, I saw that they covered themes to the point of explaining how to produce such weapons material. At the words "means of mass destruction" I closed the books; and I hid the discovery in a window nook, behind the bedsprings of a metal bed frame that belonged to us. My conscience in questions of discernment advised me to treat the matter and my landlord with discretion; although there was no doubt that the landlord had misled me somehow when he assigned this cellar to me for the move. I complied with the appointed moving date, and one day I revealed my discovery to the appropriate authorities. The factual report in my hands explained that the objects left in our cellar were supposed to have belonged to a student who emigrated to the West before the Berlin Wall fell. As the seals showed, the books came from the library of the GDR Military Academy; and the prior, benevolent landlord of the emigre was the Protestant Church. I found it difficult not to seek a meaning. On the day the authorities had chosen to examine my discovery in the cellar, I announced to the construction supervisor in a timely fashion the status of my efforts. He was pleased with the quiet style of my treatment of the facts and was present at the examination of the material. To my amazement the supervisor admitted to the authorities in my presence that the discovery in my cellar was an opportunity to ask himself and them whether there was possibly some connection to an inaccessible room they had noticed in the cellar. For example, whether poison gas could be stored in it, and so on. Obviously the explicit assumption gained the expectant attention of those in the cellar, which did not disappear after the authorities quickly declared the anxiety for practically unfounded. The investigation into this room had demonstrated that it was not to be found in any of the floor plans. The construction office had tried to find out what purpose the enclosed and completely sand-filled room might have served; but no reasonable explanation was forthcoming. We were astonished to hear that the authorities recommended we forget the whole matter for financial reasons. They appropriated the discovery I had shown them: for "disposal," as they said. And they anxiously insisted that the discovery was almost inconsequential. While the authorities were leaving, they advised the construction supervisor to explore by means of a "deep bore" what actually and whether even there was something hidden in the sand of the enclosed room. The construction supervisor, an architect in a white suit with a black bow tie, answered: "I'd rather not." And that ended more or less the encounter in the cellar. The enclosed room was not opened. If I want, I can still confirm that right now. But the question, to which this hidden story about the phenomenon of our house is supposed to be dedicated, has become all but invisible. And it has not even been stated that the house is supposed to have been owned by Jews, and that its owners in the GDR had donated it as a gift to the Protestant Church. What, in God's name, does the room in the cellar conceal. Ah, where are you, the possible speech in Germany.

Berlin, March 1995

Translated by Marc Silberman

Marc Silberman

Gert Neuman: Bio-bibliography

Born in 1942 in East Prussia (Heilsberg, today in Poland), Neumann —whose father was killed in the war—fled with his mother and two siblings to Munich in 1945. In 1946 his mother joined the land reform movement ("Neubauer") in the Soviet Occupation Zone and moved with the children to a farm in Mecklenburg. From 1949-51 they lived in Halle, and in 1951 they moved to Hohen-Neuendorf, a northern suburb of Berlin, where Neumann completed the middle school and then began an apprenticeship as tractor mechanic/driver at a collective farm (LPG) in the neighboring village of Schönfließ (1957-59). He volunteered for the army as a construction recruit in 1960, and after completing his two-year stint, worked in a series of farming jobs. He joined the socialist party (SED) in 1963 and was admitted in 1967 to the Johannes R. Becher Institute for Literature in Leipzig; in May 1969 he was exmatriculated from the Institute and kicked out of the party owing to his "eclectic, anti-socialist attitude." Thereafter Neumann held various positions in Leipzig as janitor or mechanic (department store, hospital, theater, and a church meeting house called "Oratorium"; during this time he assumed the surname of his wife, Heidemarie Härtl). In 1988 he moved to Berlin as a free-lance writer, where he still lives, and now works as a book dealer. Neumann's texts were virtually unknown to the public in the GDR. Only a few poems and short prose texts were published in the eighties in underground *samizdat* journals like *Anschlag* (Leipzig), *Schaden* (Berlin), and *Glasnot* (Berlin). Neumann was also a contributing editor of the journal *Anschlag* (1984-89) and together with Dietrich Oltmanns and his wife Härtl helped found in June 1987 the underground journal *Zweite Person* (Neumann left the editorial board after the first issues). Arrested twice by the Stasi and threatened with a prison sentence for having published books in West Germany, Neumann gained a reputation as one of the foremost literary dissidents in the alternative scene and peace circles of the GDR during the 1980s.

Recipient of a writer's prize from the Academy of Arts in West Berlin, 1982
Writer-in-residence in Ansbach as recipient of the city's Lyon's Club Prize (1990)
Recipient of the annual literary prize of the Schiller Foundation (Weimar), 1992
Recipient of the international writer's prize from the Robert Bosch Foundation (one-year residency in Ardeche, France, 1992-93)
Fellow of the Stiftung Literaturfonds (Darmstadt, 1995)
Fellow of the Stiftung Kulturfonds (Schloß Wiepersdorf, 1996)

Books authored by Neumann (by date of publication):

Die Schuld der Worte. Poetry and prose texts. Frankfurt/Main: Fischer, 1979. Reprint Rostock: Hinstorff, 1989.

Elf Uhr. Diary novel. Frankfurt/Main: Fischer, 1981. Reprint Rostock: Hinstorff, 1990.

Die Klandestinität der Kesselreiniger. Novel. Frankfurt/Main: Fischer, 1989.

Übungen jenseits der Möglichkeit. Prose and poetry. Frankfurt/Main: Koren und Debes, 1991.

Artists' editions (numbered, bibliophile editions with original graphics; signed by Neumann and the artists):

Übungen jenseits der Möglichkeit. Prose. (Two editions with graphics by different artists under the same title.) Berlin: Edition Maldoror, 1991 and 1992. The essay (written 1974-85) consists of

17 numbered prose texts and appeared as well in *Übungen* (1991), 27-57.

Produktionsgewässer. Prose. Berlin: Edition Maldoror,1993.

Rauch. Berlin: Edition Maldoror, 1993. Includes "Die Namen" (3-4), "Gesang" (7-11), "Poesiebeweis" (poem, 12), "Rauch" (15-16), "Die Burgen" (19-20), "Vom Bowling" (23-41).

Das nabeloonische Chaos. Prose. Berlin: Edition Maldoror, 1993. Includes also "Karl-Heinz Jakobs brieflich im Gespräch mit Gert Neumann".

Sprechen in Deutschland. Prose and poetry. Berlin: Edition Maldoror, 1993. Includes "Ausstand (Eine Rede)" (3-12), "Sprechen in Deutschland" (13-20), "Erfahren und Zernutzen" (21-27), "Triftig" (poem, 28), "Die "Dimension Bitterfeld" (29-40).

Feindselig. Prose. Berlin: Edition Quartre en Samisdat (= Maldoror), 1993.

Deuterosen. Prose. *Dschamp* 12. Berlin: Galerie auf Zeit, 1995.

Tunnelrede. Prose and poetry. Berlin: Edition Maldoror, 1996. Includes "Berührt" (poem, 3), "Illumination" (4-7), "Tunnelrede" (8-24), "Verdunkelung" (25-39).

Poetry and short prose (alphabetical list by title):
[some of these entries were published before 1990 in GDR underground publications not listed here; the date of composition is indicated in parentheses immediately after the title, if available; *Herzattacke* is a quarterly journal edited by Maximilian Barck at Edition Maldoror]

"Allein" (poem, 1989). *Herzattacke* 4 (1993): 102. Also in *Übungen* (1991), 78.

"Anfangstext einer Lesung" (September 1984), in Andreas Koziol and Rainer Schedlinksi, eds. *Abriß der Ariadnefabrik*. Berlin: Galrev, 1990. 146-48.

"auf Adam Michnik" (poem, 1984). *Übungen* (1991), 26.

"Aus einem Brief." *Die Schuld der Worte* (1979), 97-103.

"Ausstand. Eine Rede". *Herzattacke* 2-3 (1991): 329-43, *Übungen* (1991), 158-67, and *Sprechen in Deutschland* (1993), 13-20.

"Berührt" (poem, 1990). *Herzattacke* 4 (1993): 14. Also in *Übungen* (1991), 157, and *Tunnelrede* (1996), 3.

"Beschreibung einer Scheiterung." *Die Schuld der Worte* (1979), 12-13.

"Bewegt" (poem). In Klaus Michael and Thomas Wohlfahrt, eds. *Vogel oder Käfig sein. Kunst und Literatur in der DDR 1979-1989*. Berlin: Galrev, 1991, 185.

"Brief an Adam Michnik." In Thomas Beckermann, ed. *Reise durch die Gegenwart: Ein Lesebuch der Collection*. Frankfurt/Main: S. Fischer, 1987, 343-355. Same as part 17 of "Übungen jenseits der Möglichkeit" (see below) and excerpted also as "Der Dialog mit den Dingen. Aus einem Brief an Adam Michnik," *Ästhetik und Kommunikation* 65/66 (1986/87): 109-112.

"Brief in das Gefängnis" (1983). In Klaus Michael and Thomas Wohlfahrt, eds. *Vogel oder Käfig sein. Kunst und Literatur in der DDR 1979-1989*. Berlin: Galrev, 1991, 101-106.

"Brief in die DDR" (July 1990). *Übungen* (1991), 129-31.

"Brief ohne Antwort" (1986). *Übungen* (1991), 60-72, and *Herzattacke* 3 (1994): 40-54.

"Briefrede" (1982). *Übungen* (1991), 7-11.

"Das Buch des Lesens" (1989). *Manuskripte* 106 (December, 1989): 74-75. Also in *Neue Rundschau* 100.4 (1989): 19-23, *Übungen* (1991), 73-77, and *Herzattacke* 1 (1993): 144-52.

"Die Burgen." *Die Schuld der Worte* (1979), 64-66. Also in Hans Bender, ed. *Spiele ohne Ende: Erzählungen aus 100 Jahre S. Fischer*. Frankfurt/Main: S. Fischer, 1986, 689-690, and *Rauch* (1993), 19-20.

"Deuterosen" (September 1995). Original version in *Dschamp 12*. Berlin: Galerie auf Zeit, 1995. Revised version (with "Brief an den Herausgeber") in *Herzattacke* 4 (Berlin, 1995): 293-302. Also in *Moosbrand* (Berlin, 1995): 113-119, *Ostragehege* 1.4 (Leipzig, 1996): 24-27, and set to music by Thomas Buchholz and performed at Kloster Michaelstein near Halle in July 1996 (Leipzig: Musikverlag Ebert, 1996).

"Die Dimension Bitterfeld" (May 1992). *Glanz und Elend* 1 (Zeitschrift für Kultur und Kritik, September 1992): 27-31. Also in *Sprache im technischen Zeitalter* 124 (December 1992): 455-63, *Herzattacke* 4 (1992): 37-56, *Salz* 69 (Salzburg, September-October 1992): 23-32, and *Sprechen in Deutschland* (1993), 29-40.

"E-dur" (1985), in Egmont Hesse, ed. *Sprache und Antwort: Stimmen und Texte einer anderen Literatur aus der DDR*. Frankfurt/Main: Fischer, 1988, 125-27. Also in *Übungen* (1991), 57-59.

"Erfahren und Zernutzen," in Herbert Witt, ed. *Poetik des Widerstandes: Versuch einer Annäherung.* Symposium am 25. und 26. Oktober 1991 in Leipzig. Leipzig: Friedrich-Ebert-Stiftung, 1992, 9-15 (two additional, untitled statements, 88-93 and 126-131). Also in *Herzattacke* 2 (1992): 253-264, *Manuskripte* 116 (June 1992): 76-77, and *Sprechen in Deutschland* (1993), 21-27.

"Eröffnungstext der Lesung 'und all so ist Sprache'" (with Wolfgang Hilbig in Berlin, February 1994). *Herzattacke* 2 (1994): 337-38.

"Die Ethik der Sätze" (October 1989). *Manuskripte* 106 (Graz, 1989): 71-73. Also in *Kontext* 3 (1990): 14-17, and *Übungen* (1991), 94-98.

"Feindselig" (October 1993). Also in *Herzattacke* 1 (1994): 397-401.

"Gesang." *Die Schuld der Worte* (1979), 61-63. Also in *Rauch* (1993), 7-11.

"Hoppetanz" (interview by letter with Karl-Heinz Jakobs, July 1992). *Herzattacke* 4 (1992): 59-82. Also under the title "Karl-Heinz Jakobs brieflich im Gespräch mit Gert Neumann" in *Das nabeloonische Chaos* (1993).

"Illumination" (December 1992). *Herzattacke* 1 (1994): 159-160. Also in *Tunnelrede* (1996), 4-7.

"Im Karree" (poem, 1983). *Herzattacke* 4 (1993): 249. Also in *Übungen* (1991), 12.

"Klandestin" (poem, 1992). In Hendrik Liersch, ed. *Retsina für Vauo.* Berlin: Corvinus Presse, 1995. n.p. (Limited, signed graphic arts edition).

"Medium Weiß" (November 1989 - February 1990). *Kontext* 3 (1990): 17-22. Also in *Manuskripte* 107 (März 1990): 67-69, Heinz Ludwig Arnold, ed. *Die andere Sprache*. Sonderband *Text und Kritik*. Munich: Edition Text und Kritik, 1990, 215-20, *Übungen* (1991), 99-106, and *Herzattacke* 1 (1993): 158-68.

"Die Möglichkeiten zur Transzendenz." *Die Schuld der Worte* (1979), 71-73

"Das nabeloonische Chaos" (1990/91). *Übungen* (1991), 140-156. Also in *Herzattacke 4* (1993): 131-51, and *Das nabeloonische Chaos* (1993). Also under the title "Gespräch und Widerstand: Das nabeloonische Chaos," in Ernest Wichner and Herbert Wiesner, eds. *"Literaturentwicklungsprozesse": Die Zensur der Literatur in der DDR*. Frankfurt/Main: Suhrkamp, 1993, 144-62 [plus letter to the Minister of Culture, November 3, 1979, 163-65].

"Die Namen." *Die Schuld der Worte* (1979), 7-8. Also in *Rauch* (1993), 3-4.

"Notwendig." *Die Schuld der Worte* (1979), 111-153.

"Passacaglia" (August 1989). *Kontext* 3 (1990): 7-10. Also in *Übungen* (1991), 83-88, and *Herzattacke* 2 (1994): 9-16.

"Pastorale." *Die Schuld der Worte* (1979), 90-96. Also in Thomas Beckermann, ed. *Reise durch die Gegenwart: Ein Lesebuch der Collection*. Frankfurt/Main: S. Fischer, 1987, 332-337.

"Poesiebeweis" (poem). Die Schuld der Worte (1979), 89. Also in *Rauch* (1993), 12.

"Produktionsgewässer" (September 1989 - September 1990). *Übungen* (1991), 115-28. Also in *Herzattacke* 2 (1993): 74-92, and *Produktionsgewässer* (1993).

"Rauch." *Die Schuld der Worte* (1979), 14-15. Also in Egmont Hesse, ed. *Sprache und Antwort: Stimmen und Texte einer anderen Literatur aus der DDR.* Frankfurt/Main: Fischer, 1988, 123-24, and *Rauch* (1993), 15-16.

"Die Rechte des Erzählens" (January 1997). *Herzattacke* 1 (1997): ?. Also in *Monatshefte* (Madison, 1997).

"Die Reportagen." *Die Schuld der Worte* (1979), 16-60.

"Die Schuld der Worte" (September 1989; not the same as the 1979 book collection). *Kontext* 3 (1990): 11-14. Also in *Übungen* (1991), 89-93.

"Sehr geehrter Herr Höpcke" (letter of 18 January 1989 concerning the publication of the novel *Die Klandestinität der Kesselreiniger*). *Übungen* (1991), 79-82.

"Sprechen in Deutschland." (Eröffnungstext einer Lesung in Frankfurt am Main, December 1991). *Neue deutsche Literatur* 6 (1992): 112-18. Also in *Der Prokurist* 9 (Vienna, 1992): 107-115, *Herzattacke* 1 (1992): 209-222, and *Sprechen in Deutschland* (1993), 13-20.

"Die Stimme des Schweigens" (1983). *Neue Rundschau* 94.1 (1983): 83-87. Also in *Herzattacke* 4 (1994): 69-74, and *Übungen* (1991), 21-25.

"Sturztrunk. Eine Rede" (September 1990). *Sprache im technischen Zeitalter* 116 (December 1990): 315-20. Also in *Kontext* 12 (November/December 1990): 39-44, *Herzattacke* 4 (1990): 206-218, *Neue deutsche Literatur* 12 (1990): 86-92, and *Übungen* (1991), 132-39.

"Tabu" (poem). In Egmont Hesse, ed. *Sprache und Antwort:*

Stimmen und Texte einer anderen Literatur aus der DDR. Frankfurt/Main: Fischer, 1988, 128, and in Klaus Michael and Thomas Wohlfahrt, eds. *Vogel oder Käfig sein. Kunst und Literatur in der DDR 1979-1989.* Berlin: Galrev, 1991, 100.

"Die Terrasse." *Die Schuld der Worte* (1979), 67-70.

"Die Tiefe war eigentlich genannt..." *Niemandsland* 2.5 (Berlin, 1988): 74.

"Triptychon." *Die Schuld der Worte* (1979), 9-11.

"Tunnelrede" (1994). Herzattacke 4 (1994): 305-316. Also in *Tunnelrede* (1996), 8-24.

"Toccata" (April 1990). *Sondeur* 3 (1990): 52-56. Also in *Übungen* (1991), 107-14.

"Triftig" (poem, 1991). *Herzattacke* 3 (1992): 264. Also in *Sprechen in Deutschland* (1993), 28.

"Übungen jenseits der Möglichkeiten." *Neue Rundschau* 97.2/3 (1986): 49-63 (16 parts). Also in *Übungen* (1991), 27-57 (includes part 17 "Brief an Adam Michnik"), and *Übungen* (artists editions, 1991 and 1992).

"Die Umgebung des Textes." (Eröffnungstext einer Lesung im Brecht-Zentrum Berlin, June 1991). Inge Gellert, ed. *Nach Brecht. Ein Almanach.* Berlin: Argon, 1992, 18-20.

"Unverhoffte Feier" (poem). In Klaus Michael and Thomas Wohlfahrt, eds. *Vogel oder Käfig sein. Kunst und Literatur in der DDR 1979-1989.* Berlin: Galrev, 1991, 101.

"Das Urteil der Mechanismen." *Neue Rundschau* 99.2 (1988): 5-25 (accompanied by photos of Tamara Bauer).

"Die Verdunkelung" (March 1995). *E-Dit* (Leipzig 1995). Also in *Herzattacke* 4 (1996): 141-48, *Tunnelrede* (1996), 25-39, and translated into English by Marc Silberman as "Blackout" in Jost Hermand and Marc Silberman, eds., *Contentious Memories: Looking Back at the GDR*. New York and Frankfurt/Main: Peter Lang, 1997.

"Die Versammlung." *Die Schuld der Worte* (1979), 104-110.

"Versuche eines gültigen Sprechens: Gespräch Herbert M. Debes - Gert Neumann" (June 1989). *Verwendung* 9 (Beiheft, January 1990): 1- 10. (The supplement also includes "Passacaglia," "Die Schuld der Worte," and "Die Ethik der Sätze".)

"Vom Bowling." *Die Schuld der Worte* (1979), 74-88. Also in *Rauch* (1993), 23-41.

"Weitersprechen." In Ulrich Janetzki and Wolfgang Rath, eds. *Tendenz Freisprache: Texte zu einer Poetik der achtziger Jahre*. Frankfurt/Main: Suhrkamp, 1991, 147-150.

"Die Wörter des reinen Denkens" (Eröffnungstext einer Lesung, December 1984). *Neue Rundschau* 96.2 (1985): 144-51. Also in Andreas Koziol and Rainer Schedlinksi, eds. *Abriß der Ariadnefabrik*. Berlin: Galrev, 1990. 249-54, Klaus Michael and Thomas Wohlfahrt, eds. *Vogel oder Käfig sein. Kunst und Literatur in der DDR 1979-1989*. Berlin: Galrev, 1991, and *Übungen* (1991), 185-191.

"Zweiter Februar 1978." *Neue Rundschau* 91.2/3 (1980): 236-47 (excerpt from *Elf Uhr*). Also in Thomas Beckermann, ed. *Reise durch die Gegenwart: Ein Lesebuch der Collection*. Frankfurt/Main: S. Fischer, 1987, 338-342.

Other pertinent texts (by date of publication):

Hanns-Josef Ortheil, "Die Sprache des Widerstands" (1981). In Ortheil, *Schauprozesse: Beiträge zur Kultur der 80er Jahre.* Munich: Piper, 1990, 129-139 (originally published in *Merkur*).

Theo Mechtenberg, "Literatur als Plädoyer für eine zweite Wirklichkeit: Anmerkungen zum poetologischen Programm von Gert Neumann, Wolfgang Hilbig und Wolfgang Hegewald." *Deutschland Archiv* 19.3 (1986): 285-93.

Egmont Hesse, "Geheimsprache 'Klandestinität': Gespräch mit Gert Neumann" (January 1984). *Neue Rundschau* 98.2 (1987): 5-20. Also under the title "Das Gespräch befindet sich da, wo man es sucht," in Egmont Hesse, ed. *Sprache und Antwort: Stimmen und Texte einer anderen Literatur aus der DDR.* Frankfurt/Main: Fischer, 1988, 139-144.

Thomas Beckermann, "Die Diktatur repräsentiert das Abwesende nicht: Essay on Monika Maron, Wolfgang Hilbig and Gert Neumann." In Arthur Williams, Stuart Parkes, Roland Smith, eds. *German Literature at a Time of Change 1989-1990: German Unity and German Identity in Literary Perspective.* Bern: Peter Lang, 1989, 97-116.

Antonia Grünenberg, "In den Räumen der Sprache: Gedankenbilder zur Literatur Gert Neumanns." In Heinz-Ludwig Arnold, ed. *Die andere Sprache.* Sonderband *Text und Kritik.* Munich: Edition Text und Kritik, 1990, 206-213

Ernest Wichner and Herbert Wiesner, eds. *Zensur in der DDR: Geschichte, Praxis und "Ästhetik" der Behinderung von Literatur.* Exhibition catalogue. Berlin: Literaturhaus, 1991. Documentation of 1979-81 correspondence concerning the publication of *Elf Uhr* between Neumann and the Cultural Ministry (Klaus Höpke, Kurt Hager), 169-75.

Jürgen Egyptien, "Scheherazade, ewiger Umgang und Klandestinität: Anmerkungen zur poetologischen Praxis und zu den Erzähltheorien von Hanns-Josef Ortheil, Gerhard Köpf und Gert Neumann." *Text und Kritik* 113 (Munich 1992).

Colin Grant, "Gert Neumann." Chapter 3.1. in C. Grant, *Literary Communication from Consensus to Rupture: Practice and Theory in Honecker's GDR.* Amsterdam and Atlanta: Rodopi, 1995, 138-152.

Joachim Walther, *Sicherungsbereich Literatur: Schriftsteller und Staatssicherheit in der Deutschen Demokratischen Republik.* Berlin: Ch. Links, 1996. On the operations against Neumann, see 406-408 and 413-422.

Marc Silberman

Whose Story Is This?
Rewriting the Literary History of the GDR

After the collapse of 1989 the GDR has grown more attractive as an object of historical interest. As past phenomena its cultural institutions now seem to cohere in an extraordinarily complex system of relations between art, artists, and power. While the posteriority resulting from German (re)unification may well mark the boundary to this experience of growing distance, it also extends a line from the past to the present and beyond. Vestiges of the old and the not-yet-new accompany the process of forgetting that constitutes memory, the looking-back with which we are concerned. Though the GDR is said to be a closed chapter historically after German unification, it is no less part of Germany's postwar history with consequences for the way we—as specialists of GDR cultural history—judge and narrate the present. In other words, rather than sequestering the GDR within a separate history during its forty-year existence, I want to examine here continuity and commonality in the broader German context.

Yet, at the same time that the GDR is to be rescued from the status of an "anomaly" in German history, I do not wish simply to neutralize its alterity by integrating it into a seamless narrative of postwar evolution. The subtitle of my contribution—"Rewriting the Literary History of the GDR"—picks up on this notion of looking back. It refers to the determining moment of the end of the Cold War as the impetus to rethink, to rehistoricize the GDR. This is a process taking place in the social science and humanistic disciplines. Indeed, among German historians the collapse of the GDR and Germany's unification have brought forth different contours of twentieth-century German history, exposing suddenly the need for new narrative strategies and leading to a controversy about the status of the Third Reich that is sometimes referred to as the "kleiner Historikerstreit."[1] For literary historians the challenge to rethink issues and categories, while less spectacular, is no less imperative, but—as I intend to elaborate here—there are problems specific to the discipline and the internal history of "germanistische Literaturwissenschaft" which we ought to consider. Because the (re)writing of literary history takes place within the functional relations and social structure of our academic institutions, our effort to produce meaning is also part of a larger power struggle for control of or access to knowledge. By proposing connections to historical knowledge, it reinforces the construction of experience and memory, at the very least documenting and perhaps even intervening in the ongoing discursive event. In this vein the main title of my contribution—"Whose Story Is This?"—is an intentionally polemical question about ownership and responsibility. A more accurate formulation of the question might be: "has the past changed?" My answer to both questions leads me to a position many might consider hopelessly old-fashioned or even empirically discredited. To anticipate my conclusion, then, I will be arguing that my place as a literary historian looking back on the GDR can only be within ideology.

Let's remember that literary historians and critics are generally in the business of reorganizing the canon, inflating certain texts at the expense of others and producing multiple meanings. So what is the urgency to reconsider the literary history of the GDR, particularly in view of the fact that there already exist respectable surveys? I suggest that the rapid disappearance of the systemic structures of literary life in the GDR has made its literature into a historical phenomenon much more quickly than is usually the case with the passage of time—a potentially advantageous situation for literary historians because it can foreground the historicity of our own judgments. It should become clear that hierarchies of quality and achievement are retrospective constructions validated by the context of those who judge. Moreover, the sudden historicity of the concept "GDR literature" poses an especially interesting problem, both as a productive category and as an impediment. This changed context exposes other contradictions and continuities. The relations between institutions, authors, and the GDR reading public as well as between authors and their cultural (re)sources must be rethought. We, in turn, as contemporary readers enter a different relationship to the texts with our newly acquired hindsight. On the one hand, this position vis-à-vis history assumes an open attitude toward its changeability; on the other, it can engender an attitude of moral and aesthetic superiority that assumes rather than problematizes the position of the GDR writer and reader in their historical context.

This background helps explain typical responses and their shortcomings in the initial retrospective view of GDR literature by critics and literary historians. I will mention only three representative ones. For some the confrontation with the dystopian reality of existing socialism has generated disenchantment, even dismissive rejection of the entirety. Accusations of guilt by association and self-congratulatory, a posteriori claims of early prescience are not unusual but lack a serious engagement with literary historiography. On the contrary, this operation simply transforms the GDR into a new kind of Other in a process that is supposed to help create a post-Wall German identity. Another popular response is nostalgia. The memory of the former utopian promise of socialism has generated "Ostalgie," counterbalanced on the other side by a growing "Westalgie" for the presumably less complicated, pre-1990 Cold-War certainties. The hope for change that fueled past utopian thought gives way to the fear of loss and a sentimental attachment to the past. In both cases the discourse of loss goes hand in hand with a yearning for the (mythical) golden age when literary history and political affiliations seemed to be more stable. For literary historians drawn to utopian thought GDR literature can be examined as a repository of past dreams that have lost their imaginative power and acquired now historical power. That is, utopian narratives assume their proper status as fictions of possible but failed alternative histories. The mission then would be to retrieve from literary texts the history of utopian potential *and* its lack of realization in order to uncover the impossible ideals identified with socialism in the GDR.[2] A third popular and especially interesting response to the cultural paradigm change is a kind of public self-flagellation with appeals to "Trauerarbeit" and "Vergangenheitsbewältigung." Coming to terms with the past is a process that appropriately acknowledges rifts as well as continuities and that offers counter narratives for what retrospectively come to be seen as world-political events and representative traditions. That these specific German phrases are already associated with a rich, complex historicization of the Third Reich and the Holocaust gives me pause when they are applied to the GDR as a new object of attention, especially when their persistent repetition seems to be more a ritualistic gesture than a serious engagement with the resistances or ruptures that individual memory opposes to public images and discourses.

For this task the literary historian needs the most refined tools of the trade to trace and describe the complexity of contradictory contexts and developments. In what follows I do not intend to tell my own grand narrative of GDR literature but rather to suggest the ambiguity of its telling by examining the obstacles, typologies, and strategies pertinent to such an undertaking. What should emerge will be neither a counter literary history of buried texts nor a testament to what remains ("was bleibt") but a reflection on the writing of literary history, for I find that GDR literature offers an especially salient object for illustrating how we construct tradition and how we endorse values that define continuity. The privileged position of being witness to world-changing events should motivate theoretical consciousness, and the course of recent German history has made it imperative to rethink methodological assumptions. At the same time the rapid flow of events and surprising turns thwart generalizations and highlight clichés. Essential for the undertaking, however, is our agreement from the start about three premises. First, contrary to the state-propagated image of harmony, the GDR was not a homogeneous society in which individual and social interests coincided. Second, the GDR was characterized by an economy of shortage that undermined the whole idea of planning at the heart of the socialist system, including in the ideological sphere; as a result, the popular image of totalitarian, centralized control must at least acknowledge the considerable room for resistance and various forms of accommodation created by individuals. Finally, literary history is concerned with values and how they are established but not with moral judgments.

Let me start with the big issues and proceed deductively. The project of literary history is said to represent literary production and reception through its national, chronological, and/or genre-specific characteristics and is driven by cognitive, often even narcissistic and self-affirming interests.[3] The resulting narratives, contributions to an endless chain of retellings, are of course only an approximation of an ideal representation, yet the project is significant because it makes visible the process of history and historicization. The process consists of collecting and ordering: selecting texts and data, positing relations among them, and criticizing or commenting on them. Literary history, in other words, is a construction based on the definition of its object, on the linking of this object to other areas of social or artistic life, and on criteria of evaluation. In the context of GDR literature each of these terms is open to legitimate questioning. How do we define the object of interest, GDR literature? How do we weigh the relative autonomy of literary production and reception in a system where one political party explicitly established the framework for all ideological activity? And what constraints do the epistemological implications of a reflection theory of literature such as socialist realism imply for the evaluation of art?

Narrative histories of literature always rely on abstract, retrospective concepts to order and analyze their material, otherwise there would be no way to convey complex meanings. Until recently, the cognitive framework of literary historiography derived from the Enlightenment notion of history's progressive unfolding with a morally charged understanding of literature's relation to utility, truth, and beauty. Only in the 1960s, largely in response to the challenge of structuralism, did the discourse of literary history begin to question its own premises. The concept of literature, for example, was broadened so that the issue of data selection came to the fore. The question of voice—who could speak and who was heard—intermingled with issues of class (popular forms of literature), gender (the effort to recuperate women's writing), and race or nation (the position of exile and migrant literatures). The inequality inscribed in traditional or politicized definitions of literature is in its own way especially pertinent for the GDR but also in the post-1989 discussions about the GDR, if one recalls the German proclivity to forget or obliterate the histories of its "others." Related to the vagaries of constituting the canon is the issue of literary change. Contrary to the traditional grounding of the autonomy of literary communication on the basis of poetological axioms or phenomenological evidence (works or texts), sociologically grounded models of structural change began in the 1960s to treat literary communication as a particular (sub)system of social interaction. As I will try to show, the intersection of systems theory with social history in the 1970s became the most popular approach to GDR literary history and in large measure still defines it.

A further challenge to the discourse of literary history concerns the authority of its linear construction, with or without a causal structure. Riding on the theory waves in the 1970s and 1980s formalism and deconstruction asserted themselves as potent players in the field, proposing other analytical figures such as spirals, oscillations, rhizoms, or knots to describe the landscape of literary activity. In the meantime literary historians in general seem to have assumed a posture of ontological modesty vis-à-vis the tradition of grand narratives, often shifting the focus synchronically by expanding the breadth of the textual base or relying intuitively on a collage approach of loosely connected insights and analyses. It has been argued that literary history, like all historiography, has recourse to an organizing notion or unity, even if the goal is no longer a totalizing one.[4] In my view GDR literary history has suffered precisely from rigidly teleological organizing schemes, that is, it arranges material retrospectively from a predetermined endpoint, assuming that meanings can be fixed and then proceeding to establish that fixed meaning. Indeed, one of the more widespread perspectives on GDR literature even now reads it in a kind of one-way, reverse causality from the failure of socialism. At the very least a reciprocal approach is more adequate in order to understand both "the work in its time" as well as "its present meaning as history," that is, an approach open to the notion that literature is propelled by the writer's as well as the reader's fantasy. Finally, rethinking literary change and continuity has thrown into question accepted models of periodization. The passage of literary temporality is often arbitrarily divided into years without reference to content (literature of the twenties or fifties) or derived from socio-political events (Weimar or fascist literature), from intellectual history ("Empfindsamkeit," decadence), from philosophy (Enlightenment literature), or from art historical terminology ("Jugendstil," impressionism). This coding of literature devalues its inherent aesthetic properties as secondary or as an epiphenomenon of some hierarchically more important activity. GDR literary histories present an especially egregious example of such attempts at periodization, measured by decades or political hiatuses and changes in regime (e.g., 1945, 1961, 1971), by party congresses and meetings of the Writers Union, or by generational cohorts of fifteen-year duration. Yet GDR writers did not produce texts in direct response to political events and cultural political guidelines. An approach to periodization that attends to the way texts, often written or reworked over years, anticipated, accompanied, challenged, or engaged existential questions would begin to devise other continuities and breaks. And these textual aspects are to be discovered not only or primarily in content or plot but also in structures, forms, references, poetic language, etc.

Needless to say, the problematization of literary history does not obviate the need to pursue synthesizing retrospectives. Without the selectivity of a literary canon the evaluation of genres, authors, and individual works can not proceed, and without historicizing periods and phases comparisons become all but impossible. The point is to define our expectations and limitations when contemplating the past, to recognize how this activity might renew the sense of our own reading presence as a sequel, if not exactly the culmination of a genealogy. With this in mind, it is useful to turn to the tradition of GDR literary historiography in both East and West Germany prior to 1990.

While we may agree in the abstract that the text corpus called "GDR literature" is now constituted in its entirety with the collapse of the GDR, I am not so sure what specifically it should describe. Is a GDR text defined by political geography, that is, by the birthplace of the author, by the author's place of residence, by the place where the text is written, by the place where it is published, or by some combination of these factors? When we speak of GDR literature, do we mean literature *in* the GDR, *from* the GDR, *about* the GDR? *for* GDR readers? or affirmative socialist-realist writing? or texts written under the constraints imposed by the SED and the Stasi? Was GDR literature simply an abstraction of cultural functionaries who in the tradition of Leninist vanguardism wanted to eliminate difference in their own camp by circumscribing the enemy? What about the underground literature of the eighties, the Prenzlauer Berg writers who, on the one hand, refused any identity at all with the GDR state or its literary tradition, but, on the other hand, can only be understood in their individual and group identity with reference to the GDR? And what about the writers who left or were expelled in the wake of the Biermann affair in 1976? While we can probably agree from a different historical perspective on the category of exile writer for those like Brecht, Seghers, and Zweig, who returned and continued to write in the GDR, it becomes problematic in the case of "die Wegegangenen."[5] Among those who left legally, some returned and others chose not to. Some continued to write in West Germany about GDR topics or experiences, while others found new issues. When, if ever, did these "Weggegangene" cross the border out of GDR literature, and into what space did they enter from the perspective of literary history? Clearly there is no simple answer, since the concept of "GDR literature" defined by political geography immediately raises questions of inclusion and exclusion that do not correspond to literary distinctions, and depending on how the boundaries are drawn, that is, depending on the implicit or explicit cognitive interests of those who draw the lines, the results will come into focus in various ways. Certainly we can agree, though, that there is no *a priori* reason for maintaining such a concept of GDR literature.

One way to clarify the stakes of this definition is to recall the Cold-War discussions about the unity of German literature or "wieviele deutsche Literaturen gibt es?" Of course, this was mainly a West German or western discussion because in the GDR the issue was subsumed under the notion of "sozialistisches Erbe" or "sozialistische Nationalkultur." Nonetheless, it is worthwhile to remember the differing stages of the discussion in east and west. For instance, in the Soviet Zone there were at least rhetorical efforts in the immediate postwar period among occupation authorities, German functionaries, and writers to revive the Popular-Front politics of the thirties under the banner of antifascism and humanism, appealing to progressive writers and intellectuals in both east and west regardless of political affiliation.[6] Even after the two German states were established in 1949 and Cold-War realities had shifted their priorities from cooperation to confrontation, in the GDR the notion of a common "deutsche Kulturnation" continued to echo in official pronouncements far into the sixties. Yet for politicians and literary historians on both sides of the border, the divergence of the two German literatures during the fifties and sixties was a de facto reality. For the one side literature "hinter dem Eisernen Vorhang" was pure propaganda serving the party; for the other literature produced under capitalism was "revanchistisch-imperialistischer Schund."

The GDR head of state, Walter Ulbricht, was invoking already in 1956 the automony of "einer sozialistischen deutschen Nationalkultur" in the GDR, and at the same time the cultural minister, Johannes R. Becher, introduced his utopian idea of a "Literaturgesellschaft" to describe the new shape that the community of readers and writers would take.[7] Thus, the foundations of a specific "GDR literature" emerged fairly early but notably without geographical restriction. In these early years the imposing presence of exile writers in the East, who during the Third Reich had sustained German culture without regard for national boundaries, excluded any kind of particularism. This is an important point because at no time did the concept of GDR literature appeal to a nationalist agenda. On the contrary, while the establishment of the GDR state rested clearly on its delimitation from the Federal Republic, especially after the signing of the mutual recognition treaty in 1972, all claims for national unity and German national identity were dropped in favor of socialist identity as a substitute nationality.[8] Nonetheless, as a tool of cultural policy "GDR literature" became an excuse to legitimate state intervention because literature *in* the GDR was defined politically and ideologically from the beginning.[9] Officially, that is, for the party and cultural functionaries, it was primarily a pedagogical tool for mass indoctrination, molding the consciousness that would support the dominant Marxist world view. The underdeveloped aspects of civil society helped preserve this late nineteenth-century ideal of proletarian culture and education that regarded the class-conscious worker as a reader, perhaps even as a writer, and the word as the vehicle for raising class consciousness. Thus, cultural policy insisted on the existence of GDR literature based on a hypostacized social experience and a biologistic projection of proletarian reality, but at the same time its mechanical, Leninist model relegated writers to function as a relay between the vanguard party and the recalcitrant readers.

For many literary critics, writers, and readers, however, GDR literature was seen as a seismograph that both formulated *and* formed attitudes toward life in the GDR. More often than not, this "Lebensgefühl" deviated in essential ways from the official consensus view, yet many writers continued to take advantage of the logocentric nature of traditional communistic movements that grant those who use words a special social status. In this capacity they could assume the unusual roles both of "educator of the princes" and mouthpiece of the people. With the construction of the Berlin Wall in the early 1960s and the party's acceptance of détente in the early 1970s, the growing collective identification with "unsere Literatur" seemed to indicate more than just a rhetorical flourish on the part of writers and readers. To be sure, distinctions should be made here between public and private expressions of sentiment, between various periods in an individual writer's development and identity with the goals of the GDR state, and between writer intentionality and the complicated, somewhat defiant sense of a "Wir-Gefühl" that evolved in the literary reception process.[10] In any case, by 1970 the respected literary scholar Claus Träger from Leipzig was arguing in a strong polemic for the separate trajectories of two German literatures in two German states, and characteristically volume 11 (1976) of the East German *Geschichte der deutschen Literatur von den Anfängen bis zur Gegenwart* was devoted exclusively to GDR literature.[11] Both were indebted essentially to Marxist versions of intellectual history or *Geistesgeschichte* that traced the historical progress of the GDR state in the evolution of its "Poesie."[12] Meanwhile, another group of influential literary scholars was beginning to critique exactly the dominant GDR model of literary history that reduced literature to a cognitive function subject to ideological regulation and interpretation. The shift to what became known in the course of the 1970s as the communicative-functional model focused on the subjective side of the writer and the aesthetic affects of the text, positing a communicative collectivity of equal partners who write and read.[13] The shift brought forth some astonishingly sensitive textual analyses but is interesting in our context for two metatheoretical reasons. First, it allowed a de-ideologization of literary criticism because the assumptions and philosophical coordinates of the entire Marxist system were no longer explicit or even under debate. Second, it led to a depoliticization of literary history because the reception model based on an idealized concept of equality between writer and reader obviated the need to acknowledge or regulate political conflict in literary texts or the reading process. Thus, while the fixed meanings of Marxist critique were abandoned, the assumption that writer and reader were equal partners in the process of semiotic decoding still relied on the assumption that literature accurately represents "reality," something external to the representation itself.

What, then, was the status of "GDR literature" in the GDR? It is remarkable that in late November 1989, the "Für unser Land" initiative launched by Christa Wolf and other prominent writers and intellectuals was couched in an appeal to antifascist and humanistic ideals of solidarity identified with the GDR state but not with national loyalty.[14] The lack of popular resonance to this call for self-determination within the GDR demonstrates the fundamental contradiction of the reform movement: it needed the protection of the Wall to guarantee the statehood in which the project of democratization could unfold. This is another way of asking whether from the perspective of literary history GDR literature actually existed, since the state—its sovereignty and its border— was buttressed by what for the majority was a symbol of illegitimacy: the Wall. To come to grips with these differing kinds of attitudes internal to the GDR I suggest that we regard "GDR literature" as an invention based on an imagined collectivity and as such a vehicle of historical experience. Rather than foregrounding an illusionary or unreal quality this definition emphasizes the constructedness of the category "GDR literature" and of the reality it contains. This discursive formation, in the Foucauldian sense, refers as much to moments of affiliation and establishment as disavowel, exclusion, and contestation. From this perspective GDR literature becomes a trope for belonging, bordering, and commitment vis-à-vis the GDR, and the task of the literary historian is to analyze how writings and readings managed the tensions they formulated and produced.

In West Germany the discursive formation "GDR literature" was a different invention and had a different function. Although Hans Magnus Enzensberger had already insisted in 1959 on the existence of two German literatures and Hans Mayer's 1967 discussion of postwar literary developments drew a fine line between east and west, it was not until the early 1970s that GDR literature entered the public consciousness in the West.[15] The connection to the larger issues of "Ostpolitik" and the recognition of the GDR's sovereign borders in 1972 needs no further comment. In this context, however, it is interesting to note how from a juridical perspective the notion of "Kulturnation" migrated from east to west. While the GDR constitutionally eliminated all references to Germany and thereby relinquished the hope and rhetoric of unification, the Constitutional Court of the Federal Republic explicitly interpreted the phrase "zwei Staaten einer [deutschen] Nation" in the 1972 treaty to mean that linguistic and cultural unity was the legal foundation of future political unification.[16] Nonetheless, precisely the perceived alterity of GDR literature gave rise to the extended discussion in the West about two German literatures in the 1970s, and for literary scholars this discussion derived less from political or legal conventions than from an analysis of literary history. Their point of departure insisted on understanding GDR literature from its own context of production and reception. In other words the GDR was seen as representing a new or different system of discourse, and texts therefore entered a different discursive context. Just scanning the volume or chapter titles of the pertinent literary histories published in West Germany during the 1970s and 1980s reveals how this view dominated scholarly opinion.[17] Moreover, with the institutional establishment of GDR studies in western academies and universities an impressive list of scholarly introductions and teaching anthologies devoted exclusively to GDR literature began to emerge around the same time.[18] To varying degrees all of these approaches shared the conviction that cultural tradition, political and economic conditions, and literary-theoretical principles distinguished GDR literature in a fundamental way from other German-language literature. Less frequently were textual aspects and writers' intentions, not to speak of reading strategies, the basis of such particularism.

The sudden turn to GDR literature in the 1970s on the part of western literary scholars can be attributed to the coincidence of three factors. First, the generational shift identified with the baby-boom phenomenon was accompanied in the late 1960s and early 1970s by a search for alternative politics. Particularly at the universities students and young scholars in German studies who had been mobilized by the antiwar movement projected into the GDR the unfolding of a political energy that in their own social configuration seemed frozen in Cold-War antinomies and burdened by continuities from the Third Reich. Domestic capitalism was seen to be in crisis during the seventies, and this fueled the belief in scenarios of convergence (capitalism would whither away) or the revolutionary victory of socialism. Today these views seem naive and apocalyptic while they also account in part for the modest critical skill and rather vague rhetoric of utopian Marxism that marks much of the early GDR scholarship. Second, and directly related to the first point, was the influence of theoretical innovations in the field of Germanistik during the 1970s. Marxism, ideology critique, and literary sociology all operated with a derivative model of social evolution and literary development based on the analysis of socially critical motifs, life histories, and political phenomena as reflected in literary texts. Like no other corpus in German literary history did GDR literature seem to lend itself to such social-historical narratives. The programmatic functionalization of literature by state cultural policy and institutions on the one hand made it seem easy to describe the conjunctures of the literary system, but on the other it evinced a one-sided dependency on official discourse for periodization and for evaluating literary developments.[19] A third factor related to the ascendancy of GDR literary studies was its status as information. Since historians and other social scientists in the West had only limited access to their usual sources in the GDR like individuals, archives, statistics, and quotidian experience, literature itself became a compensatory informant about everyday life. As a consequence, general descriptions of social and political contextualization were more important than traditional textual analysis, but at the same time this tendency camouflaged the lack of knowledge about the real conditions under which GDR literature was produced and read. Moreover, the ever narrower focus of scholarly attention on politically critical authors (who never were in the majority but who in the West always enjoyed the bonus of authenticity) skewered the perception of literature *tout court* as the counter public sphere in a system that made no allowance for critical media.

In the course of the 1970s, then, GDR literature established itself for literary history as an independent category. The discussion on two German literatures gained momentum, and the number slowly hypertrophied, first from two to four, including Austria and Switzerland, then to five, including literature written by German-language minorities ("auslandsdeutsche Literatur," for example, in Romania or Israel), and then even to six, including literature written by non-Germans in Germany ("Gastarbeiterliteratur" and "Migrantenliteratur"). There were, however, counter arguments advanced for the unity of German literature despite political and cultural differentiation between the East and the West. Besides obvious factors like a common language and tradition, systemic and market features were identified that undermined strict distinctions, for example, the ongoing presence of non-marxist authors who published in the GDR, or the publication only in the West of works by authors living in the GDR. In addition, some writers who left the GDR for the West after 1976 continued to be published in the East as well. Important for literary scholars were convergence theories that became popular among sociologists and political scientists after the mid-seventies as an analytical model for highly complex industrial societies like East and West Germany, and their work on political elites and social stratification suggested parallel structures as well in the respective cultural spheres.[20] Furthermore the cultural exchanges in the wake of détente led to a growing popular reception of GDR writers in the West (although relatively it remained a small sampling), which suggested in turn that they were addressing analogous problems with familiar writing strategies. Ironically, then, by the early 1980s GDR literature as an independent phenomenon had become institutionalized in the West at the very time when its alterity began to be questioned. GDR writers began to leave because literary communication was becoming largely dysfunctional for them. Symptomatically, two of the earliest and most vociferous proponents of the separation thesis, Hans Mayer and Fritz J. Raddatz, revised their views around this time.[21]   Wolfgang Emmerich's authoritative *Kleine Literaturgeschichte der DDR* (first published in 1981) was oriented toward the thesis of a gradual rapprochement of modernist themes and forms in the literature of the entire German-speaking world.[22] And prominent writers from both parts of Germany—for example, those who participated in the "Berliner Begegnung zur Friedensforschung" organized by Stephan Hermlin in December 1981 in response to the growing threat to world civilization by nuclear arms—stressed their self-identity as *German* authors.[23] In other words, a growing consensus among the literary historians posited the existence of a "GDR literature" characterized by its homogeneity in every respect during the 1950s and 1960s, but since the early 1970s this conventional image had become increasingly untenable.

With the collapse of the GDR in 1989 its literature immediately became the object of renewed controversy with striking twists and inversions. In a kind of proxy war for a larger systemic critique the writers and their works variously seemed to display the worst complicity and the most admirable courage. Now the position of one, unified German literature was most forcefully argued by those who dismissed the entire postwar tradition as affirmative and provincial, claiming that in both east and west literature had been falsely politicized and driven by utopian illusions ("Gesinnungsästhetik"). The polemical, public debate of 1990/91 has already gone down in history under the indicative title of "der deutsch-deutsche Literaturstreit," accurately suggesting the extension of the Cold-War melodrama of absolute loyalties.[24]

Meanwhile, the residue of the two-literatures position flickered up in the agony of "Abwicklung," the administrative process of dismantling institutions of the former socialist system. The discovery and defense of (new) unarticulated identities in the two-year struggle to unify the two Academies of Art in East and West Berlin or in the as yet still undecided future of the two German PEN Centers offer classic examples of how binary thinking (victim/victimized; betrayer/ betrayed; consent/critique) has less to do with morality, as is often claimed, than discrediting alternatives and erasing issues as trivial, naive, and illegitimate by appealing to experience and historical lessons. For the purposes of literary scholarship these debates—mainly engaged in the culture pages of the major newspapers—do not offer much direction. Under the pressure of maintaining or increasing readership, daily news tends to promote sensationalist revelations and scandalous denunciations rather than critically reflecting on assumptions and cognitive interests. If anything, the debates helped articulate real, lived ressentiments and in this respect they may enter literary histories that aim at investigating larger discursive struggles for power and authority in the cultural sphere.

Two temporary conclusions can be made at this point. First, a fundamental difference for the literary developments in East and West Germany was the understanding of autonomy among writers. In the West writers (authors and critics) could assume their constitutionally guaranteed freedom of expression, even when it was under attack, as well as the relative indifference to their practice of writing on the part of the state (and public). In the East, however, the entire sphere of cultural production served the ideological needs of the party. The writer worked, so to speak, under state commission, whether under accommodation or in defiance, and as a result the party and the public embued words and texts with a special power. Second, GDR literature was not simply the product of repression but, as in the West, a heterogenous configuration that fulfilled many functions, which in themselves gradually changed over time. Cultural activity did take place in a closed, protected system with its own rules, although even here the fixation at all levels on the West and the ready access to Western media undermined the practice of regulation. There were, however, a variety of responses on the part of writers to this situation beyond straightforward acquiescence. Some were broken and resigned, some left or were forced to leave, others "dropped out" by creating a putative alternative space, still others developed hyper-sensitive nerves, learning how to use a specific kind of imagination to formulate tensions and contradictions.

I alluded at the outset to the ongoing work of GDR literary historians and, before concluding with a summary of future directions and tasks, I would like to review briefly several contributions that have appeared since the collapse of the GDR. Among the anthologies *Verrat an der Kunst? Rückblicke auf die DDR-Literatur* (1993) in the title already implies the widespread approach of settling the accounts.[25] The formulation of the main title as a question does leave open the possibility of a "yes" or "no" response, but more significant is the presumed consensus about the "essence" of art, that there is some kind of pure aesthetic language or form or function against which betrayal can be measured. The title's "Rückblicke," rereadings from a post-1990 perspective of over twentyfive generally well-known, even popular GDR works (from poems to novels to dramas to essays), thematizes the present distance from past judgments. Because the authors (who include not only GDR specialists or literary scholars) were not expected to apply a common set of criteria, the various aspects they use to ground their revaluations and the uneven, sometimes contradictory manner of argumentation result in an agreeably differentiated image of production and reception in the GDR. Not intended as a synthesizing literary history, it nonetheless highlights important strategies for such an undertaking. For example, the literary qualities and popularity of Hermann Kant's novel *Die Aula* are not measured against his career as a party functionary; writers like Uwe Johnson and Günter Kunert, who left the GDR, or Adolf Endler, whose writing was hardly known there, are represented along with "canonical" names; and the extensive coverage given to underground writing of the 1980s points both to a reassessment of its importance and to how it was integrated into the literary landscape despite its exhibitionist gesture of refusal to participate.

A second anthology, the collection *Das bleibt: Deutsche Gedichte 1945-1995* edited by Jörg Drews, is a reader and therefore of interest in so far as it reveals how the process of canonization is proceeding in one genre.[26] The provocative, even provoking title, with its polemical reference to Christa Wolf's novella "Was bleibt" (1990) and the dismissive discussion about GDR literature it engendered, echoes the same triage principle alluded to in the title of the above-mentioned anthology, in this instance invigorated by a dose of ignorance. In the editor's lengthy, appended essay that details the selection criteria for poems from all the German-speaking countries, the reader finds the following comment: "Spannend wird es übrigens obendrein sein, wenn die Lyrik der DDR nach und nach noch einmal und unter veränderten Bedingungen zur Kenntnis genommen wird..." (259). Despite the pretension of presenting a balance sheet, Drews expresses here in the *future* tense his expectations for GDR poetry, admitting that—contrary to the reader's inference from the volume's title—he has not yet begun to sift through the material. Logically, then, his discussion of postwar poetry focuses exclusively on debates and theoretical issues from West Germany, Austria, and Switzerland, while the important hiatuses in the GDR development are not acknowledged, and therefore the "proper" poems could not be chosen to represent them. The relatively generous selection of GDR poems included in the anthology can not compensate for this willful, symptomatic blindness.

Three historical treatments of GDR literature have appeared as well in the past three years. Ralf Schnell's 1993 *Geschichte der deutschsprachigen Literatur seit 1945* is the least interesting of them both in its scope and approach.[27] Half of the volume is devoted to West German developments from 1949-89 in which much of the material comes from Schnell's 1986 volume *Die*

Literatur der Bundesrepublik (Metzler). Two short appendixes treat the literature of Switzerland and of Austria respectively, while two introductory chapters discuss general issues of literary life and the constitution of two literatures in Germany during the immediate postwar period 1945-49. The remaining quarter of the volume is devoted to GDR literature from 1949-89 in the traditional West German pattern of the 1980s: a chapter on cultural policy followed by cursory chapters on each of three periods divided by the building of the Wall in 1961 and the Biermann expatriation in 1976. Indeed, the author states explicitly in the forward that he is aiming for a social-historical survey of the two German literatures (X) and proceeds then to update previous attempts with similar hybrid results: a small selection of representative texts are "read" within a socio-political context, and literary life is presented as a social institution controlled by functionaries. Meanwhile the entire project of examining how this socio-political context is described and evaluated remains unexplored and unquestioned.

The 1994 *Geschichte der deutschen Literatur von 1945 bis zur Gegenwart*, edited by Wilfried Barner, is a curiously amphibious project.[28] Conceived in the late 1970s, the eight contributing authors had largely completed drafts of their chapters by November 1989, when suddenly the entire span of their historiography was thrown into a new light. Although the basic organizing principles remained the same, a logistical postponement of the publication deadline allowed for revisions and additional chapters on post-1989 shifts in the literary landscape. The result is a history of postwar German-language literature based on lessons drawn from shortcomings of predecessors that were adapted to the timely "present" position of a newly engendered closure to the postwar period. Its most striking feature is the synchronic approach that distinguishes West German, Austrian, and Swiss literature on the one hand and GDR literature on the other in their independent lines of development but also in their shared areas of interest. This unified perspective breaks down the material by means of relatively neutral, arbitrary periods measured by decades, and each decade is then surveyed in the East and the West so that the commonalities and mutual dependencies are foregrounded. Within each decade the presentation maintains the traditional approach of describing first the changes in the respective literary system followed by discussions of pertinent developments in the three main genres (prose, poetry, and drama as well as radio plays in West Germany) with brief reference to textual exponents and short author portraits. Although the authors' West German bias is sometimes visible (e.g., gaps or lack of clarity concerning the GDR's "structure of literary communication" or the imbalance in the treatment of the rich tradition of GDR radio plays), the volume's synthetic approach succeeds in establishing or suggesting new connections and comparisons between the respective systemic specificities of the postwar German literatures.

Wolfgang Emmerich's third, expanded and revised edition of the *Kleine Literaturgeschichte der DDR* (1996) is by far the most significant contribution to recent literary history of the GDR.[29] The earlier editions of 1981 and 1989 had already established him as one of the best informed and most discriminating GDR specialists in West Germany. A careful comparison of the nuanced shifts in accent and evaluation over fifteen years could in fact reveal much about changes in GDR literary historiography. This kind of treatment is, however, unfeasible in our context. Suffice it to note that the new edition is almost double in length, updating and extending the previous edition through the collapse of the GDR and unification into the mid-nineties. With over a hundred pages of bibliography, tabular chronologies, and an index, it will remain for the foreseeable future the standard, most informed overview of GDR literary developments. Since 1990 Emmerich has been a vocal and sensible advocate of rethinking and revising GDR literary historiography. Thus it is all the more remarkable to read in the opening pages to the new edition that on the one hand he has taken the step from what he calls an earlier mythologization to a historicization of GDR literature (9), while on the other his fundamental thesis and approach remain unchanged (18-19).[30]

Although he emphasizes that his perspective now is less absolute, not so unconditional, more sensitive and more skeptical than before, the same teleology of increasing autonomy and subjectivity that characterized his previous work guides his new judgments. From this perspective the forty-year history of GDR literature traces a progressive evolution from a pre-modern, closed society under the extra-literary control of dogmatic censorship that produced works of socialist realism to modern forms of resistance and systemic critique that culminated in experimental and avantgarde aesthetics.

Emmerich has repeatedly criticized reductive, teleological projections invested in GDR literature, as he does again in the introduction to this volume (17). Yet he himself invokes a fairly crude reflection theory of aesthetic value schooled on Adorno's and Horkheimer's notion of modernism as counter discourse. Thus, while the GDR's premodern socialism preserved "backward" forms of social life that were not yet instrumentalized like in the highly rationalized capitalist world, at the same time the repressive rule of the party and cultural policy produced more alienation and dissociation of the self than anything comparable in the West. In other words, the aesthetic emancipation of GDR literature obtains from a caricature of affirmative, socialist-realist mass culture that allegedly dominated GDR writing in the 1950s and 1960s and then gradually gave way to the critical (13), better (15), interesting (26) GDR literature of the 1970s and 1980s.[31] In this equation modern literature directly reflects the crisis of the social process of modernization, but the equation also raises questions unposed and unanswered by Emmerich about the supposed convergence of GDR literature with modernism in the 1980s. Was it merely a local GDR phenomenon, a "catching up" with the most advanced cultural forms already achieved in the capitalist West, or was it an escapist reaction to ubiquitous stagnation? If it was an expression of the more general fragmentation in advanced industrial societies, were GDR writers and citizens especially susceptible to such alienation, and if so, why did it become especially visible there?

Emmerich's ideology of modernist emancipation is augmented

by another, symptomatic feature of the new edition. Citing Bernhard Greiner (see note 19 above), he rejects the overtly political orientation of previous GDR scholarship, including his own, and gives priority now to the individual work of art as an aesthetic creation, to GDR literature *as* literature (27). I find this apology deceptive, since in practice Emmerich does continue to demonstrate, as in previous editions, that politics and cultural policy impacted literary production and reception in essential ways, now in fact with even more expansive background offered on the role of censorship and Stasi manipulation. Thus, his tendentious goal of purging historical and political considerations in order to salvage the aesthetic means or forms beyond specific meaning contradicts the very contours and cognitive interest of his own project.

An argument based on the binaries of politics/aesthetics or content/form strikes me in any case as a distinctly regressive gesture on Emmerich's part. To posit literature's "real" function in the realm of aesthetic form misconstrues the shift in discursive coordinates of cultural criticism. The optimistic dream of transforming the natural world for the masses is a view that dominated the political imagination in both the East and the West. With its dissipation the structure of its cultural discourse has also become a casualty of the Cold War. The similarities between modern forms of culture and organization—capitalism, socialism, fascism—emerge now in high relief.[32] They shared goals of mass production, mass transportation, mass housing, and mass loyalty and they sought comparable technological solutions to achieve them. They also produced similar cultural forms—monumental architecture, heroic imagery, constructivist principles—and similar social problems—rust belts, pollution, underemployment, alienation. There were fundamental differences in how these socio-political systems squandered human and natural resources or in how they controlled access to power, but they also constitute the shared past out of which the new globalization of art and culture has been emerging. Thus, it is important to recognize that aesthetic structures can be filled with essentially whatever content serves a specific purpose, and art may aim to mobilize (political) ideas, but it more directly mobilizes fantasy and desire. The global economy of advanced capitalism confronts us with a new cultural paradigm: autonomous history disappears, traditional regimes of political power no longer function, and national boundaries become superfluous in a mediatized world with ubiquitous digitalized communications ports and internationalized modes of consumerism.

This is the point where literary historiography of the GDR must now take the lead. The writing of literary history is always "in process," the process of telling a story that involves questions of judgment about the past and principles of weighing individual differences in order to establish larger lines or periods of evolution. When treating the literature of postwar Germany either common-alities or differences will emerge as more significant, depending on the methodological premises. Beyond such generalities it is possible to draw some consequences from past achievements and shortcomings that indicate tendencies at least for the immediate future. For example, because historiographical research during the last two decades has stressed the separate literary systems in East and West Germany, investigating complementary and compensatory aspects of their distinctive conditions and varying processes of development suggests itself. This might include attention to the dynamics of how literary groups and centers of literary activity formed or to generational shifts and relations of mentoring in both east and west. Common generational experiences such as war trauma, hopes for a new beginning, and authors' self-understanding as well as changing attitudes toward the status of elite and popular culture, toward metropolitan and regional identities could be compared. New criteria for periodization should be tested. For example, rather than considering GDR literature as an aberration or detour within the modernist paradigm, one could examine the earlier anti-modern turn over the entire spectrum of German literature around 1930 that extended through 1960 with distinctive accents determined by exile, inner emigration, the east/west split, etc. Alternately, one could situate GDR literature within a longer

German or even international tradition of working-class literature, of politically engaged writing that would include a critical and serious treatment of socialist realism as a subsystem in its own right with artistic languages, genres, and distinct trajectories in the various arts. Genre investigations promise fruitful new insights too. For example, a comparative investigation of lyric poetry and the work on poetic language during the fifties in both east and west might identify telling resemblances insofar as silences and the relation to tradition is concerned.   Also, comparing the nonsynchronous introduction of operative literary forms in East and West German literature could foreground the different function or relation to popular traditions in the respective contexts (e.g., traces of "Heimat" nostalgia in GDR production novels of the 1950s, or the revival of a "cult of the hero" in West German political literature of the 1960s). Finally, larger issues like the symmetrical refusal to engage a language of national discourse and the complementary displacement of the idea of "Germanness" into the opposition capitalism/socialism expose deeper layers of historically shared experience.

Such a list must remain partial and reflects my own interests, of course, yet it also suggests not a reduction or thinning out of the canon of GDR literature but its expansion as well as a more intensive focus on the earlier postwar period, especially before the 1960s. Access to new archive material, different typologies and categories, renaming and recharacterizing movements and periods, these are the tasks before us that will help us understand GDR literature as the imagined invention I mentioned earlier. Moreover, to accept Wolfgang Emmerich's justified call for a plurality of approaches does not mean that the collapse of socialism liberated us from Cold-War ideologies in order to deliver us into some kind of natural, non-ideological state of pluralism. Recent epistemological critiques have undermined the familiar notion of ideology as false consciousness because it assumes there exists a privileged position from which the truth can be known. But is there a place outside of ideology from which one might recognize the rationale and historical meaning of GDR literature and not immediately be branded as partisan and/or naive? The postmodern answer advises us to renounce the very notion of extra-ideological reality (in itself an ideological gesture) because everything is fictional, symbolic, discursive. I suggest instead that we must maintain the impossible position of distinguishing ideology from reality while at the same time recognizing how ideology is already at work in everything we experience as "reality."[33] Many theories of human activity seek to explain the fundamental tension or antagonism I am describing: cultural anthropology founded on violence, Freudian psychoanalysis rooted in the repressed, Marxism grounded in class struggle, etc. In contradistinction to them I suggest that we should understand ideology as this very epistemological gap. Irreducible to any totalizing or final explanation, the empty place called ideology in fact constitutes the very means by which we are able to conceptualize what we do, that is, separating the imagined from reality, relating text and context. What consequence follows from situating ourselves in this empty place called ideology? At the risk of sounding all too petty, it means for me that as literary historian I must constantly remain aware of this connecting particle "and," because it is the crucial element that defines boundaries and allows literary historiography to proceed. In short, I must understand the options, perspective, foreknowledge, and interest I bring to my work, or, to repeat: whose story is this?

Notes

1   See Michael Geyer and Konrad H. Jarausch, "Great Men and Postmodern Ruptures: Overcoming the 'Belatedness' of German Historiography," *German Studies Review* 18.2 (May 1995): 260, or note the title of Julia Hell, Loren Kruger, and Katie Trumpener, "Dossier: Socialist Realism and East German Modernism - Another Historians' Debate," *Rethinking Marxism* 7.3 (Fall 1994): 37-44.

2   This would be a kind of cultural archaeology indebted to Walter Benjamin's approach in the *Passagenwerk*; see Benjamin, *Gesammelte Schriften* V:1-2 (Frankfurt/Main, 1982).

3   The genealogy of the literary historical project in conjunction with the rise of European nationalisms in the nineteenth century is especially pertinent in Germany. For background, see Jürgen Fohrmann, *Das Projekt der deutschen Literaturgeschichte: Entstehung und Scheitern einer nationalen Poesiegeschichtschreibung zwischen Humanismus und Deutschem Kaiserreich* (Stuttgart, 1989), especially Part II: "Nation als Subjekt der Entelechie" (69-129); for a briefer overview, see Jost Hermand, "Die nationalliberale Welle," Hermand, *Geschichte der Germanistik* (Reinbek, 1994), 41-53.

4   See Jürgen Fohrmann, "Über das Schreiben von Literaturgeschichte," Peter J. Brenner, ed., *Geist, Geld und Wissenschaft: Arbeits- und Darstellungsformen von Literaturwissenschaft* (Frankfurt/Main, 1993), 180.

5   The category of "exile" has been applied to or claimed by those writers who left or were expelled from the GDR, for example, see Frank Goyke und Andreas Sinakowski, eds., *Jetzt wohin? Deutsche Literatur im deutschen Exil: Gespräche und Texte* (Berlin, 1990).

6   The discussions on the licensing of the "Kulturbund" by the Soviet Military Administration reveal the strategies for maintaining a united front; see Magdalene Heider, *Politik— Kultur—Kulturbund: Zur Gründungs- und Frühgeschichte des Kulturbunds zur demokratischen Erneuerung Deutschlands 1945-1954 in der SBZ/DDR* (Köln, 1993), especially chapter 6 (75-88). On the rapid deterioration of this unity, which already became visible by 1947, see Anneli Hartmann and Wolfram Eggeling, "Kontroverse Ost/West: Der I. Deutsche Schriftstellerkongreß: *ein* Beginn des kalten Krieges," *Internationales Archiv für Sozialgeschichte der deutschen Literatur* 17.1 (1992): 66-92.

7   See Walter Ulbricht, "Fragen der neuen deutschen Nationalliteratur: Aus der Diskussionsrede auf dem IV. Deutschen Schriftstellerkongress vom 9. bis 14. Januar 1956 in Berlin," Walter Ulbricht, *Zur Geschichte der deutschen Arbeiterbewegung: Aus Reden und Aufsätzen* 5 (Berlin, 1964), 590-99 (here 593). On Becher's notion of "Literaturgesellschaft," see "Von der Größe unserer Literatur: Rede auf dem IV. Schriftstellerkongreß der DDR," (1956), Johannes R. Becher, *Gesammelte Werke* 18 (Publizistik 4) (Berlin and Weimar, 1981), 499-534, especially 521.

8   Changes in wording of the GDR constitution reflected this shift in the official rhetoric of nation-building while avoiding the component of nation. In the 1968 constitution the GDR was defined as a "sozialistischer Staat deutscher Nation," and in the 1974 revision all references to "deutsch" were dropped, so that the GDR became "ein sozialistischer Staat der Arbeiter und Bauern." As a result the names of all institutions and agencies with the word "deutsch" were changed (e.g., Akademie der Künste der DDR), and the text of the national anthem, penned by Johannes R. Becher ("Deutschland, einig Vaterland"), was prohibited from being sung publically.

9   Ursula Heukenkamp draws attention to the fact that Georg Lukács's participation in the unsuccessful Hungarian reform movement in 1956 and Becher's death in 1958 made it easier for party functionaries to engage in this kind of political reductionism because the two most authoritative voices that had argued for literature's relative autonomy no longer were to be heard. Heukenkamp's article touches on some of the same issues I am concerned with here; see "*Eine* Geschichte oder *viele* Geschichten der deutschen Literatur seit 1945? Gründe und Gegengründe," *Zeitschrift für Germanistik* 5.1 (1995): 22-37, here 31.

10 On the collective identity of a "Wir-Gefühl," see my essay "Speaking with Silence: Intellectuals and the New Germany," *German Politics and Society* 29 (Summer 1993), 83-103 (here

95).

11 Claus Träger, "Zweierlei Geschichte - zweierlei Literatur: Einige Aspekte zur literarischen Situation in Deutschland," Träger, *Studien zur Literaturtheorie und vergleichenden Literaturgeschichte* (Leipzig, 1970), 346-372. Volume 11 of the official GDR literary history was edited by a scholarly collective at the Akademie der Wissenschaften under the direction of Horst Haase (Berlin, 1976); volume 12 focused on literature of the FRG.

12 Rainer Rosenberg, who was a member of the editorial committee and participating author of the GDR's *Geschichte der deutschen Literatur* called this approach retrospectively "eine marxistisch umgestülpte Geistesgeschichte" in Rosenberg, "Zur Geschichte der Literaturwissenschaft in der DDR," *Zeitschrift für Germanistik*, 1.2 (1991): 252.

13 See, for example, Manfred Naumann, ed., *Gesellschaft - Literatur - Lesen: Literaturrezeption in theoretischer Sicht* (Berlin und Weimar, 1973), Dieter Schlenstedt, ed., *Funktion der Literatur: Aspekte—Probleme—Aufgaben* (Berlin, 1975), and Dieter Schlenstedt, *Wirkungsästhetische Analysen: Poetologie und Prosa in der neueren DDR-Literatur* (Berlin, 1979).

14 "Für unser Land," Volker Gransow and Konrad H. Jarausch, eds., *Die deutsche Vereinigung: Dokumente zu Bürgerbewegung, Annäherung und Beitritt* (Köln, 1991), 100-101.

15 Enzensberger's apodictic comment appeared in a review of Uwe Johnson's novel *Mutmaßungen über Jakob*, which he regarded on the contrary as an example of "gesamtdeutsche" literature. The reference is quoted in Ursula Heukenkamp, "Ortsgebundenheit: Die DDR-Literatur als Variante des Regionalismus in der deutschen Nachkriegsliteratur," *Weimarer Beiträge* 42.1 (1996): 32 (note 9), and the original is to be found in Enzensberger, *Einzelheiten* (Frankfurt/Main, 1962), 234-39; Hans Mayer, "Über die Einheit der deutschen Literatur," Mayer, *Zur deutschen Literatur der Zeit:*

Zusammenhänge, Schriftsteller, Bücher (Reinbek, 1967), 344-57.

16 See Helmut Peitsch, "West German Writers and 9 November 1989," Arthur Williams, Stuart Parker, and Roland Smith , eds., *German Literature at a Time of Change 1989-1990* (Bern, 1991), 151 (note 21).

17 See, for example, Kindler's *Geschichte der Gegenwartsliteratur* (1971-76) with four volumes on the literatures of the FRG, Austria, Switzerland, and the GDR; Fischer Verlag's *Sozialgeschichte der deutschen Literatur von 1918 bis zur Gegenwart* (1981) treats the GDR separately from the FRG, which in this case includes Switzerland and Austria, apparently because the latter belong to the same marketing system; volume 3 (Part 2) on the period 1945-80 of Athenäum's *Geschichte der deutschen Literatur vom 18. Jahrhundert bis zur Gegenwart* (1984) has separate sections for the GDR and the FRG; Hanser Verlag's *Sozialgeschichte der deutschen Literatur* has a separate volume (volume 11, 1983) on the GDR. For background on the discussion of "two German literatures," see the early survey of positions in Eberhard Mannack, *Zwei deutsche Literaturen?* (Kronberg/Ts., 1977), the useful report by Jörg Schönert, "Identität und Alterität zweier literarischer Kulturen in der Bundesrepublik und DDR als Problem einer interkulturellen Germanistik," Alois Wierlacher, ed., *Das Fremde und das Eigene: Prolegomena zu einer interkulturellen Germanistik* (München, 1985), 212-33 (with bibliography), and the most recent contribution to the debate by Rainer Rosenberg (a literary historian from the GDR), "Was war DDR-Literatur? Die Diskussion um den Gegenstand in der Literaturwissenschaft der Bundesrepublik Deutschland," *Zeitschrift für Germanistik* 5.1 (1995): 9-21.

18 For the most complete overview, see the extensive bibliography (especially section 4 on anthologies and section 7 on surveys of GDR literature) in the most recent, revised, third edition of Wolfgang Emmerich, *Kleine Geschichte der*

DDR (Leipzig, 1996).

19 In a "Forschungsbericht" published in 1983 already and frequently cited since 1990 Bernhard Greiner summarized the deficits of this kind of approach to GDR literature in five theses; see "DDR-Literatur als Problem der Literaturwissenschaft," Paul Gerhard Klussmann and Heinrich Mohr, eds., *Probleme deutscher Identität. Jahrbuch zur Literatur in der DDR* 3 (Bonn, 1983), 233 - 262.

20 The theoretical and empirical work on convergence theories was mainly centered—although not confined to—a group of scholars in West Berlin around Peter C. Ludz and later Hartmut Zimmermann. For a general, critical overview, see Gerd Meyer, "Die westdeutsche DDR- und Deutschlandforschung im Umbruch: Probleme und Perspektiven in den Sozialwissenschaften," *Deutschland-Archiv* 3 (1992): 273-85.

21 On Mayer's and Raddatz's revision, see Theo Buck, "Deutsche Literatur, deutsche Literaturen? Zur Frage der Einheit der deutschen Literatur seit 1945," Heinz Ludwig Arnold, ed., *Bestandsaufnahme Gegenwartsliteratur*. Sonderband *Text und Kritik* (München, 1988): 188 (note 21).

22 Wolfgang Emmerich, *Kleine Literaturgeschichte der DDR*. 1st edition (Darmstadt und Neuwied, 1981).

23 For representative expressions of German self-identity, see Günter Grass's novel, *Kopfgeburten oder Die Deutschen sterben aus* (Darmstadt and Neuwied, 1980), and speeches by Martin Walser, "Über Deutschland reden (Ein Bericht)," Walser, *Über Deutschland reden* (Frankfurt/Main, 1989), 76-100, by Stephan Hermlin, "In den Kämpfen dieser Zeit: Rede vor der VIII. Schriftstellerkongreß der DDR am 30. Mai 1978", Hermlin, *Aufsätze. Reportage. Reden. Interviews* (München, 1980), 123-35 (here 126), and even by the President of the Writers Union, Hermann Kant, "Rede," *X. Schriftstellerkongreß der DDR: Plenum* (Berlin and Weimar, 1988), 21-52 (here 31).

24 See the volume of collected essays with bibliography under this title, Karl Deiritz and Hannes Krauss, eds., *Der deutsch-deutsche Literaturstreit oder "Freunde, es spricht sich schlecht mit gebundener Zunge": Analysen und Materialien* (Hamburg and Zürich, 1991). On the "melodramatic conflict ... of Cold War discourse," see Hell, Kruger, and Trumpener,41.

25 Karl Deiritz und Hannes Krauss, eds., *Verrat an der Kunst? Rückblicke auf die DDR-Literatur* (Berlin, 1993).

26 Jörg Drews, ed., *Das bleibt: Deutsche Gedichte 1945-1995* (Leipzig, 1995).

27 Ralf Schnell, *Geschichte der deutschsprachigen Literatur seit 1945* (Stuttgart and Weimar, 1993).

28 Wilfried Barner, ed., *Geschichte der deutschen Literatur von 1945 bis zur Gegenwart* (München, 1994). The eight contributing authors are Wilfried Barner, Alexander von Bormann, Manfred Durzak, Anne Hartmann, Manfred Karnick, Thomas Koebner, Lothar Köhn, and Jürgen Schröder.

29 Emmerich, *Kleine Literaturgeschichte der DDR*; the first edition was published in 1981, the second in Spring 1989.

30 See Emmerich's various contributions to conference proceedings, which by and large repeat similar considerations brought together in the introductory chapter of the new *Kleine Literaturgeschichte* (11-28), e.g., "Do We Need to Rewrite German Literary History Since 1945? A German Perspective," Friederike Eigler and Peter C. Pfeiffer, eds., *Cultural Transformations in the New Germany: American and German Perspectives* (Columbia, SC, 1993), 117-131, reprinted in German as "Für eine andere Wahrnehmung der DDR-Literatur. Neue Kontexte, neue Pragdigmen, ein neuer Kanon," Emmerich, *Die andere deutsche Literatur: Aufsätze zur Literatur aus der DDR* (Opladen, 1994), 190-207 as well as in a slightly earlier version in Arthur Goodbody and Dennis Tate, eds., *Geist und Macht: Writers and the State in the GDR*. Special issue of *The German Monitor* (Amsterdam/Atlanta, 1992), 7-22. Emmerich's collection of previously published

essays from the mid-1980s to the early 1990s, *Die andere Literatur*, reflects this ongoing reflection process.

31 For a similar critique of Emmerich based already on his 1989 version of the *Kleine Literaturgeschichte der DDR*, see Hell, Kruger, and Trumpener, 38-39.

32 This was the topic of a major European exhibit co-produced in London, Barcelona, and Berlin; see "Kunst und Macht im Europa der Diktatoren 1930 bis 1945," exhibit at the Deutsches Historisches Museum (Berlin, 1996); the catalog under the same title was edited by David Britt (Stuttgart, 1996).

33 For a dense but well-argued critique of the status of ideology today, see Slavoj Žižek, "The Spectre of Ideology," Žižek, ed., Mapping Ideology (London and New York, 1994), 1-33. Although I have extracted it from his Lacanian framework, I am indebted to his elaboration of ideology as an empty place, especially p. 17 and 28.

Jay Rosellini

Response

Although I do not normally find it difficult to critique other people's writings, this is a special case. This coming January, it will be 25 years since I first met Marc on a wintry day in Bloomington. We by no means agreed about everything, but our ways of thinking about culture and politics were very similar—or so it seemed at the time. I well remember how Marc, when a young visiting assistant professor, was chastised by a senior faculty member for hanging a "communist" poster on his office wall. (I think that it had a Brecht poem on it, either "Lob des Revolutionärs" or "Die unbesiegliche Inschrift.") Now he seems to embrace the challenges and new paradigm of the global economic and cultural marketplace as a creative stimulus, whereas I am frozen in time, as it were. Despite all that I have learned and experienced in the past quarter-century, I still believe that the "Enlightenment Project" is relevant for today's world. This of course affects the way in which I view the literary and political history of the GDR. I find myself between a rock and a hard place, because I reject both Emmerich's new re-primatization of esthetics and Marc's new and improved totalitarianism theory that sees only minor differences between capitalism, socialism, and fascism. I also find little solace in the standpoint of someone like George Steiner, who rejects the "nihilistic merriments of deconstruction and post-modernity" but proposes a return to metaphysics as an alternative to the humanities, that, in his words, "do not, as a rule, humanize."[1] One explanation for my fossilization might be an autobiographical one. Without boring you with an account of "German Lessons" analogous to Alice Kaplan's "French Lessons,"[2] I should at least point out that Marc grew up in an academic household, whereas I lived in a house without books, music, or art. I am still suffering from a severe case of *Ungleichzeitigkeit*. You might be wondering why I have bothered to go into this at all. I think that I felt it was necessary because although Marc stated in his last sentence that as a literary historian, he must "constantly remain aware of the options, perspective, fore-knowledge, and interest" that he brings to his work, these things were not articulated directly in his paper.

Whose story is this, anyway? It is ours in the sense that we are Germanists, but neither of us is German, although we both are capable of the "double optics" of which John McCarthy and Jeffrey Sammons have spoken.[3] I do wonder, as Marc says himself, why it is so "urgent" to reconsider the literary history of the GDR. Reconsidering the history of GDR Studies in the US, a task to be undertaken by the graduate student collective later this afternoon, is quite a different matter, and an important one. I predict that most of the myriad revisionist publications that have appeared in the past seven years will be relegated to the dust bin of literary history or studied by future generations of literary sociologists as examples of personal vendettas or political polemics. This of course will depend to a great extent on coming historical developments. If Francis Fukuyama's thesis about the "end of history"[4] proves to be absolutely wrong—and events in places like Bosnia, Iraq, and Rwanda point in this direction—, our assessment of the failed "socialist experiment" (not my term) and its accompanying cultural production could be very different. For now, I find Marc's description of the three typical responses to the shift quite accurate. Those who reject forty years of complex reality *in toto* are in all likelihood burying part of their own identity to keep it from the scrutiny of others. Those who engage in "public self-flagellation" may well be opportunists hoping for crumbs from the table of the new powers that be. Those who examine GDR literature as a "repository of past dreams" are easily the most sympathetic, although this assessment is doubtless colored by my belief that most human beings need some kind of *telos* in their lives. (I am thinking of a *telos* that goes beyond a home theater with surround sound and two dozen sports and shopping channels.) If the present German *telos*, namely material prosperity, were to ebb away—and it is actually doing that already for certain sectors of society—, it will again become kosher to speak of utopias. One minor criticism of

Marc's categorizations would be that utopian narratives are not always fictions of "failed" alternative histories. The Enlightenment is one example of a utopia whose realization has been spatially and temporally fragmented. Its complete history has not yet been written, and it may never be finished (please indulge my utopian streak, if you can).

The attitude toward the idea of utopia and the preservation of memory might prove to be the most useful categories when attempting to find the proper place for GDR literature in German literary history. Both can be traced back to the need to transcend the immediate present, and such a need of course stems from a complete or partial dissatisfaction with and alienation from that present. (This was a very German phenomenon long before 1945.) In the case of post-fascist Germany, most writers of any stature quickly realized that the old German dream of true democracy would not be put into practice in the context of the Cold War. In addition, the apparent triumph of repression over *Trauerarbeit* meant that literature had to take over the task of preserving the memory of recent horrors. Seen against this backdrop, there are many similarities between Christa Wolf and Günter Grass, Günter de Bruyn and Martin Walser, Jürgen Fuchs and Günter Wallraff, Wolf Biermann and Erich Fried, Erika Runge and Maxie Wander, Günter Kunert and Hans Magnus Enzensberger, Volker Braun and Heinar Kipphardt, Irmtraud Morgner and Ingeborg Bachmann, etc. (One can imagine why I have not paired Heiner Müller with anyone.)   As you may have noticed, this list contains only one writer whose political coming-of-age happened after 1968, namely Jürgen Fuchs. I readily admit that the younger generations of GDR authors are much more difficult to pigeonhole. Actually, the division undertaken by the authors and editors of *Hansers Sozialgeschichte* [5] might have staying power: The year 1968, in which the hopes for a post-Soviet *and* post-capitalistic Europe were first raised, then dashed, will, in my view, be seen as perhaps more significant than the year 1989. Our new world order—in economics, politics, and culture—was born in 1968 and merely came to the fore in 1989. Lest this sound too Hegelian, I hasten to add that the life experiences of real people between 1968 and 1989 should not be brushed aside as mere historical footnotes.

This brings me to the question of morality. Marc has emphasized that literary history is concerned with "values," but not with "moral judgments." He characterizes a "morally charged understanding of literature's relation to truth and beauty" as a thing of the past. I myself am not a disciple of Shaftesbury, who linked ethical and esthetic judgment, simply because the ethical is much more important to me. When I castigated Peter Hacks for his slander of the just-expatriated Biermann,[6] my motive was moral indignation. This indignation clearly was related to utopian dreams: I expected more of someone who, at least on the surface, was striving for a just society. The relationship between talent and character is hardly a new theme, but any literary scholar who made it one of the underpinnings of his history of GDR literature would be justified in doing so. I would add just one proviso: This should not be done only when looking to the east, but also when examining the literary life *westlich der Elbe*. It will no longer do to excoriate Grass for his critique of the new Germany and simultaneously celebrate Ernst Jünger as the "grand old man of German letters."[7] In a similar vein, those who criticize Christa Wolf's lack of civil courage should also warn of the dangers inherent in the recent pronouncements of Handke and Strauß. The "empty place" that interests me is not ideology, but the place in which the left is willing and able to speak of moral values, just as the left is finally attempting to say something meaningful about the concept of *Heimat*. A history of GDR literature is as good a place as any to start.

My vision of our "work" is a bit different than Marc's, at least as it is articulated in his final paragraph. Rather than "relating literature to its context," I strive to delve into the essence of the entire context by beginning with an analysis of one sector of this context, namely, the literary one. This is partly the result of my professional training, but it is also a product of the realization that the rise of specialization has rendered a *Gesamtschau* almost impossible. Literature is one of the few sectors where all aspects of our private and social being can be examined and related to each other. If I believed in conspiracy theories, I would think that the chronic underfunding of "logocentric" humanities departments is meant as an attack on that last bastion of non-specialization. Jacob Grimm's defense of the "Wert der ungenauen Wissenschaften" at the first meeting of Germanists in Frankfurt in 1846[8] is perhaps the first signpost on the way to German Studies as much more than literary or linguistic scholarship. My proclivity for this model motivates me to recommend the short history of GDR literature found in the 1995 volume *German Cultural Studies. An Introduction* edited by Rob Burns.[9] Here, no apology is made for the utilization of historical and political milestones as points of departure for literary analysis. I sympathize with the editor's conviction, taken from Raymond Williams, that the view of culture as a "'whole way of life,' the entire mental and material habitat of a distinct people or social group," provides more insight into the "general system" than an exclusive focus on *E-Kultur*.[10] The British Germanists who contributed to this volume stumble here and there, but their cultural studies orientation could well be the most fruitful one when dealing with "the little state that couldn't."

Notes

1   George Steiner, commencement address at Kenyon College [1996], excerpted in *The Chronicle of Higher Education*, June 21, 1996, B6.
2   Alice Kaplan, *French Lessons* (Chicago and London 1993).
3   John A. McCarthy, "Double Optics: The Americanization of Germanistik—The Germanization of Americans," in *The Future of Germanistik in the USA* (Nashville 1996), ed. John A. McCarthy and Katrin Schneider, 1ff.
4   Francis Fukuyama, *The End of History and the Last Man* (New York 1992).

5   Gegenwartsliteratur seit 1968, ed. Klaus Briegleb and Sigrid Weigel (München/Wien 1992), *Hansers Sozialgeschichte der deutschen Literatur vom 16. Jahrhundert bis zur Gegenwart,* Band 12. All of GDR literature is treated in one volume, i.e., Band 11.

6   Jay Rosellini, *Wolf Biermann* (München 1992), 89.

7   Not all of the many responses to the author's 100th birthday were positive, but the outpouring had a clear subtext, namely that Jünger is a truly incomparable figure worthy of our attention.

8   Cited in Johannes Janota, "Einleitung," *Eine Wissenschaft etabliert sich,* ed. J. Janota (Tübingen 1980), 8. (*Deutsche Texte,* ed. Gotthart Wunberg: *Texte zur Wissenschafts-geschichte der Germanistik III.)*

9   *German Cultural Studies. An Introduction* (Oxford/New York 1995). The chapter on GDR literature, entitled "The Failed Socialist Experiment: Culture in the GDR," was written by the well-known specialists Axel Goodbody, Dennis Tate, and Ian Wallace.

10 Rob Burns, "Introduction," *German Cultural Studies. An Introduction,* 1.

Julia Hell

Critical Orthodoxies, Old and New, or The Fantasy of a Pure Voice: Christa Wolf

Since 1989, those of us who specialize in the GDR have been in the process of rewriting its literary and cultural history.[1] Already a new story is emerging, one that sees East German literature as the gradual development of an authentic feminist modernism. For instance, in 1995, Oxford University Press published a volume entitled *German Cultural Studies*. The chapter on the GDR locates the story of East German literature in a teleology of convergence: according to the authors of this piece, the differences between the cultures of East and West Germany gradually faded as both literatures became more concerned with questions of women's emancipation, peace, and ecology. At the same time, East German literature is "modernized." By this I mean the authors' idea that "from the late 1960s, the GDR's leading writers began to learn from and use the literary strategies of modernism."[2] In the ensuing period, the argument continues, a genuine "cultural identity" materialized. This Golden Age in comparison to the period preceding it is marked by the emergence of an "authentic narrative voice of female authors."[3]

A similar account can be found in Barbara Einhorn's book *Cinderella Goes To Market* (1993),[4] and in recent articles by Dorothea Boeck,[5] and Allison Lewis.[6] The former East German literary critic Ursula Heukenkamp is most explicit in this attempt to "redeem" East German literature through its women's literature. Polemically arguing against a characterization of GDR literature as "regional literature, child of the provinces, in the middle of modernity," Heukenkamp concludes her discussion with an emphatic defense of East Germany's women's literature. The argument runs as follows: because the GDR's early literature responded exclusively to the expectations of East Germany's cultural politics, today this moralizing and didactic non-art is rightfully forgotten; although the literature of the 1960s sketched a new model of communication, it too, was flawed because of its utopian dimension. Developing in the 1970s, women's literature overcomes this flaw: it is pragmatic, not utopian - and therefore, still valid.[7]

This view of East German literature as the slow emergence of a (feminist) modernism is not new. It basically follows Wolfgang Emmerich's periodization of GDR culture into the pre-modern, modern, and postmodern. Like feminist critics before '89, the post-89 version merely foregrounds what remained implicit in Emmerich's story, namely the centrality of Christa Wolf's writing, in particular the pivotal position occupied by her 1968 novel *Nachdenken Über Christa T.*. There is thus a strong continuity, a strong commitment to the following core ideas: first, the privileging of modernism and the concomitant investment in the period from the sixties to the mid-eighties as the Golden Age of East German literature; second, the overt rejection or simple neglect of the GDR's early literature, the "dark" and embarrassing ages of socialist realism; third, the reliance on an underlying teleology. What I mean by that is: Emmerich saw the emancipation of the authors' voice from the GDR's official political and aesthetic discourse in the writers' increasing mastery of modernist techniques and growing awareness of the dialectic of enlightenment. Similarly, in the emergence of a feminist consciousness and its autonomous feminine aesthetic, these post-89 critics find a growing liberation from the official patriarchal ideology. The core notion of these stories is modernism's "authentic voice," a voice that succeeded in establishing a critical distance toward the GDR's dominant ideology. In all accounts, this voice is derived from Christa Wolf's concept of subjective authenticity which Wolf defined as a speaking position based on experience,[8] this difficult attempt of "saying 'I'"—to quote from Christa T.[9]

Of course, there are alternative accounts. Bernd Hüppauf, for instance, argues that the GDR's "nineteenth-century" political universe corresponded to a nineteenth-century aesthetics lacking the wordplay and negativity typical for the literature of the West.[10] This argument is as reductionist as the new kind of post-89 historiography which characterizes the GDR as premodern, as another German *Sonderweg*.[11] But I don't want to discuss this revival of modernization theory and its problems here. Instead, I want to discuss the emergence of a feminine voice with respect to the critics' prime example, Christa Wolf.

Not surprisingly, critics do not agree on how to understand the components of this literary historical event—how they understand authenticity, or feminine, or even voice. Among the literature mentioned above, we can discern three different takes: For Barbara Einhorn, "authenticity" means the portrayal of women's "real" lives under socialism.[12] The emergence of a female narrator is understood on two different levels: 1) within a liberal framework as the opposition between the monoperspective of socialist realism and a form of writing that introduces multiple perspectives; 2) in terms of a gendered opposition between the universal and the particular, that is the female narrator is pictured as a counterpart to socialist realism's universal male narrator. Sometimes, the notion of "feminine writing" props up, yet remains untheorized. Other critics work more explicitly with this concept. Sonja Hilzinger for instance isolates the increasing "subjectivization of narration"[13] as one of the first signs of a new feminine aesthetic. After this initial break with the monoperspective of (socialist) realism,[14] Cassandra's "alien" voice is then later conceptualized as the eruption of the semiotic into the symbolic order. This is a quote from Hilzinger:

> Voice stands in for the female body which is not realized
> but rather repressed in the act of speaking, or narrating—
> just like eroticism, sexuality, femininity in general.[15]

A recent essay by Löwy and Sayre will serve as the last example. In this essay, the authors trace Wolf's "Marxist/feminist utopia" throughout her entire work. Wolf, they write, equates instrumental rationality with patriarchy. In their account, subjective authenticity is then but an epiphenomenon of that underlying philosophical paradigm, the literary expression of a philosophy of modernity as increasing alienation.[16] *Subjective authenticity is thus variously conceptualized as a break with socialist realism and the appropriation of voice on the part of a young woman author, as a marxist feminism in the tradition of German romantic anticapitalism, or as another way of writing altogether.* These elements are all present in Wolf's work—indeed, Wolf would be the first to agree to that.

In my reading of voice in Wolf, I nevertheless propose to leave aside the relationship between *Kulturpolitik* and actual literary practice, and between marxist discourse and feminist critique for a moment. Instead I want to concentrate on a different level, the level of unconscious fantasies about the body and about voice. My overarching argument is, first, that the GDR's dominant ideological discourse, that of antifascism, took the form of a family narrative, a paternal narrative organized around the figure of the father as antifascist hero. Second, Wolf is the writer most thoroughly implicated in this discourse: she accepted this ideological story as the framework of her early writing, and she contributed to its writing in her own novels—novels which often revolve around a young woman, the figure of the daughter. So far, what I am describing here is known to everyone familiar with Wolf's work and her interviews: the post-war family romance of replacing "real," i.e. fascist parents, with new communist fathers and mothers.[17] But I am not so much interested in this part of the story. What I want to draw attention to is what happens once this framework is in place, namely, 1) the production of fantasies about the post-fascist subject's body, and, 2) the production of fantasies about her post-fascist voice. Both, fantasies about body and fantasies about voice, involve processes of identification with parental figures, and both involve a specific concept of the communist's body as a sublime body.

Before continuing with my argument, I want to emphasize three things: first, Wolf is not the only writer involved in this project—what I am analyzing is a cultural discourse, not the idiosyncrasies of one particular author. Other authors—Brigitte Reimann, Dieter Noll, and Irmtraut Morgner, to name only three—participate in this paternal narrative. However, what makes Wolf's contribution unique is the fact that, starting with "Moskauer Novelle" (1961), her texts explore the post-fascist body's voice, an exploration which eventually has significant repercussions for the process of narration itself. In Wolf's texts, voice becomes the symptom of the body and its relationship to the past. Second, this approach makes it imperative to return to Wolf's early texts, to abandon this neat separation of dark and golden ages. And third, this is not a psychobiography—I make no claim about the author Christa Wolf and her psyche.[18] I am reading fantasies inscribed in literary texts and aesthetic essays—what their relationship to Christa Wolf's fantasies is a mystery, to us as readers, and most probably to Wolf herself. Finally, a point about procedure: in this article, I will first focus on two texts, "Moskauer Novelle" (1961) and *Kassandra* (1983) with a brief digression through *Der geteilte Himmel* (1963). That is of course a bit of a chronological leap, but a leap that has its advantages: while it forces me to leave out a lot of intermediate arguments, it will clarify the argument. Only then will I return to the text which the story of feminist modernism is based on, *Nachdenken über Christa T.*, discussing it from a new vantage point, the focus on the connection between (un-)conscious fantasies about body and voice.

I. Paternal Narratives, Post-Fascist Bodies, and A Post-Fascist Voice:

First, the term paternal narratives. As has often been pointed out, the Literaturstreit—the controversy in the summer of 1990 around Wolf's *Was bleibt*—was also a controversy about the GDR.[19] The categories which have since been used are familiar: the rather simplistic notion of *Unrechtsstaat*; dictatorship, the designation agreed upon by the parliamentary committee on GDR history; and, finally, the notion of totalitarianism. This category informs, for instance, Sigrid Meuschel's highly influential *Legitimation und Parteiherrschaft in der DDR*. Meuschel argues that all attempts to increase the autonomy of economic, cultural, and social processes were blocked by the SED, resulting in complete social immobilization.[20]The arguments against this version of totalitarianism theory are familiar: first, emphasizing state repression, this version of totalitarianism cannot account for the intricate pattern of conformity and resistance characterizing the GDR. Second, this approach collapses *project* and reality, the SED's political-ideological program and its actual effects. In contrast to Meuschel, Claude Lefort theorizes totalitarianism as a political-ideological project, involving the propagation of a one-party rule, and a fantasy of social homogeneity. This social fantasy is metaphorically embodied in the notion of the People-as-One *and* in the image of the leader's *body*. This theory draws our attention to the issue of the representation of power: under the ancien regime, the king's body represented the body politic and its center; in democratic societies, power is no longer linked to the body, the locus of power is empty. The various movements of post-democratic totalitarianism, Lefort argues, can be understood as attempts to revitalize the body's *symbolic* function and to *re-present the center*.[21]

What does this mean for post-war Germany? Following the collapse of National Socialism and its political imaginary, organized around Hitler's body, the locus of power was empty. For the SED, reconstruction involved creating a new symbolic order, and the center of this new order was constructed by deploying a *symbolic politics of paternity*, a cultural discourse centered around the Antifascist Father. This discourse characterizes the political speeches and essays of the immediate post-war period; but, above all, it is developed in literature. Between 1945 and 59, Willi Bredel, Hans Marchwitza, Anna Seghers, and Otto Gotsche published several novels which told the GDR's pre-history as a family narrative, focusing on the lineage from father to son.[22]

These foundational narratives, or fictions of the antifascist father display the male body as a sublime body. Re-surfacing in the discussions of Socialist Realism after 1945, the notion of the sublime came to designate the "image of unlimited power." The following is a Soviet quote from 1950 calling for a literature centered around images of Soviet leaders:

> The sublime beauty of the leaders . . . is the basis for the coinciding of the 'beautiful' and the 'true' in the art of socialist realism.[23]

Slavoj Zizek theorizes this *sublime* body as the *communist leader's "split" body*. Like the body of the medieval king, the communist's body is divided into the sublime and the material, the mystical and the organic. Its sublime part is linked to a transcendent truth— Stalinism's "Laws of History." And it is contained by what Zizek calls a "transient material envelopment,"[24] that part of the body which functions as mere material support, and which needs to be constantly steeled. In the East German narratives, the *sublime communist body* takes on two different forms: on the one hand, there is the "hardened," disciplined and ascetic body, an imagery that focuses on sheer physical strength. Bredel's and Tschesno-Hell's *Thälmann* films come to mind, or the monumental sculptures representing the communist pantheon dispersed throughout the former Eastern bloc, and now discarded to the graveyards of socialist realism.[25] On the other hand, the communist body becomes a body-in-pain, a sublime body resisting under torture. Thus, Otto Gotsche's *Fahne von Kriwoj Rog* (1959), for instance, culminates in a series of torture scenes. Excerpts from this novel which was commissioned for the 40th anniversary of the Bolshevic Revolution were published in Neue deutsche Literatur. They were introduced by Christa Wolf, and arranged to focus on these torture scenes.[26] Let me quote two passages from this novel, exemplifying these two versions of the sublime communist body, and the idea of a split body:

> His body stiffened rebelliously . . . The stout man of

medium height made a fist . . . and raised it to greet the comrades to whom his letter was addressed across thousands of kilometers (DF/16).

The next quote refers to the scene when Brosowski is tortured by the SA:

They turned Brosowski like a spindle around himself, so that his joints cracked and blood spilled from his mouth. He remained silent.
Did he weaken once?—No. He could say that with a good conscience. His body might fail, his arms, legs, hearing— he did not fail.
He was hanging like a ball of tangled ropes on the wall, he moaned, drawn-out and dangling from the window frame, his dislocated joints swollen and red, he no longer possessed a body.
What remained of it was the Communist Brosowski. Ribs, bones, sinews—they no longer belonged to him. They could take it and trample it, they could burn it and break it and hang it. Only the brain was still there, and the thoughts—they belonged to the Communist Brosowski. And he remained silent.[27]

The latter quote seemingly contradicts the idea of a split body ("he no longer possessed a body"). But let me point to this other level of contradiction, the contradiction between what is stated and what is represented. The entire segment draws its affective power from the minutely executed *representation* of a body-in-pain, a representation bordering in its effect, I would argue, on sadism. Far from eliminating this material body—again: "he no longer possessed a body"—the text creates and deploys the body-in-pain and its horrifying dismemberment as the indispensable support of Brosowski, the communist.

What happens in the transition from this foundational literature to the literature of the early 1960s, that is in the transition from the literature of the fathers to the literature of the sons and daughters? And what happens in the transition from the ideological fantasy of the father's sublime body to the fantasy of the post-fascist body? Being a communist means having a communist body, a body which is more than a mere material support. On the territory of East Germany's history, this fantasy takes on a specific form: the material part of the communist's transcendent body is fantasized as non-sexual, the fascist body as sexual. Why this focus on sexuality?

The armored body of the antifascist fighter, the very incarnation of the military avantgarde, was created as an attempt to establish firm boundaries against feminine sexuality. Not in Theweleit's sense as a phobic reaction, but rather as a reaction against femininity as that which represents castration, that is, *weakness*, or *defeat*.[28] The emergence of the postfascist body with the GDR's *Aufbaugeneration* introduces that generation's own problematic. In the narratives of this generation, the sexual body is no longer a signifier of weakness; instead, it signifies an "impure" past, replacing the dichotomy of weakness versus strength with that of purity versus impurity. There is thus, on the one hand, a continuity along a specific register of fantasy, where the body is imagined along the lines of sexuality. On the other hand, there is, I would argue, a carry-over of National Socialist discourses on "purity"—of the people, of the body.

What do I base this reading on? The texts I have in mind— novels like Brigitte Reimann's *Ankunft im Alltag*, Dieter Noll's *Werner Holt. Roman einer Heimkehr*, Wolf's "Moskauer Novelle" and *Der geteilte Himmel*, but also some of the so-called *Produktionsromane*[29]—all revolve around a conflict between their young protagonists and their "new" parental figures. The conflict extends into what at first seems only an insignificant sub-plot, the novels' love story. It is on the level of this apparent sub-plot and its fantasies about the body, not on the level of the protagonists' changing consciousness, that we can trace the novels' link to the paternal narrative of antifascism. I am thus changing the level of

analysis from political discourse to that of conscious and
unconscious fantasies. In these texts, sexuality as that part of
subjectivity which is tied most inextricably to the fascist past has to
be split off, contained. Or, in terms of plot, the story of forbidden
love has to come to an end.

How do Wolf's texts fit into this? "Moskauer Novelle" (1961)
thematizes the transition from a National Socialist to a communist
father figure; it positions its female protagonist as daughter; and
narrates a conflict with these "new" parental figures, a conflict
which involves the story of forbidden love. And the resolution of
this conflict generates the fantasy of a pure body, "cleansed" of its
past. Let me argue this in more detail, starting with a brief synopsis
of the text: "Moskauer Novelle" focuses on Vera and her trip to the
Soviet Union in 1959. The delegation's translator, Pawel Koschkin,
is a former officer of the Red army who fought in Germany in 1945.
Vera and Pawel met in 1945 and it was Pawel's influence that
turned her into a communist. During the trip in '59, they resume
their relationship. This involves massive guilt on Vera's part, not
only because she is married, but also because of her Nationalist
Socialist past. The story of their relationship and Vera's decision to
return to Germany is framed by two scenes, conversations between
Vera and two figures representing the older generation; Vera's Party
school instructor Walter Kernten, who happens to be the
delegation's leader, and Lidia Worochinowa, a Soviet doctor.

Vera's love story and the story of her past are connected
through a discourse on disciplining the body. With Pawel, Vera is
forced to remember her past, since he is the one who knows her as
this sixteen-year-old girl, "mired in fanaticism."[30] For Vera, being
in love is dangerous, and desire generates anxiety, an anxiety which
is associated with the experience of losing control over her
emotions. The story is one of regaining this control.

And this is the important aspect: Regaining control over the
body of the past becomes tied to maintaining control over this
body's voice. In a conversation with Pawel, Vera tells him that the
most difficult thing to control is the impulse to sing Nazi songs:

'The songs were the worst,' she told Pawel. 'They were very difficult to forget. *Can you imagine suspiciously watching every sound that wants to escape your lips* (MO/166).

In the passage where this quote occurs, Wolf creates an analogy between guarding one's voice and guarding one's body, both involving the strictest discipline.

Let us pursue this topic of singing. When Vera and Pawel sleep together, the narrative suddenly veers into socialist realist kitsch, and the topic of sexuality itself vanishes. In this context, we encounter Vera singing. During a visit to a collective farm, Vera starts singing a German folk song about love. The logic informing this scene is, on the one hand, the granting of absolution: Vera is absolved of her guilt, because the delegation's sojourn at the collective farm has explicitly reconciled Germans and Russians; on the other hand, the love song thematizes the elimination of a "body out of control," translates desire into sentimental kitsch.

Through the issue of Vera's song, the *post-fascist body* is linked to a "new" voice born in the very process of Vera's final separation from her past. Reaffirming her new voice, this narrative segment closes with yet another scene thematizing singing. Sitting in a train which takes them back to Moscow, a few members of Vera's delegation start humming German and Russian songs until finally they all join together in singing "Brüder, zur Sonne, zur Freiheit!" After a brief interval of silence, Walter Kernten tells them about his years in Buchenwald, and about a clandestine meeting of the communist cell. This meeting, he tells them, ended with the very same song. Like the previous scene, this one rethematizes the issue of guilt, reconciliation, and redemption—this time a reconciliation between the antifascist hero and the generation of former Hitler Youth members, sealed by the repetition of a specific song. In my view, this passage with its focus on the shared song finalizes the *realignment of voice from National Socialism to Communism*, from the fascist father of the past to the communist father of the present.

My reading of Wolf's text is informed by the following: Freudian theory stresses the origins of the ego in a *bodily ego*. And certain psychoanalytic theorists link the very first awareness of a bodily ego to voice. Before the Lacanian mirror stage, in which the visual experience of a Gestalt provides the infant with a first (illusory) experience of wholeness, there is what Didier Anzieu calls the *"acoustic mirror"*: the experience of a bodily ego, of the first defining boundaries, in the mimesis of another's voice. Voice originates as mimesis, both the mimesis of the infants own bodily sounds and the voice of the other, it is tied to bodily sensations and the first experience of bodily wholeness.[31] The imaginary unity of mother and child, is recreated in the "Übereinstimmung" of Vera's voice with Kernten's.[32] Vera's new postfascist voice represents a voice in mimesis of its superego, located in the communist Walter Kernten. Posing the problem of identity in terms of voice focuses identity around the archaic emergence of *the first contours of a bodily ego in the acoustic mirror*. This focus accounts for the connection which the text establishes between *(post-fascist) voice and (post-fascist) body*. In "Moskauer Novelle," the realignment of Vera's voice from the fascist father to the communist father/mother finalizes the transition from the sexual body of the past to the asexual body of the present: just as the *post-fascist body* is produced through the splitting off of sexuality as the part of subjectivity linked to the past, the *post-fascist voice* emerges from a replacement of the songs of the past by the songs of the present—and from the substitution of the father of the past by a father/mother of the present.

One last point about this novella: The fact that "Moskauer Novelle" thematizes this early connection between bodily ego and voice forces us to modify the earlier statement that Vera's "new" voice arises out of a separation from the body. This logic of a voice "purified" of desire collides with the paradoxical nature voice: voice belongs to both the realm of the body and the realm of language. Psychoanalytic discussions of the *singing* voice as *voix-corps* or body voice, related to the lost jouissance of the imaginary, and the thesis that voice has a "corporal source, a source in the organic and in excitation," leads to an understanding of voice as always carrying the trace of the body, its fantasies, and its desires.[33] We thus have to read Vera's new voice as highly ambiguous, at once the marker of a sublime postfascist body, whose "fragile materiality"[34] has been submitted to the strictest discipline, and the very trace of this material body, the proof of its indelible presence.

Wolf's first text thus inextricably links body and voice. Before discussing these issues with respect to *Kassandra*, I will briefly sketch the ways in which body and voice are implicated in *Der geteilte Himmel* (1963). Wolf's second novel narrates the building of the wall and the subsequent division of Germany as both love story and Rita's novel of formation. In this text, the sexual body is displaced onto Manfred, the protagonist's lover, who leaves for the West. Recovering from the separation means repressing the memories of this body, memories which flood Rita's consciousness. Like her previous narrative, *Der geteilte Himmel* thus participates in the fantasy of the postfascist body. It also participates in the fantasy of a new voice. In this text, this fantasy has to be read symptomatically: you might remember that the text alternates between first and third person, between Rita/"I" and Rita/"she." Traditionally, this split has been read as the first timid departure from socialist realism, and the first emergence of "subjective authenticity." I read this split voice on the level of the text's unconscious fantasies about body and voice: the new voice—Rita's "I"/"she"—arises out of the split from the sexual body, the separation from Manfred, her lover. The fascist body as the sexual body is displaced onto this masculine figure, while Rita emerges with a "pure" body—and a new, a "pure" voice. But this is only one level on which to read this divided voice. The other level concerns a different split: the passage which celebrates Rita's recovery, her ability to finally say "I," centrally involves a dream in which Rita finds herself at home, next to Wendland, Manfred's rival. This is not the foreshadowing of a solution along the lines of an alternative love story—Rita with Wendland, the communist, not Manfred, the nihilist—but Rita's recovery as both daughter—"she"—and son: "I." Rita as one of the many young liberated women of the '60s—think about the women figures in the censored films of 1965, for instance Kurt Maetzig's *Das Kaninchen bin ich* or Frank Beyer's *Spur der Steine*; and Rita as the paternal narrative's archetypical figure of the "son." Rita's "I/she" is also an "I/he."

One last observation about *Der geteilte Himmel*, and the sudden change from "I" to "she" borrowed from Büchner. My final thesis is that the text's split narrative voice is formed mimetically and that this mimesis involves the author Anna Seghers. I propose to understand this particular kind of acoustic mirror in the following way: as her essays on Seghers show, Wolf takes over Seghers' own literary-historical paradigm of the opposition between Goethe, the classicist, on the one hand, and authors such as Hölderlin, Lenz, Kleist, Büchner, and Günderrode, on the other hand. Wolf defines the author Seghers from the pre-GDR era as a non-classical author, on the side of the "younger generation."[35] It is this author that Wolf comes to identify with against what she constructs as Seghers, the "classical national author."[36] Seghers' generational schema, in my view, constitutes the very foundation upon which Wolf elaborates her notion of subjective authenticity. And that notion is primarily developed through Wolf's reading of Seghers' *Ausflug der toten Mädchen*.

In her reading of this text, Wolf foregrounds writing as a *process of coming to terms with a personal experience*, and she foregrounds the highly distinct *voice* that transmits this process. In later essays, she adds another dimension, the connection between the therapeutic function of writing and the party line: the process of writing becomes a process of overcoming a personal crisis of "belief," while "overcoming through narrating" becomes equated with "pulling oneself together." Wolf thus writes herself into the ideological narrative of the family both on the level of her novels, but also on the level of the definition of her own authorship, developing her "new" voice within a generational paradigm. I argued for a double reading of the split narrative voice in *Der geteilte Himmel*: "I"/"she" and "I"/"he"—the female protagonist as woman and as man. This basic constellation recurs on the level of narration itself: by elaborating on Büchner's characteristic narrative mode, Wolf takes up a particular position in Seghers' generational paradigm of German literary history, she takes up the position of the "son."

Wolf's texts from the late 1950s to the 1970s thus form a fabric centrally concerned with the question of voice. By this I mean *the speaking position Wolf elaborates, which consists of the following three elements*: the increasing use of first-person narration; the notion that modern prose should be a process of working through a crisis that is simultaneously personal and political; and, finally, the ethico-political dimension always present in this existential crisis, the struggle against resignation as an imperative sustaining all writing. The author's early *literary* texts add a specific dimension to this whole complex of voice, the fantasy of a *pure voice* linked to a *purified body*. Throughout Wolf's essayistic reflections, the voice of the author Anna Seghers is drawn into this web through the story which mourns the Jewish mother, Seghers' "Ausflug der toten Mädchen." The privileging of this particular text signifies, I would argue, that the voice which is derived from Seghers as the non-canonical author carries yet another meaning, that of the *purity of the (Jewish) victim*. We thus find, on the level of aesthetic theory as well as on the level of narrative practice, an identification with the victim of National Socialism, a gesture which I am inclined to read as the indirect, but nevertheless urgent mimesis of a "pure," a non-fascist voice. Yet what is striking is the lack of a literary text written in the first-person, the "I"—a topic I will come back to later.

II. Kassandra or, The Body-in-Pain[37]

What happens in *Kassandra*, we might want to ask, in the story of the Trojan war told by Cassandra, the king's daughter? How can we approach this text to gain insight into the topic of body and voice?

Kassandra, such is my contention, is a deliberate reflection on East Germany's paternal narrative, a conscious exploration into its power and its fantasies. I propose to start with one of the major problems encountered by critics trying to read *Kassandra* as an example of "feminine writing": Any reading that sees *Kassandra* celebrating feminine sexuality and the body runs up against the thick layer of anxiety and pain that is also part of this text. Wolf tells Cassandra's story as the daughter's disillusionment with the idealized father. The confrontations between daughter and king take the form of Cassandra's moments of "madness," scenes which organize the entire narrative. The following quote refers to the very first time Cassandra's aline voice appears:

> [M]y legs, which were as much out of my control as all my other limbs, jerked and danced with a disreputable, unseemly delight . . . They were out of control, everything in me was out of control, I was uncontrollable.[38]

In this scene, the erotic side of the act is foregrounded, it plays on the text's epigraph—Sappho's "limb-loosing love" (glieder-schüttelnde Liebe). The second major scene describing Cassandra's attack foregrounds not pleasure but pain. This level of pain, even terror, is very pronounced, the outburst is described as a "dreadful torment," a "dismembering," where "all my members [were set] to [] rattling and hurling about" (C/59; K/70). How should we read this contradiction, the celebration of the erotic and the experience of pain? I would propose to read these moments of "madness" as an instance of hysterical theatre. These are the aspects of the notion of hysteria that I want to foreground: From a classically Freudian view, the "nucleus of hysteria" is the idea of the conversion of psychic conflict into bodily symptoms,[39] and the reenactment of a repressed incestuous fantasy. Jean Laplanche explicitly theorizes hysteria as a communication "made in the privileged area of the body," understanding it as a "mise-en-scène" or fantasy scenario.[40] We also need to recall Freud's belated insight into the bisexuality of the hysterical scene: the conflict produced by the desire for both father and mother, a constellation which then also involves both a feminine and masculine identification.[41] These aspects are condensed in Gregorio Kohon's notion of the "hysterical stage." Kohon understands the term both in Laplanche's sense, i.e., stage as a fantasy scenario, and as a developmental stage, stage as that moment when the subject becomes "fixed" or paralyzed by her inability to change from the mother as primary object to the father. The hysterical scene is then a moment which enacts the conflict between desire for the mother and desire for the father, between masculine and feminine identification.[42]

In *Kassandra*, the incestuous content of Cassandra's outbursts is made rather explicit. But how can I argue the contradictory identification of Cassandra as both feminine and masculine? To answer this question, I will return to the second outburst, the one in which Wolf foregrounds pain. After her attack, Cassandra retreats into "madness," which she calls "[b]lack milk" (ibid.). How should we read this scene of torture with its allusion to Celan's metaphor? I would argue that in this image of *the body-in-pain*, we re-encounter the iconic image of the antifascist hero, the sublime body of the communist under torture—the image I mentioned above: "They turned Brosowski like a spindle around himself, so that his joints cracked and blood spilled from his mouth." In her painful spectacle, that is my thesis, Cassandra enacts the identification with the antifascist father. Like Rita, Cassandra is both *daughter and son*.

So far, I have focused on the body—against the obvious presence of voice in these scenes. Let me propose my reading of this "alien" voice. First and foremost, the voice of Cassandra, the speaker, has to be kept separate from the voice that erupts from Cassandra's body. Furthermore, rather than reading the latter as a genuine expression of femininity, or the feminine body, a historically contextualized reading ought to understand this "alien" voice as part of the entire problematic of voice that unfolds in Wolf's work—the connection of voice to the postfascist present and the fascist past, its link to the (post)-fascist body. Thus what *Kassandra* stages in these outbursts is not some "true" voice of the feminine outside of the symbolic order, but instead a very idiosyncratic utopia, the *utopia of the pure voice of the sexual body*. Or, to put it differently, the voice of the "truth" of experience expressed in the immediacy of a link between the sexual body and its voice. It is a connection located *outside of any ideological inscription*. In her outbursts, Cassandra reconnects voice to a sexual body. This is a utopia of immediacy that escapes for one fleeting moment from the threat that Wolf associates with the sexual body throughout her entire work: the determination of the body by the fascist past. And in a most paradoxical move, in this utopian voice, feminine sexuality becomes the very locus of purity.[43]

Second, this voice is a symptom, the result of a conflict between feminine and masculine identifications, between the daughter's Oedipal identification with the mother's desire and her identification with the icon of antifascism, the sublime tortured body of the antifascist hero. Seen from this perspective, Cassandra's outburst is a moment of "hysterical resistance," the "effect and testimony of a failed interpellation into the symbolic order"[44]—to quote Zizek.

Resistance against what? First and foremost, simply against being a daughter. Second, the association of *sexual body* and *voice of experience*, I would argue, constitutes an act of resistance against the very subject position created by Wolf herself, that of the post-fascist daughter. Resistance against this daughter who embodies the postfascist body and its "purified" voice. But it is important to recognize that *the utopian image of a sexual body linked to an authentic voice does not cancel the image of the antifascist hero as a layer of identification*. On the contrary, the utopia of another body/another voice can only safely be deployed *against the very backdrop of the identification with the father of antifascism*.

Let us return to the voice of the subject of enunciation, the "I" of Cassandra, the narrator. Cassandra the speaker is characterized by the desire to suppress all feeling in order to achieve one ultimate end—to be witness to the destruction. What characterizes the position from which Cassandra speaks is, from the beginning, the separation from Aeneas. In contrast to Cassandra, the subject of the outbursts, Cassandra the narrator thus once again speaks from the *position of the sublime postfascist body*. This is a body linked to a higher mission—to testify—and again it is a body "purified" of its materiality. Yet even that body is ultimately overcome in death: "With the story, I go to my death" (C/3; K/5; TA) is the sentence which opens Cassandra's testimony to the destruction of Troy. What it tells us is that Cassandra's "I" is ultimately based on the radical fantasy of a voice soon to be separated from its body.

It is this fantasy which finally frees Wolf from the constraints that had prevented her from using "I." Thus, for the first time, Wolf fully appropriates the speaking position which she analyzed as Seghers' own, creating a narrator who is in the process of overcoming the post-fascist body, this body which will forever tie Wolf's protagonists to their fascist past. We now have to ask: what are the particular conditions that allow this appropriation, this full mimesis, of Seghers' voice? In her lectures, Wolf establishes a strong parallel between Cassandra as the one who bears witness to the destruction of Troy, and Wolf herself as the author whose duty it is to bear witness to the possible destruction of Europe. And with respect to this duty, an even stronger parallel surfaces between the heating up of the Cold War in the 1980s and the rise of National Socialism in the 1930s. What are the processes of identification underlying this analogy? I understand Cassandra, the narrator of her story, as a variation on those "young German authors" who "dropped out," "died insane," or by suicide—Kleist, Büchner, Lenz, Bürger, Günderrode, names from Seghers' list.[45]German reality—now and then—pushes its intellectuals to their death. Cassandra is the daughter in the Oedipal drama of an ideological narrative who chooses death. She thus speaks within Seghers' literary-historical framework, and she remembers from a speaking position developed on the basis of Seghers' work, speaks in what Wolf called Seghers' tone. But the "stance" has changed: Cassandra has resigned—like

Günderrode, she decides to die. In her mimetic approach to her protagonist, Wolf situates herself as a daughter vis-...-vis Seghers. But what allows her to finally use the first person, the "I" so anxiously avoided in her previous texts? Significant here is the gesture implied in the equation between Cold War and National Socialism, Troy and East Germany: Cassandra's account is a testimony to a catastrophe similar to that of the last war, or more precisely, similar to the Holocaust. In my view, the use of first-person narrative here is overdetermined: Cassandra's going to her death is a gesture of identification with the Jewish victim on her way to the "slaughterhouse," a term from the novel. This last aspect makes *Kassandra* the most densely layered text on the GDR's dominant legitimatory discourse, the discourse of antifascism—and *not* Wolf's most "feminist" text, if we mean by feminist the option of being outside the GDR's symbolic order.

But there are other implications of this reading. First, what I have been arguing undermines the teleological narrative constructed by many of Wolf's critics—and by herself.[46] The story of subjective authenticity is not the story of a feminine voice progressively liberating itself from the GDR's official discourse. This idea only works if we limit our reading to the level of the text's relationship to the GDR's official *Kulturpolitik*, its normative aesthetics, or to the political discourse inscribed in the text or derived from other sources. If we abandon this level of analysis and instead focus on the level of (un-)conscious fantasies, a different picture emerges: the picture of Wolf's work as deeply implicated in the GDR's founding narrative. But that does not make Wolf's work any less compelling. Second, I started with the pivotal position that *Christa T.* occupies in the new, and the old story of East German literature. Obviously my reading of voice in Wolf's texts unsettles that narrative: *Christa T.* as the point of emergence of a feminist modernism does not work. But then what does work?

III. *Nachdenken Über Christa T.* or, The Other Woman's Exquisite Corpse

Let us approach the text anew focusing on this nexus of (post-fascist) body and voice. To readers familiar with the book, the following components naturally come to mind: the split between narrator and character, Wolf's famous statement that in creating her character, Christa T., she was suddenly confronted with herself; Christa T.'s equally famous attempt of saying "I";[47] "Krischan's" spontaneous trumpet call; the author's desperate struggle to re-assert her intentions against Western "misreadings" of the novel as an expression of her "resignation";[48] and, of course, the diseased, the dead body.[49] The problem that this novel raises for us is how to read the connection between post-fascist body/voice and death—or the corpse of Christa T.. I will begin by pointing to the obvious links between this text and the antifascist narrative as I outlined it above. There is, first, the confrontation between Christa T. and the director of her school, again an iconographic figure of antifascism, "a survivor, one of the old crowd" (CT/103; N/116), that ties *Nachdenken über Christa T.* to the paternal narrative. This conversation concludes with a conciliatory gesture. This passage presents the novels' core issue—Christa T.'s refusal to accept "real existing socialism" as the goal, her insistence to see socialism as a project of self-realization, not as a system[50]—as a generational conflict. Second, Wolf explicitly introduces the topic of "The New Man" in this third novel. With respect to the Nazi past, this New Man is defined in terms familiar from our previous readings. Writing about the 1950s, the narrator states:

> We were fully occupied with making ourselves unassailable . . . Not only to admit into our minds nothing extraneous-and all sorts of things we considered extraneous; also to let nothing extraneous well up from inside of ourselves, and if it did so-a doubt, a suspicion, observations, questions-then not to let it show. . . .

The idea of perfection had taken hold of our minds . . . and from the rostrums at meetings came in addition a great impatience: verily, I say unto you, you shall be with me today in paradise! Oh, we had a presentiment of it . . . we were . . . arguing whether or not our paradise would have atom-powered heating . . . Who, but who would be worthy to inhabit it? Only the very purest, that seemed a certainty. So we subjected ourselves afresh to our spiritual exercises (CT/50 and 52; N/61 and 62-63; emphasis mine; TA).

Only the purest—Christa T. takes for granted the fantasy of post-fascist body, the embodied transition from Nazi past to present: "[T]o make the precise and sharp cut-off separating "ourselves" from "the others," once and for all, that would save us (CT/27; N/36)."[51] *But what about this New Man and the future?* Kornelia Hauser argues that Christa T. responds to a petrified socialism with an alternative form of productivity, a productivity that relies on her female body. This particular version of a "concrete future," however, turns out to be a trap, a return to traditional modes of femininity.[52] Reproduction turns the post-fascist body into a diseased body, links giving birth to death. Christa T. is the novel of a crisis, a crisis lived on the level of the post-fascist body. This crisis is formulated primarily with respect to Christa T.'s story of "forbidden love" (CT/158; N/176). Like her decision to become a mother, this passionate relationship is her attempt to "break out of the dead center in which she'd planted herself" (CT/157; N/175), to escape the "unused feelings" that are beginning "to poison her" (CT/156; N/174). Here, the fantasy of the daughter's post-fascist body is as tenuous a construct as it was in "Moskauer Novelle" and in *Der geteilte Himmel*. In *Nachdenken über Christa T.* the ideological fantasy of the daughter's post-fascist body is transformed along the register of a re-sexualized female body—"solutions" that do not work. Instead, the body becomes corpse. But what exactly is this corpse?

Let us first look at the relationship between narrator and character. The dominant reading of this relationship is one which sees it in terms of transference. For Alison Lewis this "transference of desire" confers authorship on the text's "other" woman, allowing her to "transgress the boundaries of the socially permissible."[53] Like other critics, she understands this constellation as a means to subvert censorship. This particular reading finds support in Wolf's own statements, for instance her use of the term "medium of transference" for her protagonist.[54] But is that really all that is involved in this constellation? The question is rhetorical, and the notion of melancholia, I contend, provides us with a better starting point to investigate the complexities involved in this narrative arrangement. I will, for the moment, simply assume that Christa T. is indeed Christa T. Melancholia, Freud taught us, is the result of failed mourning. Unable to separate from the lost object, the subject incorporates it—the object becomes part of the self.[55] Ostensibly, the text is written to save Christa T. from being forgotten. But then the narrator tells us that she, Christa T., has always been there, inside:

> I'd never realized that for years her image in my mind has
> not changed; and there's no hope of her changing. Not a
> person or thing in the world can make her dark fuzzy hair
> go gray as mine will (CT/4; N/10; TA).

What is preserved in this memory? What has been lost? A young woman who is different from others, whose spontaneous scream has the power to lift the sky (CT/10; N/17). Chapter One opens with Christa T.'s "scream," and it closes with the narrator losing her, but she tells us: "The ingenuous open heart preserves one's ability to say 'I' to a stranger, until a time comes when this strange 'I' returns and enters 'me' again" (CT/14; N/22). This foreign I inhabiting the narrator is preserved in one particular image, or rather in a series of images. This series begins with what we later recognize as the fragment of a particularly vivid memory, the image of Christa T. at the beach running after a red and white ball (CT/4; N/9). For the narrator, Christa T. incarnates the very desire to live amidst, or rather, against petrified conditions; she represents the transgressive utopian potential of the figure of the young woman that I mentioned in the context of *Der geteilte Himmel*. Unlike Rita, however, Christa T. partakes in this association of feminine sexuality and transgression, feminine sexuality and utopia that we find in the women protagonists of *Spur der Steine* or *Das Kaninchen bin ich*.

But by the end of the narrative, this figure invested with the reformist energies of the early 1960s will be lost, transformed into a corpse. Moreover, this loss cannot be spoken—and to that extent, censorship is indeed constitutive of the text. The writing of melancholia comes to a full stop: *Nachdenken über Christa T.* ends in 1962, a year after the building of the wall (an event understood as a caesura potentially leading to reforms) and three years before the 11th Plenum which so radically undercut the burgeoning avantgarde of the early 1960s.[56]

A loss that cannot be spoken, a process of mourning that cannot fully articulate what it lost results in what Nicolas Abraham and Maria Torok call cryptic mourning:

> The words that cannot be uttered, the scenes that cannot be recalled, the tears that cannot be shed—everything will be swallowed along with the trauma that led to the loss. Swallowed and preserved. Inexpressible mourning erects a secret tomb inside the subject. Reconstituted from the memories of words, scenes, and affects, the objectal correlative of the loss is buried alive in the crypt as a full-fledged person, complete with its own topography. The crypt also includes the actual or supposed traumas that made introjection impracticable. A whole world of unconscious fantasy is created, one that leads its own separate and concealed existence.[57]

The analysts give us the example of a young boy who keeps his sister "alive." The "carrier of a crypt," he comes to identify with her.[58] When the "cryptophoric"[59] subject speaks, Abraham and Torok argue, we hear the voice of the object, an object which "carries the ego as its mask."[60] At the origin of this mechanism lies not only an "undisclosable grief,"[61] but a secret that needs to be guarded at all cost:

> Crypts are constructed only when the shameful secret is the love object's doing and when that object also functions for the subject as ego ideal. It is therefore the object's secret that needs to be kept.[62]

The result of this process is a particular fantasy, the fantasy of the "exquisite corpse,"[63] at once preserved and hidden away. And it needs to be preserved because

> [t]he imago along with its external embodiment in the object, was set up as the repository of hope; the desires it forbade would be realized one day.

According to Abraham and Torok, the "imago retains the valuable thing whose lack cripples the ego."[64] The melancholic's work is directed at one goal: to revive this exquisite corpse.[65]

We are now in a position to read another series of images that the narrator gathers toward the end of the novel, especially in the pivotal 19th chapter. This chapter starts with the effort to produce a memory long forgotten: the narrator who observes Christa T. early in the morning as the latter writes the crucial sentence—"The Big Hope or, The Difficulty of Saying 'I'" (CT/169; N/188). This scene has a predecessor: in chapter 17, the narrator tells us about her stay in Christa T.'s house *after her friend's death*. As she descends to the living room she feels a ghostly presence as if her friend were sitting in her chair writing.[66] This house built to provide a space for Christa T.'s writing, but also representing a risk (the risk of Christa T. "burying herself" (CT/151; N/168)), this house has indeed turned into a tomb, I would argue, a crypt preserving an exquisite corpse.

What is contained in the image of Christa T. writing? Why does it have to be encrypted, and concealed? In both passages, we encounter the word "secret," both times tied to the issue of voice and writing. Christa T.'s secret is that wants to write, and that her writing is connected to her trumpet call:

> That morning, the first of the New Year, when she was so wide awake and I was so sleepy, we might have talked about many things, but my mind was too much at rest. I was cradled in the certainty that much was still reversible and attainable . . . An untidy confidence seized me; I believed that all would be well. Only her face as she leaned over the sheet of paper, seemed strange. Yes, I said, the way one says things, between sleeping and waking, which one doesn't ordinarily say: the same face. I once saw you blowing a trumpet, eighteen years ago (CT/169; N/189).

This image establishes a contrast between narrator and character, the one believing in the possibility of reform—the other appearing "alien": alien to this order that might be reformed, alien as she works to transform a scream into writing.

At the end of the novel, Christa T. is still the figure who refuses to arrive anywhere (CT/170; N/189), invested in the idea of a "time when real changes were being made" (CT/174; N/194). And the crisis is overcome by reformulating the historical mission that the sublime communist body incarnates as a socialism that is a "way to ourselves" (CT/30; N/40). But why then is Christa T. no longer represented as a young vibrant woman but instead appears in the guise of the exquisite corpse? The production of the exquisite corpse, Torok argues, involves a shameful secret. What constitutes this encrypted object's shameful secret? The ambiguous status of the events reported in chapter 19—fragments of memory organized into a conversation "in half sleep" (CT/170; N//190)—also pertains to the piece of paper that Christa T. leans over as the narrator watches her. This piece of paper containing the novel's core sentence ("The Big Hope, or The Difficulty of Saying 'I'") has disappeared: "When I got up I saw the piece of paper there with my own eyes; but now it has disappeared" (CT/169; N/188).[67] The only thing left are parts of a manuscript written in the third person. To say "I" is linked to Johannes R. Becher's dictum that functions as epigraph and later in a modified version as the sentence opening chapter 17: "To become oneself, with all one's strength" (CT/149; N/165). But this project, how can it be possible for a generation rooted in a past that will not go away? Again, Christa T. tells us the familiar story: "She [Christa T.] burned her old diaries, all her vows went up in smoke, and the enthusiasms one was now ashamed of, the aphorisms and songs" (CT/29; N/). Christa T. belongs to a generation that despite all its efforts to "cut itself off" from its past starts to realize that it might be impossible to "cut oneself away from oneself? (CT/27; N/36). Because, and this is the crucial part, this new version of a non-alienated socialism is in the figure of Christa T. inextricably linked to the notion of writing; and writing is inextricably linked to Christa T.'s scream, a scream that ties her to her past. The narrator tells us about Christa T.'s breakdown in 1945: "She only screamed" (CT/29; N/). And we already saw that the moment of incorporation was located in the first chapter and the image of the young woman's rebellious scream—a chapter that refers to the friends' common childhood in Nazi Germany.

Christa T. is "kept alive" as the *exquisite corpse* who would have finished the missing pages:

I would let her finish the few pages she wanted to leave us, and which, unless we are not utterly deceived, would have been news from the innermost interior, that deepest level of being which is harder to reach than the underside of the earth's crust, harder to reach than the stratosphere, because it is more closely guarded: by ourselves (CT/175; N/195; TA).

This is Christa T.'s dilemma, her paradoxical secret: this "innermost interior" is either the purest embodiment of the sublime object—the communist's historical mission reformulated in terms of the necessity of permanent transformation, or it too is rotten to the core; it is either sublime, or it is that which—like its material envelop—was potentially formed by the past. And because of this potential link to the past, it has to remain the object's shameful secret, the crypt guarded by the subject. Who is, of course, implicated herself: "If I'd been allowed to invent us, I'd have give us time" (CT/175; N/195; emphasis is mine). Moreover, as I already pointed out above, the connection which the narrator establishes in this series of images at the end of the novel between writing and screaming also introduces the potential link to the past, the link to a scream "originating" before 1945. The project of "becoming oneself" is a treacherous one, as is its writing. Christa T.'s exquisite corpse embodies that discovery.

IV. Against a "Politics of Authenticity":[68]

Re-reading the issue of voice in Wolf from a psychoanalytic angle problematizes the new story of an alternative GDR culture centered around modernism's feminine voice. The story is more complicated in the sense that in Wolf voice is a fantasy linking it to an origin in the past—and that past is the Nazi past. Moreover, that fantasy of an execrable "origin" generates a single desire: to write in a "pure" voice. This reading also sheds an entirely new light on Wolf's feminism. In the *Kassandra* lectures, but also in her most recent interviews, Wolf advocates a form of feminism that emphasizes womens' position outside of a patriarchal history of oppression: women are untouched by that history's most destructive forces. It seems to me that particular kind of feminism also strives for a position of purity—a position outside of history, outside of ideology, outside of the symbolic. As feminist critics, we should resist that desire—as do Wolf's literary texts. These texts which show the many ways in which fantasies of the body and voice are steeped in history, work against any metaphysics of an authentic, an uncontaminated voice; they also problematize the idea of a "feminine writing," indeed of a feminine subjectivity outside of the symbolic. We need to keep that in mind as we rewrite the history of East German literature and culture.

We should also keep in mind that the topic of voice and its connection to the paternal order is not limited to Wolf and her generation. In his post-89 novel *Spiegelland*, Klaus Drawert for instance writes in a section entitled "The Moment of the Damaging of the Voice":

> But I did not want to speak like my father (or my grand-father, for instance). This must have been an early feeling, which may have arisen just in time. It was the feeling of a borrowed and worthless language, a language which I resisted almost bodily, such that I unlearned it; for a shadow of perceptible invalidity and of my father's (or, for instance, my grandfather's) claim to power lay over the words, and to use this language would have been a form of submission. I forgot how to speak, and threw my father in front of everyone into a state of distress, forcing him to confront this offense: his son, his very image, without language, a blind mirror.[69]

In East Germany, voice was "damaged," not "authentic"—like everywhere else.

Notes

1 This article integrates material from my (forthcoming) book, *Post-Fascist Fantasies: Psychoanalysis, History, and the Literature of East Germany* (Durham: Duke University Press, 1997). All translations of German texts are mine unless otherwise indicated. I would like to thank Sarah Beckwith, Sibille Fischer, Toril Moi, Nancy Kaiser, and George

Steinmetz for their continuous input.

2   Axel Goodbody, Dennis Tate, Ian Wallace, "The Failed Socialist Experiment: Culture in the GDR," in *German Cultural Studies. An Introduction*, ed. Rob Burns (Oxford: Oxford University Press, 1995), p. 200.

3   Ibid., p. 167 and 164.

4   Barbara Einhorn, *Cinderella Goes to Market. Citizenship, Gender, and the Women's Movements in East Central Europe* (London: Verso, 1993).

5   Dorothea Böck, "'Ich schreibe, um herauszufinden, warum ich schreiben muß.' Frauenliteratur in der DDR zwischen Selbsterfahrung und ästhetischem Experiment," *Feministische Studien* 1 (1990), pp. 64-74.

6   Allison Lewis, "'Foiling the Censor': Reading and Transference as Feminist Strategies in the Works of Christa Wolf, Irmtraud Morgner, and Christa Moog," *The German Quarterly* 66.3 (Summer 1993), pp. 372-386.

7   Ursula Heukenkamp, "Soll das Vergessen verabredet werden? Eigenständigkeit und Eigenart der DDR-Literatur," *Aus Politik und Zeitgeschichte* B41-42/91 (October 4, 1991), p. 3.

8   See, for instance, "Subjective Authenticity. A Conversation with Hans Kaufmann," in *The Fourth Dimension*, translated by Hilary Pilkington and with an introduction by Karin McPherson (London: Verso, 1988), p. 20ff.

9   Christa Wolf, *The Quest for Christa T.*, translated by Christopher Middleton (New York: Farrar, Straus and Giroux, 1970), p. 170.

10 Bernd Hüppauf, "Moral oder Sprache. DDR-Literatur vor der Moderne," in *Literatur in der DDR. Rückblicke*, special issue of *Text + Kritik* (Munich: edition text + kritik, 1991), p. 223.

11 See, for instance, Wolfgang J. Mommsen, "Die DDR in der deutschen Geschichte," *Aus Politik und Zeitgeschehen*, B 29-30 (July 16, 1993), p. 23 and 29.

12 Barbara Einhorn; also Kornelia Hauser, *Patriarchat im Sozialismus. Soziologische Studien zu Literatur aus der DDR*

(Hamburg: Argument-Verlag, 1994).

13 Sonja Hilzinger, "Weibliches Schreiben als eine Ästhetik des Widerstands. Über Wolf's 'Kassandra'-Projekt," in *Christa Wolf. Ein Arbeitsbuch*, edited by Angela Drescher (Berlin and Weimar: Aufbau-Verlag, 1989), p. 222.

14 Sonja Hilzinger, *Kassandra. Über Christa Wolf* (Haag + Herchen: Frankfurt am Main, 1984), p. 75.

15 Sonja Hilzinger, "Weibliches Schreiben als eine Ästhetik des Widerstands," in *Christa Wolf. Ein Arbeitsbuch*, p. 223. See also Sabine Wilke, "'Wenn ich die Zeit noch habe, sollte ich von meinem Körper sprechen': Der Status des Körpers als Schauplatz der Inszenierung der Weiblichkeit," in her *"Ausgraben und Erinnern": Zur Funktion von Geschichte, und geschlechtlicher Identität in den Texten Christa Wolf's* (Wurzburg: Königshausen und Neumann, 1993), p. 163). Other essays on the novel that argue for a reading of the text in terms of feminine writing: Christiane Zehl Romero, "'Weibliches Schreiben'—Christa Wolfs *Kassandra*," *Studies in GDR Culture and Society* 8, pp. 15-27. Michael Vanhelleputte, "Christa Wolf und der Bankrott des patriarchalischen Prinzips, oder die Voraussetzungen ihres Entwurfs eines weltverändernden Feminismus," in *Christa Wolf in feministischer Sicht*, edited by Michel Vanhelleputte (Frankfurt am Main: Peter Lang, 1992), pp. 13-22; Madeline Lutjeharms, "'Doch schreiben wir weiter in den Formen, an die wir gewöhnt sind.' Überlegungen zum 'weiblichen Schreiben' aus sprachwissenschaftlicher Sicht am Beispiel der *Kassandra* von Christa Wolf," in *Christa Wolf in feministischer Sicht*, pp. 115-126; Gerhard Neumann, "Christa Wolfs *Kassandra*. Die Archäologie der weiblichen Stimme," in *Erinnerte Zukunft*, ed. Wolfram Mauser (Würzburg: Königshausen und Neumann, 1985), pp. 233-264. Heidi Gilpin, "*Cassandra*: Creating a Female Voice," in *Responses to Christa Wolf* edited by Marilyn Fries (Detroit: Wayne State, 1989), pp. 349-377.

16 Robert Sayre and Michael Löwy, "Romanticism as a Feminist
    Vision: The Quest of Christa Wolf," *New German Critique* 64
    (Winter 1995), p. 105, and p. 116-17.

17 See, for instance, her interview with Therese Hörnigk
    ("Unerledigte Widersprüche. Gespräch mit Therese Hörnigk,"
    in her *Im Dialog* (Darmstadt and Neuwied: Luchterhand
    Verlag, 1990), pp. 24 - 68), and the more recent interview with
    Günter Gaus, "'Auf mir bestehen'. Christa Wolf im Gespräch
    mit Günter Gaus," in *Akteneinsicht Christa Wolf. Zerrspiegel
    und Dialog*, edited by Hermann Vinke (Hamburg: Luchterhand
    Literaturverlag, 1993), pp. 241 - 264.

18 For a non-reductionist personal genealogy, see Toril Moi,
    Simone de Beauvoir. The Making of an Intellectual Woman
    (Oxford and Cambridge: Blackwell Publishers, 1994). What
    makes Toril Moi's contribution so unique is her insistence on
    theorizing subjectivity not exclusively as interiority, but, from
    a Bourdieuian perspective, also as social event: hence the
    chapters on Beauvoir's education, and her standing in the
    literary field as a woman author—then and now.

19 For an extensive discussion of the *Literaturstreit*, see
    Brockmann, Stephen. "Introduction: The Unification Debate,"
    New German Critique 52 (1991), pp. 3-30.

20 Sigrid Meuschel, *Legitimation und Parteiherrschaft. Zum
    Paradox von Stabilität und Revolution in der DDR 1945-1989*
    (Frankfurt am Main: Suhrkamp Verlag, 1992), p. 10.

21 Ibid., p. 305.

22 Willi Bredel, *Die Väter* (1941), *Die Söhne* (1949), *Die Enkel*
    (1953) reprinted by Dortmund: Weltkreis Verlag, 1981.
    Bredel's trilogy, for instance, ranges from 1871 to 1944. Otto
    Gotsche, *Die Fahne von Kriwoj Rog* (Halle: Mitteldeutscher
    Verlag, 1959). Hans Marchwitza, *Die Heimkehr der Kumiaks*
    (Berlin and Weimar: Aufbau Verlag, 1964); *Die Kumiaks und
    ihre Kinder* (Berlin: Verlag Tribüne, 1959); *Die Kumiaks*
    (1934) (Berlin and Weimar: Aufbau Verlag, 1965); *Die Toten
    bleiben jung* (1949) (Neuwied and Darmstadt: Luchterhand,

1981).

23 Nedoshivin, "On the Problem of the Beautiful in Soviet Art," 1950. Quoted in Leonid Heller, "A World of Prettiness: Socialist Realism and its Aesthetic Categories," *South Atlantic Quarterly* 94:3 (Summer 1995), p. 709.

24 Slavoj Zizek, *For they know not what they do. Enjoyment as a political factor* (Verso: London, 1991), p. 258. In this context, Zizek recalls Stalin's statement: "We, the Communists, are people of a special mold. We are made of special stuff" (256/57). What Zizek seems to merge are two dimensions of the sublime: the idea of unlimited power, but also the Lacanian idea of the objet a as the object of desire which is forever out of reach.

25 Article in Thomas issue

26 "Sozialistische Literatur der Gegenwart," *Neue deutsche Literatur* 7.5 (1959), pp. 3-7.

27 Otto Gotsche, *Die Fahne von Kriwoj Rog*, p. 17 and 369-370.

28 See my "At the Center an Absence: Foundationalist Narratives of the GDR and the Legitimatory Discourse of Antifascism," *Monatshefte* 84 (1992), pp. 23-45.

29 For instance, Karl Mundstock, *Helle Nächte* (1958), or Hans Marchwitza, *Roheisen* (1955).

30 Christa Wolf, "Moskauer Novelle," *An den Tag gebracht. Prosa junger Menschen*, edited by Heinz Sachs (Halle: Mitteldeutscher Verlag, 1961), p. 165. Page references from now on as MO/plus page number.

31 Didier Anzieu, "L'enveloppe sonore du Soi," *Nouvelle Revue de Psychanalyse* 13 (Spring 1976), p. . I deliberately go back to Kaja Silverman's founding texts, Anzieu and Rosolato. *The Acoustic Mirror. The Female Voice in Psychoanalysis and Cinema* (Bloomington and Indianapolis: Indiana University Press, 1988).

32 The term *Übereinstimmung* is a central term in Wolf's own discussions of her involvement in East German politics. Besides the idea of agreement, the word also carries the notion

of voices harmonizing with each other, of being in attunment.

33 Guy Rosolato, "La voix: entre corps et language," *Revue Française de Psychanalyse* 38 (1974), p. 82-83.

34 Slavoj Zizek, *For they know not what they do*, p. 260.

35 Christa Wolf, "The Shadow of a Dream: A Sketch of Karoline von Günderrode," in her *The Author's Dimension*, p. 133.

36 Christa Wolf, "Fortgesetzter Versuch," in her *Die Dimension des Autors*, vol. I, p. 345.

37 Elaine Scarry, *The Body in Pain* (New York and Oxford: Oxford UP, 1985).

38 Christa Wolf, *Cassandra. A Novel and Four Essays*, translated by Jan Van Heuck (New York: Farrar, Straus and Giroux, 1984), p. 38-37; I will quote from the novel as C/plus page number; K/plus page number refers to the following German edition: *Kassandra. Erzählung* (Darmstadt: Luchterhand Literaturverlag, 1986). Originally published in 1983, here p. 46-47. TA stands for translation amended.

39 In his previously cited report on the panel entitled "Hysteria Today" held at the 28th International Psychoanalytical Congress in Paris in 1973, Jean Laplanche reassessed the concept of hysteria, arguing for conversion as a central component ("Panel on 'Hysteria Today,'" *International Journal of Psycho-Analysis* (1974), p. 466 and 467).

40 Ibid., p. 468.

41 Ibid., p. 466. Freud added "Hysterical Phantasies and Their Relation to Bisexuality" in 1908, "Some General Remarks on Hysterical Attacks" in 1909. In the former, he wrote: "Hysterical symptoms are the expression on the one hand of a masculine unconscious sexual phantasy, and on the other hand of a feminine one." In the latter, he elaborated on the issue of identification: "The attack becomes obscured through the fact that the patient attempts to carry out the activities of both the figures who appear in the phantasy, that is to say, through *multiple identification*. Compare, for instance, the example I mentioned . . . in which a patient tore off her dress with one

hand (as the man) while she pressed it to her body with the other (as the woman)" (*The Standard Edition of the Complete Psychological Works of Sigmund Freud*, vol. IX, p. 165 and p. 230).

42 For an excellent discussion of the different aspects of the concept of hysteria, see Parveen Adams, "Symptoms and Hysteria," in her *The Emptiness of the Image. Psychoanalysis and Sexual Difference* (London and New York: Routledge, 1996), pp. 5 - 26.

43 Which it already is in *Kindheitsmuster*. See Chapter V of my *Post-Fascist Fantasies*.

44 Slavoj Zizek, *The Sublime Object of Ideology*, p. 114 and 113.

45 Anna Seghers, "Vaterlandsliebe. Rede auf dem I. Internationalen Schriftstellerkongreß zur Verteidigung der Kultur 1935," in *Die Macht der Worte. Reden - Schriften - Briefe* (Leipzig and Weimar: Gustav Kiepenheuer Verlag, 1979), p. 33.

46 See, for instance, her interview with Günter Gaus where she speaks about her life proceeding along clearly marked breaks ("Auf mir bestehen. Christa Wolf im Gespräch mit Günter Gaus," p. 257 - 258).

47 Christa Wolf, *The Quest for Christa T.*, translated by Christopher Middleton (New York: Farrar, Straus, and Giroux, 1970), p. 170. I will quote from this text as CT/plus page number; N/plus page number (here p. 188) refers to the following German edition: *Nachdenken über Christa T.* (Hamburg and Zürich: Luchterhand Literaturverlag, 1991), originally published in 1969.

48 Christa Wolf, "Notwendige Feststellung" (December 22, 1969) in *Dokumentation zu Christa Wolf "Nachdenken über Christa T."*, p. 185 - 187.

49 Karen Remmler reads this body symptomatically as the expression of the contradictions East German women had to live in her "Deciphering the Body of Memory: Writing by Former East German Women Writers," in *Postcommunism and*

the Body Politic, edited by Ellen E. Berry, special issue of *Genders* (New York and London: New York University Press, 1994), vol. 22, pp. 134 - 163.

50 Kornelia Hauser, *Patriarchat als Sozialismus*, p. 229.

51 Although the narrator already hints at the problematic nature of this act as she continues: "But how does one cut oneself away from oneself?" (CT/27; N/36).

52 Kornelia Hauser, *Patriarchat als Sozialismus*, p. 218 and 219.

53 Allison Lewis, "'Foiling the Censor'," p. 373.

54 Christa Wolf, "Tagebuchauszüge zu 'Nachdenken über Christa T." in *Dokumentation zu Christa Wolf "Nachdenken über Christa T."*, edited by Angela Drescher (Frankfurt am Main: Luchterhand Literaturverlag, 1991), p. 196.

55 Sigmund Freud, "Mourning and Melancholia," *The Standard Edition of the Complete Psychological Works of Sigmund Freud*, edited by James Strachey (London: The Hogarth), p. 249.

56 See Wolf's own assessment of the importance of this Plenum in Christa Wolf, "Erinnerungsbericht," *Kahlschlag. Das 11. Plenum des ZK der SED 1965*, edited by Günther Agde (Berlin: Aufbau Verlag, 1991), pp. 263 - 272; see also Therese Hörnigk, "Das 11. Plenum und die Folgen. Christa Wolf im politischen Diskurs der 60er," *Neue Deutsche Literatur* 10 (1990), pp. 50 - 58.

57 Maria Torok, "The Illness of Mourning and the Fantasy of the Exquisite Corpse," in Nicolas Abraham and Maria Torok, *The Shell and the Kernel*, edited, translated, and with an introduction by Nicholas T. Rand (Chicago and London: The University of Chicago Press, 1994), vol. I, p. 130.

58 Ibid., p. 130 - 31.

59 Ibid., p. 131.

60 Nicolas Abraham and Maria Torok, "'The Lost Object - Me'": Notes on Endocryptic Identification," in *The Shell and the Kernel*, vol. I, p. 141.

61 Maria Torok, "The Illness of Mourning," p. 131. Torok emphasizes again that this loss has to be of a type that prohibits it being communicated (ibid., p. 129), a condition given by censorship.

62 Ibid., p. 131.

63 Ibid., p. 118.

64 Ibid., p. 116.

65 Ibid., p. 118.

66 In the second scene, the narrator makes every effort to keep the reader in the dark about the "reality" of this scene: is this a dream, or a memory, did it, did it not take place? Was the narrator awake or asleep when it took place? The narrator thus deliberately recreates the "ghostly" atmosphere of the first scene in Chapter 17.

67 This is repeated almost verbatim on CT/172; N/192.

68 The term "politics of authenticity" is from Paul Gilroy's book on the myth of black identity (*The Black Atlantic. Modernity and Double Consciousness* (Cambridge, Massachusetts: Harvard University Press, 1993), p. 72).

69 Kurt Drawert, *Spiegelland* (Frankfurt am Main: Suhrkamp Verlag, 1992), p. 56.

Nancy Kaiser

Response

Gertrude Stein, upon returning to visit a once-familiar locale from her youth, reportedly commented: "There is no there there."[1] We might somehow share that sentiment upon revisiting the locale of subjective authenticity.

In a bold and relentlessly coherent paper, Julia Hell invites us to revisit some of our most cherished critical orthodoxies—ones long held as well as those which GDR-scholars, among others, are busily creating. The emergence-convergence histories require the linchpin of an authentic voice crying in the hegemonic wilderness in order to keep rolling. This voice has various related modalities: women's writing in the *post-Christa T.* era; a modernist (sometimes designated as feminine) aesthetic disruptive of socialist realist paradigms; resistance to the (often designated as paternal-patriarchal) official discourse, with an implied critical distance to GDR state-socialism. The authentic voice is at times positioned as vanguard, at times as external, but it is always (re)presentable in the figure of Christa Wolf.

It is not the actual person of Christa Wolf which we are being asked to revisit in Julia Hell's presentation, but her texts, read as a continuum from *Moskauer Novelle* onward, as well as Wolf's textual construction of her own position as author, which Professor Hell analyzes in Wolf's reading of Anna Seghers. Wolf's texts and her self-stylization as author are inextricably and centrally involved in the political-ideological project of the GDR, designated in the paper we have just heard as totalitarianism in Claude Lefort's terms. Julia Hell's paper investigates the extent to which all positions, including those often figured as oppositional, and all voices, including those often figured as critical, are informed by the hegemonic discourse. As we have heard, the foundational GDR narratives of the antifascist father, endowed with a sublime communist body, have a fantasy after-life in the postfascist desexualized or "pure" body endowed with a "new voice." And, since voice is never solely in opposition to a material, sexualized body but always already marked by the trace of the corporeal, any attempted mimesis of a "pure" voice is bound to fail. Wolf's texts and her appropriation of Seghers enact this failure, which is not Christa Wolf's personal failure but rather the conflict inherent to the project itself. Among Christa Wolf's literary texts, in Julia Hell's account, *Kassandra* provides scenes or stages of resistance, as well as a perhaps full mimesis of Anna Seghers's "tone." Resignation, the choice of death as eradication of the bodily trace, and the parallel drawn to the Jewish victims of National Socialism nonetheless bind the text strongly to the political-ideological project Kassandra is often read as eluding.

The argument is complex, and I have therefore highlighted points in my understanding of it. The psychoanalytic framework of analysis is essential for examining the tenacity of discursive structures, for analyzing the impossibility of getting outside or beyond. There truly is no "there" there. Yet the use of psycho-analysis in Julia Hell's paper is not essentialized, but thoroughly contextualized and historicized. It is a tool, and not an answer—a tool for understanding the multilayered and historically configured nature of voice, specifically how the foundational antifascist discourse of the GDR as a political-ideological project configures even the resisting voices.

Pondering this analysis makes Christa Wolf's texts even more interesting. It also provides a framework for reading patterns of complicity and resistance in analyzing literary texts as participants in their historical moment. I in no way hear what Professor Hell has presented as being dismissive or derogatory toward Christa Wolf or women's writing in the GDR. What she has presented makes it, not only more interesting, but also crucial that we read and reread those texts.

One question I would like to raise, however, concerns the position and possibilities for distinguishing strategies and voices of resistance within the psychoanalytic framework as it has been presented. It would seem that staging hysteria is the only model. I have long been enamored of Teresa de Lauretis's model, which draws on contemporary film theory and identifies "movement between the (represented) discursive space of the positions made available by hegemonic discourses and the space-off, the elsewhere, of those discourses."[2] My musings on the topic lead me to two questions. The first one has two parts: 1) is staging hysteria the sole voice of resistance within the psychoanalytic framework, and 2) is the limited nature of that voice and therefore the applicability of the psychoanalytic framework which allows no other position especially relevant for understanding the totalitarianism (again in Lefort's terms) that was the GDR? Phrased in somewhat different terms: is there no textual resistance to the hegemonic discourse? Phrased in de Lauretis's terms: are there traces of an "elsewhere"?

My second question, before I relinquish my priority of response to questions from the audience, concerns the further development of the generational model which Julia Hell has outlined: the foundational narratives (the literature of the fathers), the transition to the literature of the sons and daughters, and then what? Body and voice in the grandsons and granddaughters? Julia ended her paper with a quotation from Kurt Drawert. While writing this response, I recalled the opening of Kerstin Hensel's *Tanz am Kanal*, where the first-person narrator, a young girl, refuses to repeat what she is told. The German admonition is to "sprich nach" ("repeat after me"). Her father attempts to get her to say "Violine" and "sozialistisch." The young protagonist not only resists the patterns of speech, but refuses to "see" the violin at first as anything but "ein Dackel" (a dachshund).[3]

I would be interested in tracing the analysis Julia Hell has presented into texts by the following generations of writers—not as "post-modern" in Wolfgang Emmerich's triadic historical scheme, but with regard to the questions of body and voice raised by Professor Hell's work.

But I must follow my own musings myself and will gladly relinquish my priority of response to the questions and comments

I know are waiting. In the dual sense in which Jost Hermand spoke of the title and topic of this year's Wisconsin Workshop as being "Contentious Memories," I believe Julia Hell's paper to be productive. It certainly presents a challenge to critical orthodoxies. Whether it is "strittig" (disputed) remains for our discussion.

Notes

1 Gertrude Stein, *Everybody's Autobiography*, 2nd ed. (Cambridge, MA: Exact Change, 1993) 298.

2 Teresa de Lauretis, *Technologies of Gender: Essays on Theory, Film, and Fiction* (Bloomington: University of Indiana Press, 1987) 26.

3 Kerstin Hensel, *Tanz am Kanal* (Frankfurt am Main: Suhrkamp, 1994).

William Maltarich
Alan Ng
Nancy Thuleen

Literature as Contested Ground
A Retrospective of GDR Studies in the United States

Introduction

A retrospective examination of US work on GDR literature immediately comes up against a number of methodological difficulties, the first of which are matters of definition. The two most obvious questions are "What is GDR literature?" and "What is a US work?" To answer these questions would involve a complex interrogation of the role of national identity in both literary scholarship and literature, which is far beyond the scope of this project. Because our focus is on the unifying trends in the investigations by US scholars of this literature, GDR literature will be defined here as including both those works written within the German Democratic Republic and those written by authors who had moved to the West with an already established literary reputation. This definition, in turn, best describes the operative assumptions upon which US scholarship depended.

Our twofold definition of a US work used here is equally heuristic and, perhaps, equally arbitrary. In the first section, dealing with the early stages of our chronology, a US work will be any work on GDR literature based not on the nationality of the scholar, but on the location of the appearance of the work—more precisely, only articles appearing in US journals come into consideration. The remainder of this article utilizes a broader definition for a US work, focussing on the residence of the scholars. Under this definition, the publications of any scholar working in the US at the time of publication will be considered. This twofold definition gives this examination a more useful selection of material than either definition could alone. Articles published in US journals reflect the interests in the United States regardless of their origins, and the works of scholars in the US, regardless of where they were published, give a more complete picture of the results of these interests. Again, there is a historical basis for our definition; increasing communication among the growing number of participants created a geographically specific scholarly setting.

The second issue involves the organizing principle behind this examination. Although a chronological examination of US literary studies of the GDR provides useful insights into the development of the field, it leaves little room for detail and depth. On the other hand, close examination of a few exemplary studies or scholars could easily distort the picture of the US scene as a whole. Therefore a combination of views seems once again most appropriate—proceeding chronologically with more detailed analysis of important developments within each period examined. The earliest studies of the GDR are examined here in their relationship to later studies in the US, the more detailed analysis of poetry studies should help demonstrate the developments during the boom in GDR studies, and an investigation of the effect of the introduction of a feminist perspective into US work on the GDR should demonstrate the influence of this point of view in examinations of the GDR both within the US and abroad. In this respect, the following offers both an overview and specific analyses, and, although by no means all encompassing, should be representative of trends in the US throughout its encounters with "real existing socialism" as represented by the German Democratic Republic.

William Maltarich

I. The Earliest Studies of the GDR or
The Establishment of the Anti-Establishment.

Beginning in about 1986, American Germanists studying the literature of the GDR began to become self-reflexive. This trend became even more pronounced after the events of 1989/1990, events which seemed to offer the perfect opportunity for reassessment if not to demand it.[1] Though often informative and insightful, all of these retrospectives reject out of hand the work done in the 50s and 60s, work which had a large influence on the first serious GDR-scholars here in the U.S.

In the earliest U.S. retrospectives, the first generation of serious GDR scholars rejected the studies of the generation before them as hopelessly stuck in a cold-war mentality. The blindness caused by this mentality exhibits itself, so the argument goes, in the tendency to deem only the work of Brecht worthy of examination—and for most U.S. articles from the 50s and 60s this was indeed true. However, both in establishing a paradigm that would continue to be prominent throughout GDR studies and in providing a foil against which this new generation would establish its work, these early studies are quite important. An examination of articles appearing in the major U.S. Germanistik journals[2] demonstrates that the explosion in GDR studies in the early 70s was not so much a break with, but a shift in perspective from earlier studies, that the studies of Brecht made during this early period helped establish a paradigm for a GDR author long after the 70s, and that, in fact, this shift in perspective determined to a great extent the shape of U.S. studies of the GDR from the boom in the early 70s on.

Before examining the interesting case of Brecht, it seems worthwhile to point out some of the (admittedly scarce) exceptions to the sweeping condemnation of the study of GDR literature in the 50s and early 60s. First it should be noted that from very early on the periodical *Books Abroad*[3], published at the University of

Oklahoma, took notice of works published in the GDR. Although this notice took the form of (usually) brief book reviews, *Books Abroad* stands out as the only consistent source of information about GDR publications at the time. Some articles in U.S. german-istics journals also stand out as important, especially in retrospect. W.G. Marigold's 1956 article "Some Notes on the Cultural Periodicals of Post-War Germany,"[4] for example, although showing some naivete ("*Die Amerikanische Rundschau* completely avoids politics") also finds it important "to remind ourselves that some fine periodicals appear in East Germany, several of them almost completely free of noticeable political bias"[5] and gives *Sinn und Form* as a prime example.

Two much more biased examinations point to directions that would later become important in the area of GDR studies: Gustave Mathieu's "Was liest Hänschen Ost-Deutschland"[6] from 1957 and John Frey's 1953 article "Socialist Realism in East Germany"[7]. Mathieu examines readers and grammars from GDR primary schools and discovers not only an amount of political bias he finds alarming but also a heavy Russian linguistic influence (he cites the grammar's examples of weak nouns - Löwe, Mensch and Aktivist) and shows concern that the German language could eventually split, noticing with the partiality typical of the time: "Schon heute muß sich Hänschen in der DDR unter vielen Wörtern seiner Mutter-sprache etwas ganz anderes vorstellen, als diese in Wirklichkeit bedeuten."[8]   Of course, "reality" is, for Mathieu, the exclusive property of the West.   Frey's very early article in the German Quarterly is the first in a U.S. germanistic journal to examine the tenets of socialist realism, albeit with a hefty dose of cold war bravado.   Frey mentions its principles, compares this realism to others and, again typical for the time, stresses the Russian influence behind this type of fiction and its ideological implications as a rationalistic-materialistic perspective "which in these days of socialistic realism is slanted to fit the exigencies of totali-tarianism."[9]   Among the conscientious followers of this school he mentions Hermlin, Reinig and Kunert.   As was common at the time,

Frey cites Brecht and Seghers as examples of "occasionally tolerated exceptions."[10]

Of course, Brecht represented the greatest difficulty for those writing about German literature at the time because he had already been accepted as an important literary figure. Even those most willing to dismiss all literature in the East had to somehow explain Brecht's simultaneous presence there and in the canon. One method of doing this involved the very New Critical method of ignoring Brecht's politics altogether, accepting Brecht into the literary canon while rejecting his politics and other literature from the GDR. For example, in the *German Quarterly* Thomas O. Brandt wrote: "Von der Literatur der Ostzone soll mit einer einzigen Ausnahme und gelegentliche Seitenblicke hier nicht die Rede sein, und zwar aus Gründen des Wertmangels und weil ihre Phänomene sich durchaus auf einen Nenner, nämlich den politisch sich gleichbleibende beziehen."[11] As far as the single exception, Brandt writes: "Von (Brechts) politscher Einstellung—er hat sich offen zum Kommunismus bekannt—wollen wir hier absehen....Seine literarische Bedeutung bleibt vom Westen Deutschlands anerkannt. Für den Osten ist seine politische von größerer Bedeutung."[12]

Apart from the insistence on mentioning Brecht's open support of communism, Herbert Reichert takes a different, although equally representative approach, pointing out inconsistency between Brecht's (mistaken) politics and his (irreproachable) literary work. Reichert examines *Mutter Courage* and finds "that Brecht had imbued his Mutter Courage with at least some measure of free will. Such free will, incidentally, may seem inconsistent in a character created by a professed Marxist who is by rights obligated to believe in economic determinism. Marxists are, however, rather uniformly illogical in this regard...."[13] Less common is the complete rejection of Brecht based on his politics, for example Peter Heller's statement that "Everyone of Brecht's theoretical statements can and should be reduced to the level of Communist dogma."[14]

In addition to these approaches, however, we find the most interesting and most influential situation of Brecht within the GDR.

In short, these studies made Brecht into a sort of tragic hero, a great artist who shared the basic beliefs of a system to which he refused to belong completely and which in turn refused to completely accept him. For example, H.P. Boeninger's "The Dilemma of Bertolt Brecht" which appeared in 1955 in *Monatshefte*[15], stresses not only that Brecht never joined the Communist Party but also the heroic quality inherent in this stance: "To remain aloof from the group which rules the fate and minds of people in the Eastern Zone is either a display of foolhardiness or ferocious independence."[16] Boeninger stresses that such an independent thinker neither belongs nor is really welcome in the GDR and hopes for Brecht's return to the West. Two years later, Ernest Bornemann's "credo quia absurdum. An epitaph for Bertolt Brecht"[17] comes at Brecht from a similar angle. Bornemann gives a straight-ahead biography of Brecht and then comes to the crux of his argument, stating that although Brecht indeed had beliefs in common with the GDR system, his plays were more often performed and appreciated in the West. This he sees as Brecht's personal tragedy.

Finally, Peter Demetz' 1964 article "Galileo in East Berlin. Notes on the Drama of the DDR."[18] is remarkable for several reasons: It shows the first signs of Brecht's position in the GDR becoming the model for the U.S. view of "true" artists in the East, and it deals with GDR theater beyond Brecht. Demetz moves from an examination of Brecht's self-editing of Galileo for a GDR audience to an examination of Peter Hacks whom he sees following in Brecht's footsteps albeit with a bit less fury and a bit more sensuality than his predecessor. Demetz mentions specifically that Hacks, too, had been attacked in the GDR for his use of Brecht's Alienation effect, noting that the GDR establishment considered it an effective tool when used to point out the injustices in Chicago or the Third Reich, but inappropriate within a GDR context. Demetz sees a cyclical pattern of repression and relaxation in the GDR and sees Hacks as a new player in an old struggle, a struggle initiated by Brecht. This point of view, the Brecht-Paradigm of a political believer caught in a system of concrete and somewhat philistine literary politics would later dominate American views of GDR authors.[19] Such a paradigm helped to open the way for analysis of the GDR itself because this cyclical repression and relaxation, this recurring struggle, had its roots in the system as well as in rebellious or uncomfortable authors.

Another important change in the American attitude toward the GDR and its authors began to become apparent soon after Demetz' article. If early studies demonstrated a cold war mentality, studies now shifted their perspective away from a US-good, USSR-bad mentality to a general antipathy toward "The System" in both countries. In the wake of Vietnam, the cold war antithesis between the free West and totalitarian East fell apart, only to replaced by a new emphasis—If both systems were corrupt, then outsiders and opposition in either system must have been outside of and opposed to corruption. Hence those on the margins and those attacked by the system became the locus of righteousness.[20]

The first signs of this change of attitude in specific relation to the GDR appeared in the Partisan Review in 1966.[21] Eric Bentley's article "In Bahnhof Friedrichstrasse" specifically draws parallels between the evils of both the US and the GDR governments and between the opposition in both countries. For example, commenting on Ulbricht's physical appearance, Bentley writes "His violence is no more apparent from his person than Goldwater's or Johnson's." He goes on to describe the collapse of the old cold war ideology caused by the recognition that the West could not be considered the good side of the battle any more than the East. Both sides had donned the white hat and neither had proved worthy of it:

> The East, as is known, has real freedom instead of formal freedom. But that's nothing. The West has plain old Freedom, of which the capital F reaches God...This Freedom has an unambiguous meaning: that you're not in the East bloc...So do not run away with the idea that the Free in the Free University (of Berlin) means that no charge is made for tuition. On the contrary. It means that

the faculty may be Nazis but that they certainly aren't communists.[22]

Bentley demolishes the myths that both sides of the cold war propagated in order to locate the justice and righteousness within opposition on either front. "Choosing sides is not important " he writes, but staying "a thorn in the side of the government."[23] As an example of such a thorn in the side of he mentions, for the first time in the US and remarkably early, Wolf Biermann.

This change in perspective made the Brecht-Paradigm even more important. From this vantage point, it began to seem that Brecht's dilemma was the result of his belonging to the kind of opposition that would soon be a favorite object of study in the US: He stayed where his beliefs led him but also stayed true to himself, he was, in short, a member of the Opposition, an Outsider.

Of course Bentley's position did not catch on immediately—the old cold war mentality was still present, if fading, in 1966. An article by Robert Rie in the German Quarterly, "Ein amerikanischer Professor in der Zone,"[24] demonstrates this clearly. For Rie, the GDR watchtowers are built "in dem Stil KZ Wachtürme," the military uniforms look like Wehrmacht uniforms with Soviet hats, there are still traces of feudalism everywhere: "Statt der alten preußischen Königstreue, verlangen die neuen Herren unbedingte Republikstreue," and the students to whom he lectures are still "typisch preußisch in ihrer Aggressivität." It is no wonder that the view Bentley so clearly articulates in 1966 became dominant only gradually.

Around the time that Bentley's article appeared, other articles dealing with GDR works and authors more specifically appeared alongside articles such as Rie's, marking the beginning of the end of the dismissal of GDR literature on the basis of US cold-war ideology. In 1966 the German Quarterly ran a review of Erwin Strittmatter's Ole Bienkopp written by Theodore Huebener (whose The Literature of East Germany, published in 1970, was the first U.S. book to deal with the topic).[25] Also in 1966, this time in the

Germanic Review, Jerry Glenn's "An Introduction to the Poetry of Johannes Bobrowski" appeared.[26] Glenn mentions the GDR in the first paragraph and concludes that "Like many East German poets, Bobrowski laments the recent history and present condition of Mankind. But Bobrowski's poems, unlike those of most of his countrymen, are not bound to a specific doctrine or series of historical events." In other words, Bobrowski stands out because he does not conform to GDR expectations.

Between 1966 and the Boom in GDR studies which began between 1973 and 1975 (the GDR Sonderheft of Dimension appeared in 1973, in 1974 the first MLA Seminar on East Germany and the first Conway Conference took place, and 1975 brought the appearance of the GDR Bulletin) a number of books dealing with GDR literature appeared, most notably Huebener's work, John Flores' *Poetry in East Germany*, and the reader *Westen und Osten*. In general, reflection on U.S. GDR studies tends to look for its beginnings in these first works. It was, however, the work of the 50s and 60s, especially the work on Brecht and the change of perspective represented by Bentley's article that set the paradigm for work here in the United States. Thomas Fox recognized this author as oppositional hero paradigm in 1993, and only in 1993 did he see GDR studies moving away from it.[27] Fox however traced neither the roots of this paradigm, nor its implications. Many of the blind spots in the GDR work done here in the U.S. can, in retrospect, be directly related to the weaknesses in this view of GDR authors and literature. The blindness to abuses by the government in the GDR, about which David Pike complains vehemently in a letter to the GDR Bulletin in 1992,[28] stem directly from an interest in opposition in and of itself, regardless of the system opposed. The tendencies to discover opposition too readily, to see any conflict with an oversimplified view of socialist realism as a sign of dissidence, to treat the relationship between the state and the author superficially, if at all, to gloss over the distinction between author and text, and the lack of comparison between East and West German literature, all stem in part from this paradigm. In fact, until the modifications brought on by the introduction of a feminist perspective into U.S. GDR studies (a perspective readily accepted in part because of its emphasis on the woman as outsider and opposition), this paradigm and its shortcomings remained quite pervasive, as an examination of U.S. studies of East German poetry demonstrates.

Notes

1   See for example Angelika Bammer, "The American Feminist Reception of GDR Literature (With a Glance at West Germany)," *GDR Bulletin* 16.2 (1990): 18-24; David Bathrick, "Productive Mis-Reading. GDR Literature in the USA," *GDR Bulletin* 16.2 (1990): 1-6; Thomas C. Fox, "Germanistik and GDR Studies: (Re)Reading a Censored Literature," *Monatshefte*, 85.3 (1993): 284-293; Patricia Herminghouse, "Studien zur DDR-Literatur in den U.S.A. Ein Überblick," *Deutschland-Archiv* 19 (1986): 831-843.

2   The germanistic journals examined here include *Dimension, The German Quarterly, German Studies Review, Germanic Notes, The Germanic Review, Monatshefte, New German Critique, New German Review.*

3   *Books Abroad*, Norman, Oklahoma, University of Oklahoma. 1927-1976 continued after 1976 (Volume 50) as *World Literature Today.*

4   W.G. Marigold, "Some Notes on the Cultural Periodicals of Post-War Germany," *German Quarterly* 29.1(1956): 38-42.

5   Ibid., 39.

6   Gustave Mathieu, "Was liest Hänschen in Ost-Deutschland?" *German Quarterly* 30.1 (1957): 15-19.

7   John Frey, "Socialist Realism in East Germany," *German Quarterly* 26.4 (1953): 272-278.

8   Mathieu, 19.

9   Frey, 273.

10   Ibid, 276.

11 Thomas O. Brandt, "Gedanken über die zeitgenössische deutsche Dichtung," *German Quarterly* 33.1 (1960): 104.

12 Ibid., 113.

13 Herbert W. Reichert, "Hauptmann's *Frau Wolff* and Brecht's *Mutter Courage*," *German Quarterly* 34.4 (1961):446-447.

14 Peter Heller, "Nihilist into Activist: Two Phases in the Development of Bertolt Brecht," *Germanic Review* 28 (1953): 149.

15 H.P. Boeninger, "The Dilemma of Bertolt Brecht," *Monatshefte* 47 (1955): 387-392.

16 Ibid., 390-391.

17 Ernest Bornemann, "credo quia absurdum. An Epitaph for Bertolt Brecht," *Kenyon Review* 21 (1959): 169-98.

18 Peter Demetz, "Galileo in East Berlin. Notes on the Drama of the DDR," *German Quarterly* 37.3 (1964):239-245.

19 The name "Brecht-Paradigm" is somewhat misleading in that it has very little to do with Brecht himself. It has rather to do with the U.S. perception of Brecht, as a writer of merit, and his conflict within the GDR. Claims that conflict with the government proved individualism, talent, and literary merit would continue in the U.S. throughout the GDR's existence.

20 Paradoxically, the outsider/alternative position of Socialism in the United States made possible the split between those interested in Socialism as an alternative and those interested in the alternative within socialism. Both of these groups of U.S. scholars, however, it focused their attention on "oppositional" authors within the GDR, despite their different outlooks. Even those enamored with socialism paid attention almost exclusively to those authors struggling with its real existing variant. For these reasons, the shift toward outsiders and opposition is a valid description for both of these variants.

21 Eric Bentley, "In Bahnhof Friedrichstrasse," *The Partisan Review* 33.1 (1966): 97-109.

22 Ibid., 98.

23 Ibid., 103.

24 Robert Rie, "Ein amerikanischer Professor in der Zone," *German Quarterly* 39 (1966): 267-270.

25 Theodore Huebener, Theodore. "Erwin Strittmatter's *Ole Bienkopp*," *German Quarterly* 39 (1966):119-121.

26 Jerry Glenn, "An Introduction to the Poetry of Johannes Bobrowski," *Germanic Review* 41.1 (1966): 45-56.

27 Thomas C. Fox, "Germanistik and GDR Studies: (Re)Reading a Censored Literature," *Monatshefte*, Vol; 85.3 (1993): 284-293.

28 "A Letter from David Pike," *GDR Bulletin* 18.1 (Spring 1992), 45.

Alan Ng

II. The narrowing effects of specialization.
Case study: GDR poetry

We have established, on the basis of a broad bibliographical survey, that publishing activity by Americans on GDR literature increased dramatically in the middle of the 1970s. In order to be able to characterize the mass of secondary literature over the following fifteen years, we chose the subcategory of poetry as a clear focus. In addition, the way poetry was received in this country most clearly characterizes the fundamental politicization of American approaches to GDR literature. In the late 1960s, as described above, the search for oppositional literature entered an unwritten agenda of American criticism, and GDR literature became interesting as a place where the real-world effects of engaged literature could be documented. An investigation of how such an agenda was pursued by means of reading poetry—that most autonomous form of literature—best demonstrates the trends of criticism.

A survey of the work done on GDR poetry by American scholars vividly reveals this politicization of literary studies. Let me call John Flores' 1971 book, *Poetry in East Germany*, the seminal work in the field.[1] The only preceding works devoted to GDR poetry were Glenn's aforementioned 1966 article on Bobrowski, and two articles on Peter Huchel's poetry in 1968.[2] Flores' work went on to become the single most often-cited American publication by Americans writing on GDR poetry. John Flores, a graduate student at Yale with openly leftist sympathies—apparent from his introduction—, received a Fulbright grant to spend a year in Berlin in 1966 and 1967. He wrote this book under the guidance of Peter Demetz, who, as described above, had first applied Brecht's outsider role as a measure of GDR authors in 1964. Flores followed Demetz's methodological lead: "I hope to show that the writers who come into conflict with the prescribed policies, or seem to ignore them altogether, are generally the ones most worthy of discussion."[3] And his selection of poets turned out to be representative for

American interests. He gave the most attention to four first-generation poets, Stephan Hermlin, Franz Fühmann, Peter Huchel, and Johannes Bobrowski. And it was only Hermlin's, Huchel's, Bobrowski's and Brecht's later poetry that any Americans found worthy of individual studies until the late 1970s. The lone exception was Jost Hermand's 1973 article on Wolf Biermann.[4] But of these four poets, only Huchel's poetry earned any sustained interest, if one individual's four publications on Huchel in the 1980s can be called evidence of a "sustained interest."[5]

In other words, American studies of GDR poetry did not flower until around 1980, when attention focused on what we now call the "middle generation" of GDR poets—those who first entered the literary scene in the GDR after the building of the Berlin Wall. An extensive bibliographical survey provides the basis for this description of American publications on GDR poetry.[6] In terms of total numbers of American publications before 1992, the three most popular topics were the poets Günter Kunert, on whose poetry the first study appeared in 1974, then Volker Braun, starting in 1978, and Sarah Kirsch, starting in 1979. Sarah Kirsch was the poet most written on by far, with seven Americans publishing 17 studies dedicated to her poetry, at least one appearing every year from 1979 through 1992. Sex apparently mattered; six of those seven critics writing on Sarah Kirsch were women, whereas only a quarter of all the US scholars writing on GDR poetry were women (13 of 43). The most unexpected numerical finding is that there was a clear and unique peak in scholarly publications from 1980 to 1984, when more than a third of all American studies of GDR poetry were published (38 of the 95 publications).Three-quarters of those studies were on poets born between 1929 and 1939, thus the middle generation. And although the younger Prenzlauer Berg poets (chiefly Sascha Anderson) became objects of studies appearing in 1984, the "middle generation" poets remained at the center of activity through 1991. Let me round out this description by mentioning that Christine Cosentino's 21 publications between 1978 and 1991 clearly dominated the field of GDR poetry studies both in number and breadth of topics.

This numerical picture of American scholarship provides a useful background for investigating *how* Americans wrote on GDR poetry. The concentration on this particular generation of poets, and indeed the fact that 80% of all publications focused on a particular *poet*, especially in regard to his or her relationship to the GDR, is a quantitative indicator that Demetz's and Flores's poetic standards of quality, which centered on *poets*—as long as they were critical of yet still loyal to the GDR—continued into the 1980s. Qualitatively, as well, American scholars were consistent as a group, which allowed derivation of some "tenets of literary scholarship" upon which their critical methodologies depended. The first would be the centrality of the *poet* as a social and political critic who writes poems in order to achieve some intellectually defined effect upon his or her readership, or in order to communicate an argument. The other half of this communicative model of poetry assumed that the poet and "therefore" the poem are mediators of GDR society, and that the poem provides some kind of *documentation* of the personal and therefore social circumstances surrounding the poem's composition. Operating even further in the background was the assumption that a critic reads a poem *in order* to read its social origins, in this case, in order to investigate the GDR as a cultural and political entity.

Despite developments in the analytical methods applied to GDR poetry over the course of 25 years, these basic tenets, which represent a fundamentally political idea of poetry, sank further and further into what we can call the critical preconsciousness of American scholars. Back in 1973, when Jost Hermand made his self-named "kleines Plädoyer"[7] in defense of Biermann's poetry, he was very open and indeed provocative as he interrogated both Biermann's poetry and his reception in East and West in order to ask what Biermann's critical voice really had to offer as far as a "dritter Weg" for the GDR.[8] Similarly, in 1976 Jay Rosellini opens his thorough report on the 1972 cultural-political debates in the GDR with the bald statement: "In order to understand the evolution of poetry in the GDR, it is necessary to take into account the cultural policy of the Socialist Unity Party (SED)."[9] This contention seems harmless enough until one considers the path of subsequent American scholarship; then one is inclined to ask if anything *else* was necessary in order to read poetry. For example, the minority of scholars who did place their readings of GDR poetry in historical contexts larger than the GDR seemed to thereby ensure themselves a deeper analysis of the poetry. The most common such context was, of course, Brecht's legacy. In 1980 Theodore Fiedler read Günter Kunert's productive misreading of a Brecht poem, which led him to at least briefly question Kunert's communicative model of poetry: he notes the inconsistency between Kunert's "devaluation of the literal realism of literary works" with "his stated concern for the underlying relation of a work to its contemporary reality."[10] Fiedler did not mention that this inconsistency applied as well to American interpretations of GDR poetry. Richard Rundell's article from the same Brecht conference publication offers a critical commentary on reception of GDR poetry. Having started with Brecht, he is prompted to remark: "The innate ambiguity of poetic diction further complicates the question of opposition and dissent. Speculative discussions of straightforward versus deceptively compliant language and the dubious practice of reading all poetry from the DDR as 'code' are often the result."[11] But Rundell's criticism really applies to Western Cold War critics, and not to his peers in American GDR studies around 1980. Both scholars go on to read GDR poems not as any censor-proof 'code' but, like their colleagues, more as rhetorical devices designed by their poets to incite political criticism in their readers.

And that is the goal of reading that becomes consistent practice during the publication boom in the early 1980s, eclipsing the need to question the capability of poetry to perform such a function in the first place. This narrowed perspective allowed its own internally valid questions and techniques of scholarship. The clearest case is in the enthusiastic work done on Sarah Kirsch's poetry, initiated in 1979 under Christine Cosentino's prolific leadership. Kirsch's observed semantic imprecision is not sufficient to escape the critic's ability to nevertheless find the author's message in a poem. Cosentino observes: "Verunsichert stellt der Leser fest, daß selbst das Sicherste nicht mehr sicher ist." So she cleverly concludes: "Im Irritiertsein hat sich ihm die Botschaft der Kirsch erschlossen."[12] Cosentino's techniques of reading turn out to be representative for the criticism of the 80s; in general the relationship of a poem to its author's biography grounds the location of its socially critical message, and the feelings and associations that are expressed and evoked by the poetic techniques and themes are found in carefully executed close readings that focus on the dynamics of the poem-reader relationship. The underlying and unquestioned tenets of this kind of scholarship are nicely revealed by contrasting the enthusiasm of Kirsch reception with reception of Elke Erb's poetry, in which semantic play finally exceeds the careful reader's ability to find a message. Christine Cosentino strikes a clearly negative tone in 1982 as she describes the poems' lack of communicative intention and potential.[13] She openly sympathizes with and derives encouragement from Christa Wolf's similar reaction to Erb's poetry. In short, her objective description of the lack of a "Botschaft" in Erb's poetry comes across as a subjective disappointment in the course Erb chooses in regard to the possibility of a political function of poetry.

This desire to play transatlantic cheerleader and/or coach to "oppositional" GDR poets on the part of American critics, which had of course begun even before Hermand's 1973 admonishments to Biermann, became most apparent at the same time that scholarly activity peaked. The timing of the publication peak on poetry during the early 1980s, I suggest, has everything to do with the wave of emigration of poets following Biermann's *Ausbürgerung* in 1976. Whereas previous criticism identified specifically GDR internal opposition, once the poets left the GDR, the critics could and did more easily find a pan-humanist opposition to all ideological dogma in the poetry. The techniques of reading in these studies of "exile" poetry most clearly approach a kind of journalistic reduction of poetry to political commentary. Whether writing on Biermann, Kunze, Kirsch, or Kunert in the 13 such publications from 1980 to 1983, each study reads poems from before and after the poet's move in order to describe, in Jay Rosellini's words, "wie [sie] im kapitalistischen Teil Deutschlands zurechtkommen."[14] The word is measured by the deed in such studies, and the goal achieved is to measure the poet's political perspective. And most of them go on to conclude by openly speculating on the political direction the poet may take next.

Where American critics were most sensitive, therefore, was in obeying the limits of the poetologies of the poets they studied. Whether reading Brecht's Buckow Elegies, Volker Braun, or Sascha Anderson, critics responded to poetry in the way that particular poet intended, where that intention was documented by the author's biography or statements from the poet herself or himself. In general, the poetological statements of Kunert or Kunze from the mid 70s, in which their communicative models of poetry involving society, poet, poem, and reader were formulated, might as well have been the theoretical texts that unfortunately only *implicitly* founded American criticism.[15] We have here a clear case of literary theory being driven by its objects of study, and proof that exclusion of literary-theoretical or even simply methodological discussions constrains the grasp of literary criticism within the bounds of its object's internal structures.

This lack of theory is most clearly documented in the footnotes of American studies. In all the studies examined, GDR sources were cited the most or even exclusively. Sometimes only publications of the poet were cited. This focus on primary source material, and the fact that more West German critics were cited than fellow Americans, tells us that the Americans considered themselves to be more a part of the larger Western community of GDR scholarship than members of any American community. A noteworthy exception is among the publications by women. The publications on Sarah Kirsch are unique in their consistent citations of other recent American studies, all by other women. Since Sarah Kirsch was not particularly feminist herself, neither were these studies of her poetry, but nevertheless this working community is presumably explained by the uniquely strong community of feminist *Germanistik* in the US, an issue approached in the next section of this paper. Even more telling is that for all poetry studies, there was, with a very few exceptions, a universal lack of citations of works dealing with the fundamental questions of literary theory or methodology.

There was a larger context to this project: The large-scale philosophical shift during the 70s in American *Germanistik* can be summed up as a movement away from a hermetic New Critical approach towards political discourse studies in which the sociological functions and journalistic contents of literary texts become the objects of study. Even though outside of *Germanistik*, "the death of the author" was being proclaimed, in GDR studies there remained a sense of loyalty to both the circumstances of a text's composition and to its author as a human and as a political resister. This, along with the intellectual's confrontation with Cold War geopolitical dogma, made literature a tool for both sociological investigation as well as for exercising political rhetoric inside academic discourse.

The political perspective represented in American studies of GDR literature can now be restated. Except for the literary studies inspired by feminism, analyzed in the section below, no clear ideological position is apparent other than that of the outsider, continuing the tradition already described above. This same kind of universal humanism, however, characterizes the perspectives of the GDR *poets* as well, at least as they have been presented by the Americans. Although various scholars did conclude that the *poets* followed a strong Brechtian legacy, both poetically and poetologically, the scholars failed to observe that their own literary critical writings also assumed a Brechtian functionalization of literature. The shared anti-totalitarian agenda therefore reveals a project of self-identification that drove American reception of GDR literature, a project that was, however, never admitted. This lack of self-reflection, which characterized both literary critical methodology and the pursuit of personal interests in scholarship, was only countered in the much more self-reflexive development of American feminist criticism, which topic also brings us to the third stage of our retrospective of American GDR studies.

Notes

1   John Flores, *Poetry in East Germany: Adjustments, Visions, and Provocations, 1945–1970* (New Haven, 1971).

2   Ingo Seidler, "Peter Huchel und sein lyrisches Werk: Zum 65. Geburtstage am 3. April," in *Neue Deutsche Hefte* 15.1 (1968); Hans Egon Holthusen, "Natur und Geschichte in Huchels Gedicht" in Otto F. Best, ed., *Hommage für Peter Huchel: Zum 3. April 1968* (Munich, 1968).

3   Flores, p. 4.

4   Jost Hermand, "Biermanns Dilemma," in *Basis* 4 (1973).

5   Philip Dale Sweet published the following: "The Lyrical Subject in the Poetry of Peter Huchel," diss. (Univ. Michigan, 1980); "The Prophet in Peter Huchel's Poetry," in *Germanic Review* 57.1 (1982); "The Wanderer in Peter Huchel's Later Poetry," in *Publications of the Arkansas Philological Association* 10.1 (1984); "Primitivism in the Poetry of Peter Huchel," in *Germanic Notes* 18.3–4 (1987).

6   The bibliography included 95 publications, and may be published as a separate item, including tabular and graphical presentation of the data, by Alan Ng.

7   Jost Hermand, "Biermanns Dilemma," in *Basis* 4 (1973), p. 183.

8   Hermand, p. 191.

9   Jay Rosellini, "Poetry and Criticism in the GDR: The 1972 Discussion in the Context of Cultural Policy," in *New German Critique* 9 (1976), p. 153.

10   Theodore Fiedler, "The Reception of a Socialist Classic: Kunert and Biermann Read Brecht," in Betty Nance Weber,

Hubert Heinen, eds., *Bertolt Brecht: Political Theory and Literary Practice* (Athens, Georgia, 1980), p. 162.

11   Richard Rundell, "The Brechtian Influence and DDR Poetry of Political Criticism," in Betty Nance Weber, Hubert Heinen, eds., *Bertolt Brecht: Political Theory and Literary Practice* (Athens, Georgia, 1980), p. 152.

12   Christine Cosentino, "Die Lyrikerin Sarah Kirsch im Spiegel ihrer Bilder," in *Neophilologus* 63.3 (1979), p. 419.

13   Christine Cosentino, "Elke Erbs Dichtung 'Der Faden der Geduld': Roter Dada im Sozialistischen Realismus?" in *Germanic Notes* 13.1 (1982), pp. 5–8.

14   Jay Rosellini, "'des fahnenhissens bin ich müde, freund': Der Lyriker Reiner Kunze meldet sich wieder," in Margy Gerber, chief ed., *Studies in GDR culture and society 3: selected papers from the Eighth International Symposium on the German Democratic Republic* (Lanham, 1983), p. 209.

15   Compare, e.g.: Günter Kunert, "Autor und Publikum in der DDR," in Marlis Gerhardt, Gert Mattenklott, eds., *Kontext 2: Geschichte und Subjektivität* (München, 1978); Reiner Kunze, *Das weiße Gedicht. Essays* (Frankfurt/Main, 1994).

Nancy Thuleen

III. Changing Viewpoints: American Feminist Studies of GDR Women's Literature

The reception of East German women's literature by American feminist Germanists did alter the Brechtian legacy as it was previously described; scholars continued to champion the cause of the dissident or Outsider, but for American feminists this Outsider had become the woman writing about her oppression in a patriarchal society. While a lack of American poetological theory led critics to focus almost exclusively on socio-political interpretations of poetry, a near overabundance of American feminist theories made for a different kind of personal involvement on the part of American feminist Germanists. By tracing certain key developments in American feminist theory, we shall see that GDR women's literature was received here at first in the very narrow context of essentialism, but that this gradually gave way to a theoretical basis more capable of interpreting East German works within a broader framework of political, sociological, and personal contexts.

The development and expansion of feminist theory and scholarship in the USA is a well-documented event, and needs little explanation. It would be wrong to say, however, that American feminist criticism was a completely coherent and unified movement. In fact, as Angelika Bammer has described in detail,[1] one must speak of many different American feminisms, since the enormous variety in American viewpoints made for a very pluralistic feminist scene. Bammer makes a distinction between American radical, liberal, and socialist feminists active throughout the 1970's, and notes that, although liberal feminists, concerned with issues of equality and individuality, proved to be a guiding force for American-internal work, it was in many ways the socialist feminists who, believing a historical-materialistic analysis to be crucial for literary as well as economic critique, played a more important role for the research and study of East German women writers.[2]

At the same time as American feminist ideas were beginning to trickle into the GDR, a new body of women's literature was being written by younger East German authors. Like their counterparts in the US and in West Germany, the novels of East German women writers such as Christa Wolf, Irmtraud Morgner, and Maxie Wander were not only written by women, but for the most part about women's experiences and struggles in a patriarchal society. Throughout the early 1970's and up until at least 1975, however, precious little of this new women's writing reached beyond the Wall. Christa Wolf was virtually the only East German woman writer known to academics outside of specifically feminist-Germanist circles, a fact which helps to account for the extra-ordinary high percentage of articles written about her work throughout the 1970's. The limited awareness which American critics had of East German women writers can be partly explained by the relative difficulty of acquiring texts by lesser-known East German authors in America. Such writings were most certainly not exported and were painfully hard to come by, as many critics attest.[3]

In addition to the problem of availability of these texts in America, there was also, somewhat more surprisingly, an absence of feminist theory within East Germany. Why this should be the case is a fascinating question, to say the least. Bammer makes the satisfying argument that literature was preferred over theory as the public forum for political discussion and dissent in the GDR;[4] this is easily evinced by the high political involvement of writers such as Christa Wolf, and the overtly political novels of Morgner and Reimann. But American academic feminists, even within *Germanistik*, who sought above all theoretical writings about the feminist perspective, found the GDR of only peripheral interest. This indicates, however, a certain misunderstanding on the part of some early American critics as to the very position and function of literature within the socialist state. Although East German women were not theorizing per se about feminist resistance or the feminist aesthetic, the very act of writing their fictions and poems was an heroic attempt to express their struggles in concrete terms. Their avoidance of theories which might be coopted by a patriarchal society was by no means a weakness, but rather a presentation of their own imagined alternatives.

Gradually, however, the growing interest in the GDR as a field for literary studies within German departments across the nation in the early 1970's led to a convergence of feminist scholarship and GDR studies, and brought East German women's literature into sharp focus for a select number of American feminist Germanists. As noted above, most American scholars of the GDR chose to look at GDR literature as a mirror upon the society to which they had very restricted access; Patricia Herminghouse writes that East German literature served for American critics as a "window onto the workings of an otherwise closed society, a locus for the articulation of popular sentiment and the airing of political discontent, a sort of repository of critical information about the life and experiences of citizens" there.[5]

We have already discussed how American literary criticism about the GDR in the early and mid-1970's centered on the position of outsiders. There was a clear interest in and focus, for example, on dissidents, Jews, homosexuals, and especially women. The Coalition of Women in German, for example, the leading source of feminist scholarship on the Federal Republic and the GDR, was conceived at a Conference on GDR Studies in St. Louis in 1974, and by the late 1970's most major universities offered some sort of coursework dealing with significant women writers of the GDR.[6] As the number and frequency of GDR scholarly gatherings grew, feminist, Marxist and GDR scholars were brought together to mingle, share ideas, and influence one another's later work.

Certainly no one can dispute that American feminism changed greatly over the last two and a half decades. In the early 1970's, many American feminists took a rather essentialist view of sexual difference. As a result, American feminist analyses of GDR women's literature at this time often paid little attention to the political climate of the authors' state and society, and focused instead on their existence as women in a patriarchal culture. They sought, then, a feminist literature which could appeal to and help form universal bonds between women of all cultures.

Although the lack of a poetological theory, as previously argued, made American critics slavishly loyal to the intentions of the East German poets, I would like to claim that for the early 1970's reception of women's literature, the opposite held true. Strict feminist theories of 'universality' and female oppression led to a certain narrow-sightedness when interpreting East German authors: by regarding GDR women authors as expressing some 'universal' aspect of female struggles, American critics often failed to take into account the East's very different notions of feminism, equality, and oppression. In the GDR at this time, by contrast to America, when women's issues came into public discussion, the *historical* construction and *social* experience of gender were underlined. Thus the GDR women writers who chose to focus on feminist issues did so within a political and historical framework, and not out of a sense of universal sisterhood and sameness. American critics who attempted to apply East German women's writings to a universal category of "oppressed women," then, without appropriate regard for the origins of this oppression, most certainly misrepresented the authors' intentions.

Of course there are exceptions to be found. In the case of works with overtly political statements in them—works, in other words, that demanded from the reader a modicum of political and historical knowledge—American scholars were inclined to discuss the specific political ramifications of the authors' lives in a socialist state in *addition* to noting feminist concerns. Irmtraud Morgner's *Leben und Abenteuer der Trobadora Beatriz* is a prime example: even the earliest critical analyses of her 1974 novel could not help but treat the work as a document of its political and societal context, provide commentary on the political events mentioned in the text, and perhaps even consider how the text might reflect a specifically East German view of feminism.[7] But by and large, even authors as politically explosive as Christa Wolf were seen less as East German women writers than as representatives of the human woman's condition. More often than not, Wolf was treated simply as a "German" author, and the very specific political background of her writing was glossed over or ignored entirely. Her work even became a source of slogans for the 'universal' issues facing all women: "the difficulty of saying I," a phrase taken straight out of *Nachdenken über Christa T.*, has been standard jargon in many American women's studies courses over the past two decades.

Around 1975, though, a greater diversity of opinions as regards the nature of feminism and feminist discourse, which had long been growing the US, began to influence feminist GDR scholarship. Many former essentialist ideas about sexual difference had been abandoned; instead, social construction, historical basis, and biological difference were all seen to play a part in the understanding of gender. In addition, the rise of socialist feminism as a prominent method of textual criticism was proving to be quite rewarding, particularly when evaluating GDR women's writing. Suddenly scholarly articles began to appear which refer to the political system of the GDR not as any other patriarchal system, but as a specifically socialist one.[8] More importantly, there was a great hope among Western leftist intellectuals, especially feminist Germanists, that the GDR might actually be a "concrete Utopia" for their ideals, giving women the potential to function as free individuals. Although they recognized the shortcomings and pitfalls in the present GDR state, many left-leaning American critics were quick to accept these deficiencies as short-termed. Since GDR authors themselves exercised a none-too-gentle pressure towards reform, the hope for the future of a socialist feminist awareness was reinforced. Here, then, the legacy of earlier scholars, intent on championing the cause of the dissident and on critiquing the system, was reestablished, but within the framework of feminism, itself an oppositional movement.

Patricia Herminghouse has an amusingly candid take on why, exactly, American Germanists took such an interest in GDR women's literature. She, too, notes that personal involvement was common, and that often the motivation was one of socio-political ideals, even to a fault. "In the often unconscious and unreflected projection of our own political agenda onto GDR literature, however, our own critical practices became caught up in a binary scheme which limited our interpretable horizons: the GDR was 'not Wall Street,' 'not Hollywood,' 'not West Germany'; it was the potentially Utopian other of our American discontents and disillusionments."[9]

Not surprisingly, Christa Wolf was seen as the main architect and guide to this Utopia of personal and social expression.[10] Her works were an impetus to other writers and to American critics as well. Dealing largely with the possibilities for women's existence and subjectivity beyond equal rights—which were by and large a fait accompli in the GDR—Wolf's novels directly addressed, in both theoretical and literary terms, an East German feminism which, although influenced by Western ideas, differed quite entirely from American feminism. Indeed, in the long run, Socialist feminist critiques such as Christa Wolf's have proved to have a healthy reception in this country primarily because of the different perspectives such an analysis can bring to American views. To phrase the difference in Bammer's terms, while American feminists emphasized the need for a critique of the capitalist structures of their patriarchal society, GDR women writers provided a critique of the patriarchal structures of their socialist society.[11]

But the focus of critique is not the only difference between East German and American feminist reception. Several critics have noted that American feminist scholars seem extremely intent on discovering and developing a uniquely feminine aesthetic.[12] The fact that this search was more or less absent in earlier East German literature, but started to become apparent by the late seventies is, on the one hand, evidence of the East German authors' awareness of trends in Western feminism, but also proof of these authors' own attempts to critique their society by developing specifically feminine forms of writing which break with older patriarchal patterns. As such, American feminist Germanists soon turned their attention to this second generation of East German women writers. Sara Lennox, for example, is quite zealous in her praise of the Eastern women's attempts to create a feminine form of writing to express women's subjectivity: she says that in the GDR, "the visions of what women's lives might be are expressed far more creatively than in the works of any woman writing in the West."[13]

The preceding bibliographical references have documented the substantial increase in both the number and breadth of writings about GDR literature which occurred during the 1980's.   In addition, American feminist perspectives began to see an unfolding of traditional critical schemes, due in large part to the influence of feminists of color, who rejected earlier assumptions of feminine universality. The combination of this expansion with the inclusion of such new theoretical approaches as deconstructionist techniques and postmodernism makes specifying any one coherent trend in 1980's American feminist reception of GDR literature rather daunting.   One can, however, consider these new debates as evidence of the wider-ranging conception of feminism in the 1980's. Even an author such as Heiner Müller has come to be classified by many as feminist, a feminist forerunner, or, in Bathrick's terms, an anti-patriarchal author.[14] Similarly, scholars have begun to interpret older works along feminist lines, and have found in the works of authors such as Anna Seghers new realizations about the narrow categories of older scholarship. As Brandes describes: from today's perspective, Seghers' work gains "eine neue Bedeutung, die die gewohnte, ideologische Einordnung im Sinne des DDR-Sozialismus heute als problematische Enge der Interpretation erscheinen läßt."[15]   As critics gradually came to recognize this "Enge der Interpretation," in many cases there followed a collapse of the older categories of socialist versus liberal versus radical feminists.   Instead of such divisions, American feminists in *Germanistik* now usually incorporate analysis of the political and historical background of the GDR when critiquing East German authors, but the universal sufferings of women in a patriarchal state have once again become a topic of discussion. Thus, for example, in the Introduction to *Daughters of Eve*, Dorothy Rosenberg provides an intriguing mixture of socialist analysis mixed with a desire for universal sisterhood: she writes that "we were deeply affected by the universality of the issues addressed in the stories collected here. The wit, humor, stoic resignation, dignity, or despair with which these writers face familiar contradictions sends the same message to American readers as to the original GDR audience: we're not alone, we're not crazy, there is a problem and it isn't us. Our common experience as women in a postindustrial society far outweighs the cultural or political-economic differences among us."[16]

In general, then, the salient feature of American feminist criticism of East German women's literature seems to have been its willingness to approach a text from different angles, as Brandes has mentioned.[17] American critical analyses from 1975 onward treated the writings of East German women authors both as a document of a political attitude, as a universal expression of feminine conditions and concerns, and also as a sociological portrait of living conditions in the East. This multifaceted criticism, however, marked a great change from the writings of the earliest scholars, whose blind reliance on essentialist feminist ideals constrained their literary interpretations.

Notes

1   Angelika Bammer, "The American Feminist Reception of GDR Literature," in *GDR Bulletin* 16.2 (1990), pp. 18-21; Bammer, "Sozialistische Feminismen: Irmtraud Morgner und amerikanische Feministinnen in den siebziger Jahren," in Ute Brandes, ed., *Zwischen Gestern und Morgen: Schriftsteller-innen der DDR aus amerikanischer Sicht* (Berlin, 1992), pp. 237-241.

2   Bammer (1990), pp. 20-21; Bammer (1992), p. 238.

3   Ute Brandes, *Zwischen Gestern und Morgen: Schriftsteller-innen der DDR aus amerikanischer Sicht* (Berlin, 1992), pp. 9-10; see also Margy Gerber, Judith Pouget, *Literature of the German Democratic Republic in English Translation: A Bibliography* (Lanham, Maryland, 1984).

4   Bammer (1992), pp. 240-241; Bammer (1990), p. 19.

5   Patricia Herminghouse, "New Contexts for GDR Literature: An American Perspective," in Friederike Eigler, Peter C. Pfeiffer, eds., *Cultural Transformations in the New Germany: American and German Perspectives* (Columbia, South Carolina, 1993), p. 96.

6   Herminghouse, Patricia, "Studying GDR Literature in the U.S.: A Survey," in *German Issues* 3 (AICGS, 1986).

7   A prime example of this broad-ranging type of critique is Biddy Martin, "Socialist Patriarchy and the Limits of Reform: A Reading of Irmtraud Morgner's *Life and Adventures of Troubadora Beatriz as Chronicled by her Minstrel Laura*," in *Studies in Twentieth-Century Literature* 5:1 (1980).

8   The International Symposia on the GDR held in Conway, New Hampshire provided an impetus for many such analyses, as is reflected in the conference proceedings: Margy Gerber, chief ed., *Studies in GDR Culture and Society* (Lanham, New Hampshire, 1980-).

9   Herminghouse (1993), p. 94.

10   Compare Bammer (1990), p. 21.

11   Bammer (1992), p. 240.

12   See for example Sara Lennox, "Trends in Literary Theory: The Feminist Aesthetic and German Women's Writing," in *German Quarterly* 54.1 (1981) and Brandes (1992).

13   Lennox (1981), p. 70.

14   David Bathrick, "Affirmative and Negative Culture: The Avant-Garde under 'Actually Existing Socialism': The Case of the GDR," in *Social Research* 47.1 (1980).

15   Brandes (1992), p. 14.

16 Nancy Lukens, Dorothy Rosenberg, trans. and eds., *Daughters of Eve: Women's Writing from the German Democratic Republic* (Lincoln, Nebraska, 1993), p. 1.
17 Andes (1992), p. 13.

Conclusion

Overlooking the course of our retrospective, the same kind of development of critical perspective can be seen for all of American GDR studies, moving from Cold War through anti-authoritarian to the most personally relevant political agendas. Even with the benefit of a public agenda and supporting scholarly organization in the case of feminism, studies of GDR literature were always under the control of particular American fascinations with the GDR as an alternative society. In other words, Americans were not enthralled with socialism and the GDR as an alternative but with the alternative within the GDR. As quoted above, this motivation had already been named by Patricia Herminghouse in 1993. And Wolfgang Emmerich's analysis of the lack of methodological reflection in research on GDR literature appeared at the same time.[1] Our project has hopefully not merely confirmed, but provided a more specific and detailed demonstration and description of these characteristics of American GDR studies.

Germanists seeking signs of political opposition in literature found the GDR fruitful ground for a number of reasons: on the one hand, the official set of expectations for literature known as Socialist Realism allowed them to identify literature that broke the rules, opposed the state, dissented. The lack of any such open expectations and rules in the *West* made this sort of analysis far more difficult and far less attractive. On the other hand, the political force of literature on its readership, always a given in these studies, was also accepted as fact in official GDR policy. Because the government never questioned the social and political effect of literature, it never seemed necessary to question it in criticism. Was it not proof enough that the GDR government sought to employ these supposed effects, and more importantly, saw literature as dangerous enough to warrant the silencing or harassment of authors?

This need to find opposition that formed the core of the US relationship to GDR literature had something to do with biography. As quoted above from Rosenberg, Americans shared a common experience with GDR citizens, and that was as individuals in a post-industrial society. Let us add the observation that 70% of the American critics who ever published on GDR poetry were born between 1938 and 1948, and that the poets most written about were born in the 1930s. Each of those groups spent its intellectually formative years in terribly optimistic and socially critical settings, ready for revolution by the youth after '61 in the GDR and around '68 in the West. The critical literature of the GDR, then, was made to order for young Western Germanists following along later.

Broaching this subject of institutional sociology allows us a final moment of self-reflection. If our treatment of American scholarship has seemed to merely repeat the methods applied by those scholars of GDR literature, it is because we have been reading literary criticism. Criticism functions by conveying ideas, and the analysis of these ideas has been our goal. Literature, however, cannot be reduced to that function. Our finding that GDR literature was received here as a document—of biography, of opposition or of social and political conditions—demonstrates that US scholars read GDR literature as evidence of effective dissent that could strengthen the hopes of the US social critic.

Notes

1   Wolfgang Emmerich, "Do We Need to Rewrite German Literary History Since 1945? A German Perspective," transl. Peter C. Pfeiffer, in Friederike Eigler, Peter C. Pfeiffer, eds., *Cultural Transformations in the New Germany: American and German Perspectives* (Columbia, South Carolina, 1993)

Jost Hermand

Looking Back at Heiner Müller

To fail to recognize Heiner Müller's achievements as a writer would be disgraceful. And I state this not only in view of the adage "De mortuis nihil nisi bene." I state it without any qualifications, with no ifs, ands, or buts, indeed apodictically. He was—after Brecht— perhaps the greatest master of the German language. His unsparingly compact verses have an armored quality; his prose has an uncluttered concision; even his remarks in interviews, despite all their seeming casualness, usually hit the target dead center. But this was only one side of his persona. To praise him solely as a writer would be to belittle him. In all he said and wrote, Heiner Müller was simultaneously—and this constitutes his real greatness—one of the most political minds of a country which nowadays is often pilloried mercilessly, even by many formerly liberal critics.[1] To seek to save him only as a writer either from oblivion or from the ignominy that attaches to the GDR would be to serve his memory poorly. For ultimately he always sought—in the tradition of Brecht—to be taken seriously as a political thinker. But whereas Brecht could die in 1956 convinced that the socialism he aspired to would one day become social reality, Müller had to die with the awareness that this hope—in view of the overwhelming might of the West's free-market regimes—was only an illusion, one which could only "delay" the decline of humanity but not really halt it.[2]

   This stakes out an issue which goes beyond the boundaries of any purely academic discussion. Anyone who deals with Müller will necessarily be involved with the issue of the failure of the socialist experiment, with looming political, economic, and ecological catastrophes, and thus with the very survival of humankind. All these are extremely unsettling issues which many people—caught up in their own struggles for existence—would rather ignore. It was, however, Müller's greatness that he insistently forced us to confront these fundamental issues instead of allowing us the possibility of fleeing—à la Odo Marquard—into private psychological or formalist aesthetic retreats that would afford us consoling comforts.[3] Therefore I would like to avoid seeking refuge in such illusory niches and instead confront the phenomenon "Müller" as directly and candidly as possible. To that end, I have chosen a biographic-autobiographical approach which, admittedly, is not entirely risk-free. After all, the personal can easily slip into the egocentric, but it simultaneously offers the advantage of greater affinity and authenticity, which ought not to be dismissed out of hand.

It was back in the year 1957 that I first encountered the name "Heiner Müller." I had left Adenauer's Federal Republic, with its restorative, even Biedermeieresque spirit, in February of 1956, and had moved to East Berlin as a fresh-baked Ph.D. at the request of the art historian Richard Hamann in order to write a five-volume cultural history of the Wilhelminian Empire for the Akademie Verlag. It was there, in the spring of 1957, when I was just finishing the volume *Naturalism* dealing with problems of depicting the proletarian milieu of the 1890s, that I came upon a special issue of the journal *Neue deutsche Literatur* which dealt entirely with the topic "Workers and the Workers' Movement in German Literature" and also included a short drama entitled *Der Lohndrücker* by a heretofore unknown young GDR author of my age named Heiner Müller.[4] I was totally bowled over by it, discussed it with Wolfgang Heise, read it aloud to others, and was convinced that with this drama GDR-literature had come into its own for the first time. Whereas the works of former exile authors living in the GDR largely dealt with topics drawn from the history of class struggles, this young author was addressing the "objective difficulties" that hampered the GDR's industrial productivity in a manner that was breathtaking both in its causticity and in its drive toward the future. I was similarly impressed by the play *Zehn Tage, die die Welt erschütterten* by Heiner Müller and Hagen Stahl that appeared in the same year in the journal *Junge Kunst* and was then staged at the East Berlin Volksbühne that fall, in observance of the fortieth anniversary of the October Revolution.[5] The repercussions of

Khrushchev's anti-Stalin speech at the XXth Party Congress of the CPSU one year earlier had pushed aside the prescriptive aesthetics of the antiformalist campaign, enabling the Volksbühne to stage Müller's play in a style that recalled more the Expressionist-Constructivist style of Meyerhold and Eisenstein than the style of the apologists of an equally typifying but nevertheless mimetically confined Socialist Realism. Even so, this production was by no means an overwhelming success. The majority of the "Protestant, Prussian, postfascist audience," as Müller liked to call it, which was accustomed to the conventional notions of authority and therefore accepted even the GDR, was nonplussed by this play's revolutionary elan. Indeed, many audience members were openly offended by Lenin's emphatic declaration in the closing scene that revolutionaries would not be intimidated by the bourgeoisie but would stick to their course, even making use of censorship and dictatorship for the benefit of the broad masses of the populace.[6]

Fascinated by these two plays, I tried afterwards to meet Heiner Müller face to face. But before this was possible, I received in the winter of 1957-58—after the dismissal of Richard Hamann by Wilhelm Girnus, the all-powerful State Secretary for University Affairs—an order from the SED District Leadership to leave the territory of the GDR within 48 hours. Because of that I lost track of Heiner Müller's activities for a time. Returning to the former Federal Republic, I quickly realized that after two years in the GDR it would not be possible for me to stay in this other Germany either, and that I would have to go into a kind of exile. This exile I found in the fall of 1958 far from Germany, at the University of Wisconsin in Madison. Here I spent the following years in relative isolation, even though I was still working on the cultural history series for the East Berlin Akademie Verlag and still reading journals such as *Neue deutsche Literatur* and *Sinn und Form* in order to keep up to date on the latest developments in GDR literature. And the Memorial Library in Madison had all these publications, through which I learned of the difficulties Müller was getting into because of such plays as *Die Korrektur, Die*

Umsiedlerin, and then *Der Bau*. I was especially taken by his play *Der Bau*, which was based on Erik Neutsch's novel *Spur der Steine* and appeared in 1965 in *Sinn und Form*, edited by none other than Wilhelm Girnus. After the 11th Plenary of the SED, at which Heiner Müller (among others) came under fire, Girnus published one year later a "Gespräch mit Heiner Müller" in which he tried to cleanse himself of any suspicion that he agreed with the themes of this play.[7]

Unfortunately, since we had almost no graduate students in Madison at that time, I could not yet teach Müller's plays. It was not until the second half of the 1960s, when the number of students increased rapidly and—against the backdrop of student unrest—interest in German leftists of the Weimar and exile years, but also in the GDR, intensified dramatically,[8] that I gave in the fall of 1969—after my return from the boringly apolitical scene at Harvard—for the first time a seminar under the title "Post-Brechtian Drama." Besides plays by Peter Weiss and so-called documentary dramas, it dealt especially with the works of Heiner Müller, Hartmut Lange, and Volker Braun. And I well remember how the students—among them Helen Fehervary and Gunnar Huettich[9]—were enthused by these plays. Indeed, Helen Fehervary's seminar paper on "Heiner Müller's Early Brigade Plays," in which she especially emphasized their truly socialistic spirit, which contrasted sharply with the system of dependencies erected by the SED, struck me as so persuasive that I translated it in the following semester into German and published it in 1971 in the second volume of *Basis*, a yearbook for contemporary German literature that I coedited with Reinhold Grimm.[10] This was the first extensive article on Heiner Müller to appear anywhere, for he had lived during the entire 1960s in the GDR in an unofficial ban and had therefore remained almost unknown in East and West.

It was not until 1971, following the accession to power of Erich Honecker, with whom Heiner Müller had good contacts in his early years, that new possibilities opened up for him, which he immediately tried to make use of. Probably the best document of this shift is his play *Zement*, which he based on a novel by Fyodor Gladkov and wrote during these years. In its moving final scene, the White Russian traitors returning from banishment are given a second chance for a "Heimat" in the USSR. I knew nothing of this new play and was therefore quite surprised when I arrived in East Berlin on October 12, 1973, and learned from a theater poster that its premiere would take place that very evening at the Berlin Ensemble under the direction of Ruth Berghaus and Hans-Jochen Irmer. And I was even more surprised that tickets were still available, indicating how unknown among East Berlin audiences Müller had become. It was an evening I will never forget. The direction was clearly inspired by early Soviet revolutionary theater; the play's treatment of the marriage issue bore traits of radical feminism; and Müller's handling of the stagnation of development within the USSR was so openly scornful that all those who were acquainted with these problems were stunned. In contrast to theater productions in the West, this play was about real politics. On this evening, every word counted, all the more so because the first four rows were filled with the higher-ups of the SED who followed the unfolding storyline with bated breath. The oppressive silence after each scene led me to expect a disaster. But at the end, the black suits in the first four rows stood up and dutifully gave Müller, whose official rehabilitation was to take place this evening, a standing ovation that went on for fifteen minutes. There he stood on the stage in a bright red sweater, gazing down on "his" party with a stone face, the revolutionary anthem "Venceremos" resounding from behind him. I didn't dare to talk to him afterwards.

An opportunity to do so would not come about until two years later, when Helen Fehervary and Marc Silberman took me to Müller's apartment at Kissingenplatz on August 2, 1975, in order to discuss with him their translation of *Mauser*.[11] I remained rather in the background, but heard that he would spend the following fall semester at the University of Texas in Austin at the invitation of Betty Nance Weber, who had taken a lively interest in Brecht and GDR theater going back to her studies at Madison. I therefore invited Heiner Müller to take part in the 7th Wisconsin Workshop on "History in Contemporary Drama," which was scheduled for the following October in Madison, and he immediately accepted. He also encouraged me to see the production of his *Lohndrücker* at the West Berlin Schaubühne, which I did, although it struck me as completely out of place in this setting, where it did not communicate any political impulses.

During the aforementioned Wisconsin Workshop, the world premiere of his *Mauser* took place on October 21, 1975, staged by a group of young students under the direction of Jack Zipes. Müller had sent me the manuscript beforehand, and we both could hardly believe what the students had made of it. In the ensuing discussion, he enveloped himself in a cloud of cigar smoke and left the moderation mostly to me. He was all the more willing to engage in discussion on the following day at the final wrap-up of the entire Workshop, where he attempted to jolt the audience out of its academic-unpolitical attitude with cynical flippancies.[12] The general impression that Müller left behind in Madison was therefore quite a mixed one. A few had sensed something of his genius, but others he had only annoyed with his remoteness and occasional malice. And he himself must have sensed this. On November 3, when I received the transcript of the final discussion which he returned to me with handwritten emendations, I noticed that he had simply deleted some of his remarks "on Ulbricht and Weigel" that now struck him as too cynical, along with a comment disparaging Brecht's *Kaukasischer Kreidekreis* as a "Broadway-Schnulze." "Not everything that you can say in America ought to be published in the Federal Republic," he wrote as an explanation, because it would damage the GDR. Furthermore, he regretted that the final exchange had been "more of a show than a real discussion." What Müller wanted was "real controversies," that is, a genuine dialogue about politics, not scholarly explications of particular dramas. And socialized as he had been in the GDR, he was comfortable only with private settings for really frank exchanges—like the lengthy ones we had at the Ivy Inn following the Workshop.

Two months later I saw him again at the MLA convention in San Francisco, where he presented me with the first collection of his early plays published in the GDR.[13] At this convention, Betty Nance Weber presented for the first time the video recording of Müller's *Mauser*, which she had helped stage in Austin, Texas. Because of its radical feminism and the frequent personal interventions by the players involved, Müller found this staging highly original. After the video screening, Ronnie Davis, director of the San Francisco Mime Troupe, took Heiner Müller, Ginka Müller, Betty Weber, and me to an opulent dinner in Chinatown. During the meal, Müller—hardly interested in the delicacies on the table—tried to convince Davis not to stage the already "outdated" Brecht but to move on to more contemporary works by Genet and himself, preferably with black and homosexual actors. But Davis dismissed this proposal and argued that Brecht was by no means "outdated" for America, where on the contrary he had to be regularly produced and understood before advancing to other forms of political theater.[14] Afterwards he took all of us on the back of a flatbed truck across San Francisco to a so-called alternative circus, the "Pickle Family Circus," where there were no animals but people in contorted postures playing the animals. It was hilarious, and the audience laughed throughout. But even here, Müller kept his dour expression, so that I—sitting next to him—didn't dare to laugh either. I felt as if were sitting next to an author of German tragedies, perhaps a Kleist or a Hebbel, who—because of his increasingly gloomy outlook as a result of his doubts about the prospects for socialism—allowed himself no lighthearted diversions but only painkillers, such as cigars and alcohol. On the other hand, after his successes in East Berlin and his months in Texas, he felt considerably more confident than heretofore and told me, when I inquired with concern whether he had overstayed his visa: "They'll be happy if I come back at all."

And that's how it turned out. From this time on, Müller enjoyed more freedom of movement than ever before, and he was able to publish his texts with the West Berlin Rotbuch Verlag, thereby opening up a reception that was even more intense in the West than in the East. Especially at the center of attention in 1976 was his play *Mauser*, which could not be published in the East even though he had originally written it for the stages of the SED Party Schools. That year, not just *Alternative* but also *New German Critique* devoted special issues to *Mauser*.[15] The latter contained not only a translation of this play by Helen Fehervary and Marc Silberman,[16] but also the articles "'Mauser' in Austin, Texas" by Betty Nancy Weber, "'Mauser' as Learning Play" by David Bathrick and Andreas Huyssen, as well as "History and Aesthetics in Brecht and Müller" by Helen Fehervary.[17] But these publications initially had an impact only on a rather small coterie of Müller fans. For ultimately, interest in forthrightly "political" literature gradually declined in the second half of the 1970s among American as well as West German students, who turned instead to so-called New Subjectivity. While some of them still adhered to the motto "the personal is the political," others increasingly lapsed into culinary, aestheticized, or even solipsistic preoccupations.[18]

In the autumn of 1976, when at the age of 46 I arrived at the Free University in West Berlin to teach German students for the first time in my life, I was disappointed at how little interest they had in any political matters extending beyond their own personal horizons. There may have been 250 students in my seminar on "Brecht's Adaptations of World Literature," but they wanted neither to hear my views on Brecht's political outlook nor to read any of the assigned texts.[19] When I asked them what we should do instead, I always got the same answer: "Discussions!" So I suggested to them that I would invite Heiner Müller, since Brecht probably the most important adapter of themes from world literature (*Ödipus*, *Macbeth*, *Philoktet*, etc.), to discuss with him his working methods. But they weren't interested in that either, since they had never heard of Heiner Müller. When I suggested that they see *Der Lohndrücker* at the West Berlin Schaubühne, they summarily rejected my proposal on the grounds that the performance was not followed by a discussion at which they could voice "their own interests." And that was the end of it: it was a standoff between my claims to critical scholarship and general political validity versus their claims to anarchic self-fulfillment that spurned any goals going beyond the individual.

Müller was confronted with a similar situation on September 18, 1976, when he made himself available for a discussion with a relatively young audience following a performance of his play *Die Bauern*, formerly *Die Umsiedlerin*, in the foyer of the East Berlin Volksbühne. These were all East Germans who reacted to the grim mood of this play with a certain edginess, even annoyance. They asked Müller why this play, dealing with the difficulties of the early years of the GDR, was being staged nowadays, when things were so much better? "We do know," one ventured, "that you couldn't stage this play back then. But is that any reason to put it on today? Isn't it just one big ego-trip for you personally?" And Müller, in some sense unwilling to deal with questions of this sort, once again enveloped himself in a cloud of cigar smoke—as he had done back in Madison at the *Mauser* discussion—leaving it to me to give the only answer possible in a situation like this, namely that one can learn not only from current struggles but also from past struggles, as Brecht had said after the production of his *Puntila/Matti*, when the SED reproached him that this play had long since become anachronistic, since there were no longer any major landholders in the GDR.[20]

In January of 1977 I saw that the second version of Müller's play *Die Schlacht* was to have its premiere at the East Berlin Volksbühne. When I called up the box office in order to reserve a ticket, I was told by a friendly voice on the other end of the wire: "There's no need to reserve tickets for any Müller play. It's only Kotzebue's 'Deutsche Kleinstädter' that's already sold out." And indeed, the premiere was attended only by a small circle of hardcore Müller supporters. But this group experienced one of the most memorable evenings in the history of East Berlin theater. What Manfred Karge and Wolfgang Langhoff had put on the boards approached the best work of Besson and Wekwerth, indeed even

Brecht. Five brief scenes, amounting to only ten pages in the
Rotbuch edition, were staged here with such an abundance of
theatrical inspiration that it defies description. Nothing, absolutely
nothing was left untried to lend these short and simultaneously
allegorically heightened scenes a vivid theatrical power: film
screenings, pantomime, slapstick comedy, classic Greek elements,
the grotesque, pop moments, monstrosities à la Frankenstein,
recitations, parodies on religious kitsch, audience responses from
the first staging, horror components, shootouts, organ music,
parodies on the classics, death angels, revue girls, and lots more.
Despite this array of theatrical ploys, the play overall had a coherent
ferocity going far beyond any aesthetic eclecticism or superficial
collage technique.

During the performance I sat next to Müller. We were both so
engrossed by the performance that we exchanged only a few words,
and those during a scene that evoked our shared past in the Hitler
Youth. This scene presented Hitler's suicide with Schubert's
"Unfinished" playing in the background, stirring in us the memory
that 35 years earlier we had to sing to this melody the Nazi words
"Moses, du nimmst a Bad" about the "dreckige Ostjuden." By the
end we were both so drained that Müller said only: "Let's talk about
it next Tuesday. I'm going home now." When I rang the bell at his
apartment on the appointed day at 10 am, he came to the door in his
bathrobe, quickly made a cup of a coffee, and said: "I've been up all
night, translating Shakespeare. I've got to take a cold shower.
Here's my new play. Read it and tell me what you think." And
there I sat with *Leben Gundlings Friedrich von Preußen Lessings
Schlaf Traum Schrei* before me. I had 30 minutes. When he
returned to the room, I had just finished the first reading. What I
said at that moment, as he looked at me expectantly, I can no longer
precisely remember. Certainly nothing especially positive, for I still
do not know what to make of this play. But fortunately the
telephone rang at this moment. When Müller returned a short time
later, he said smiling cynically: "Even So-and-so," of whom he had
a low opinion but whom he had given the manuscript with a

strategic intent, "thinks my *Friedrich* is fine."

And then a conversation ensued that kept us glued to the table before that single cup of coffee until early evening. At first Müller blew off steam by running down in the oldest manner of literati others as well as himself. Christa Wolf's *Kindheitsmuster*, which had just appeared, he dismissed as "bourgeois kitsch." His own play *Quartett* he called a "piece of porno for the West," with which he simply aimed to make money. The *Antikenprojekt* being staged in West Berlin, which all leftists had rejected as "irrationalistic," he declared superb. And so forth. But then the conversation finally turned to *Die Schlacht*. When I pointed out to him that the Third Reich had not been simply a slaughterhouse, for it had also witnessed exile and resistance, and that without them the GDR and an author such as Heiner Müller would never have come into existence, he dismissed my challenge with a tired gesture, as if I had not grasped that this play was not just about the years between 1933 and 1945, but about the continuous slaughter and killing throughout all of human history. But then he pursued my thesis with utmost intensity, and we began to discuss fundamental questions of a possible socialist politics, with each of us by turns criticizing some of the mistaken policies of the SED. Some days later we met again, since he was not only interested in my views of the GDR but also in my evaluation of Brecht.

A short time later, I summarized some aspects of our conversations in my essay "Deutsche fressen Deutsche. Heiner Müllers 'Die Schlacht' an der Ostberliner Volksbühne," which appeared in the fall of 1978 in the *Brecht-Jahrbuch*.[21] When I taught in Bremen during the winter semester of the same year, Heiner Müller wanted to accompany Betty Weber and me to a particularly bloody staging of Hans Henny Jahnn's *Krönung Richards III.* in the city's Altes Schlachthaus, but had to cancel at the last minute. That was, for the moment, the end of our personal contacts. In 1979, I wrote my essay "Braut, Mutter oder Hure? Heiner Müllers 'Germania' und ihre Vorgeschichte," which appeared that year in my book *Sieben Arten an Deutschland zu leiden.*[22]   The same year saw the publication in *New German Critique* of an English translation of Heiner Müller's *Zement*, in which Helen Fehervary, Sue-Ellen Case, and Marc Silberman had invested much labor and love.[23] In 1980 I asked Müller to allow us to publish in the *Brecht-Jahrbuch* his text "Keuner +/- Fatzer," which he had read the preceding year at the 5th International Brecht Conference in Maryland. It contains a sentence which is of the utmost importance for his entire work: "To use Brecht without criticizing him is treason."[24] In the same *Brecht-Jahrbuch*, Helen Fehervary dealt at length with a *Zement* production in Berkeley which she and Sue-Ellen Case had staged after long discussions with Müller.[25]

I myself did not see Müller again until 1981. It was on June 13th, occasioned by a production of his play *Der Auftrag* on the studio stage of the East Berlin Volksbühne's third floor. The audience was small and consisted mostly of individuals who knew each other. Next to me sat Günter Gaus, the head of the official diplomatic representation of the Federal Republic in East Berlin; Klaus Scherpe; Dieter and Sylvia Schlenstedt; Guntram Weber, the husband of the now deceased Betty Weber; and a number of leading SED members. The text, the direction, the acting, the political message: all were of truly stunning intensity. In the smallest space imaginable, something had been achieved here which halfway satisfied even the unsatisfiable Müller. Therefore he attended almost every performance in order to engage the audience in a discussion afterwards. And so it was that evening.

When we—after a few minutes of silence to regain our composure—finally sat down with him, the following conversation opened up, which made an especially powerful impression on me—an individual who was familiar with Müller but nonetheless remained an outside observer of the GDR. The first ones to break the awkward silence and directly to address the question of the political message were the party functionaries. That they called him "Heiner" made it instantaneously clear to me just how small and tightly connected the literary scene in East Berlin was. "We are all

deeply impressed, Heiner," said one of them.   "What a play!
Almost better than *Zement*!   Based on a story by Anna
Seghers—and furthermore set against the great world-historical
background of the French Revolution and the first struggles against
imperialist colonialism. This is so much more concrete than your
works based on themes from classical antiquity. But why don't you
write plays about the GDR anymore?"

That was the kind of question Müller loved, and he hesitated
not a second to reply with a provocative edge: "Like you, I read
Neues Deutschland every day, from the first to the last page. And
what I'm told there is that we are in favor of peace—as if that
weren't something totally self-evident. As soon as you are ready to
begin dealing with the really controversial issues in *Neues
Deutschland* and open up a dialogue with the broad masses about
the objective difficulties in our state, I'll write GDR plays for you
again. Not until then. You can't expect me to begin a revolution in
cultural politics that you're afraid to start." Then he looked up and
said with a voice that mingled bitterness with pride: "It's you who
are forcing me to write world literature."

I cannot remember whether or not anyone laughed at that point.
I rather doubt it. In order to relax the tension in the air, Gaus turned
the conversation to broader questions of cultural politics, which
were far less interesting to Müller. He did not want to digress into
the realm of theory; he loved the concrete. I therefore gave him a
second chance to steer back toward politics. When someone
questioned whether highbrow literature was still capable of having
any effect in the GDR, I remarked that earlier that same day I had
seen a line of twenty people waiting to buy Stephan Hermlin's
Abendlicht at the Brecht bookstore in the Chausseestraße—and that
while the first strawberries of the season from Werder were being
sold next door. I took that as an encouraging sign. At the very
least, I had never witnessed a line of that kind in front of any
Western bookstore.

Müller immediately recognized the opening and said: "That's
how I see it, too. Look at it this way. We have two parties here in

the GDR: the SED and the writers. Our young people all read the Marxist classics and thereby develop great expectations. When they begin to make demands, however, they're rebuffed—more or less gently. That leads to feelings of frustration, and that turns them into writers. Seen in this light, we're the greatest literary talent factory in the world besides the Soviet Union. No wonder people interested in literature wait in lines in front of our bookstores. There'll never be anything of the kind in the West. On their own, they can't produce any literature worth mentioning. They survive only from our castoffs. We can lose ten authors a year to the Federal Republic without hurting, and that way they get something to read too. In the meantime, we'll have produced 100 new authors."[26]

We all knew that these words bespoke a cynicism which was directed not against the idea of socialism but against the smugness of the SED. Here was someone who wanted more, far more than what "really existed." By the late 1970s, however, this someone had stopped believing in the traditional methods of theoretical indoctrination. He therefore made use of everything that seemed to him more effective as a means of sparking change: irony, provocation, shock, all intended to counteract that "lethargy of the heart" that made it easy to accommodate to the given situation.

After this semi-official discussion, which was followed by a few private conversations, there was a longer pause in our personal contacts. From afar, I did continue to observe his writing and other activities very closely but was preoccupied during the following years with producing the two thick volumes of my *Kulturgeschichte der Bundesrepublik*.[27] I was, of course, repeatedly tempted to counter those Müller interpreters who—in the framework of the postmodernism debate of those years—totally neglected the works of his early and middle periods and dealt exclusively with works such as his *Friedrich* drama or *Die Hamletmaschine*, superimposing on them their theories of intertextuality, hybridization, ambiguity, indeed ideological ambivalence.[28] In order to stem this tide at least a little bit, I tried to show in my 1987 essay "Fridericus Rex. Das schwarze Preußen im Drama der DDR" that Müller's anti-Friedrich stance had an eminently political relevance in that it challenged the re-Prussification occurring in East Berlin during these years, which reached its high point in the restoration of Christian Daniel Rauch's Friedrich monument on Unter den Linden.[29] But any such efforts elicited only smiles from the postmodernist critics of those years, who were primarily interested in consciously dehistoricized anthropological, psychological, psychoanalytic, or textual constants, whereas they regarded political ideology as hopelessly out of date. And it cannot be denied that Müller met these tendencies halfway with texts such as *Quartett, Die Hamletmaschine, Verkommenes Ufer, Bildbeschreibung,* and so forth. But I continued to focus on other works, for example *Zement, Der Auftrag,* and *Wolokolamser Chaussee,* as well as the hope he placed on the glasnost and perestroika policies instituted by Gorbachev's reforms, which Müller even discussed with Erich Honecker.

When Frank Hörnigk asked me in 1988 to contribute to his volume *Heiner Müller Material,* which appeared on January 9, 1989, for Müller's sixtieth birthday, I immediately agreed. Since a conventional academic article with footnotes seemed inappropriate to me for such an occasion, I composed a short dialogue in which two directors, one old and one young, discuss whether, given the changed situation, it would still be worthwhile to stage a play such as *Der Lohndrücker* in East Berlin. Since they both favor the perestroika model, that is, the reconstruction of the entire society without any interruption of production, the two finally agree to demonstrate this process with Müller's "Ringofen" parable. I closed my dialogue with the same words with which the Party Secretary Schorn and the worker Balke decide at the end of Müller's *Lohndrücker* to take on this task jointly.[30]

When I came to East Berlin in February of 1988 for the huge observances of Brecht's ninetieth birthday, it was almost inevitable that I would encounter Müller again. And that happened in a highly dramatic way. When the two of us—after the presentation of the first two volumes of the monumental Berlin and Frankfurt Brecht edition—suddenly ran into each other in the foyer of the Akademie der Künste, he immediately blurted out: "Read your dialogue already. Too bad you got it all wrong. You put the major emphasis on the last scene, which seemed highly important to me when I first wrote it but has become superfluous in the meantime. I simply left it out in my staging of the play at the Deutsches Theater, which you couldn't have known about in Madison. No such confidence is possible any longer. Today one has to operate with open endings. Why don't you take a look at it. The performances may always be sold out, but we could go together this evening and sit on the steps somewhere. They won't throw me out. This Brecht brouhaha must be as boring to you as it is to me." Suddenly enflamed with anger that perhaps the postmodernists might be right with their view of Müller, I said: "If you cut the last scene, I don't want to see this production"—and turned my back to him. Wheeling around, I stepped on the foot of a silkstockinged lady behind me so forcibly that I knocked her to the floor. After Müller and Unseld had helped her back on her feet, I realized that she was Barbara Brecht. I apologized profusely and got out of there as quickly as possible.

On the same day, February 9th, I went to the Berliner Ensemble to see Müller's *Fatzer* adaptation. Still furious with him and myself for having reacted so heedlessly, the play did not speak to me. Although Ekkehard Schall did his best as Johann Fatzer, the production made a drab impression. What they staged was neither a Brecht play nor a Müller play, but something in between from which not much could be learned. Well, granted, it was directed against war and the material and psychic devastation it caused. But wasn't that message self-evident, as Müller had said of *Neues Deutschland*'s peace slogans some years earlier?

A year and a half later, I could learn of Müller's reaction to the so-called *Wende* only through television and the many interviews he gave afterwards. I initially found his stance more principled than I expected. Especially in the volume *Zur Lage der Nation* (1990), based on interviews with Frank M. Raddatz, he forthrightly professed—despite everything—his socialist past and offered a gloomy prognosis for the crisis-ridden victors of the Cold War in view of the rapidly increasingly destruction of nature and industrial overproduction. And his 1992 autobiography entitled *Krieg ohne Schlacht. Leben in zwei Diktaturen* hardly reads like a paean to the free market economy but instead culminates in the thesis that with the fall of socialism, one of the last hopes for a possible alternative to capitalism's ever more rapid suicidal course has disappeared. That he emphasized ecological aspects alongside economic ones mollified me a bit. So I sat down and wrote a lengthy essay on this book, which came out in 1993 in *Argument* under the title "Diskursive Widersprüche. Fragen an Heiner Müllers 'Auto-biographie.'"[31]

In this essay I attempted to survey the transformations which could be observed in Heiner Müller's relationship to socialism and to the GDR. In his early phase, he was oriented on Brecht—although his material had greater contemporaneity—and portrayed the basic conflicts of his dramas, such as *Der Lohndrücker* and *Die Korrektur*, in a positive way as soluble. By the early 1970s, he increasingly shifted to juxtaposing character versus character, opinion versus opinion, at times so crassly and in such an unmediated way that they could easily be read—especially because the horizon of his dramas was becoming increasingly gloomy—as spurning any ideological commitment whatsoever. As mentioned, some Western postmodernist critics have simply attempted to claim him as one of their own—given the seeming insolubility of such conflict situations, the looming darkness, as well as his occasional collaboration with Robert Wilson. But that is true only in a very superficial sense. Granted, the contradictions were there and increased over the years, but the fundamental constellations of the Cold War remained largely unaltered in most of his works. And thus he has been largely misjudged by many adherents of postmodernism or *posthistoire*, who tried to detach him from the ideological context of the GDR because they championed a global dehistoricizing of all political and socioeconomic questions.

There has been no comparable misjudgment by Müller's enemies in the West, who interpreted his texts as thoroughly

politicized attempts to halt "the aging process of socialism."[32] Thus
Richard Herzinger polemically asserted in 1992 that Müller's works
may have had "a constructive effect in the East, but only a
deconstructive effect in the West."[33] I would argue that Herzinger's
observation—even though it was meant entirely negatively—came
far closer to Müller's outlook than the views of many naive
convergence theorists. Müller was not interested in producing mere
sensationalistic stories for depoliticized theater audiences anywhere
in the world. On the contrary, he aimed to provide his audiences
with political provocations, spurring them not to yield to the
illusory hope that what really exists is necessarily what is
reasonable and auspicious. In short, he tried—under increasingly
difficult circumstances—to look the angel of history in the eye as
closely and fearlessly as possible. The results were in part
extremely gruesome, indeed even inhuman visions. I know, to
praise him solely for these visions would be misguided. But to fail
to acknowledge his unbending stance, indeed his lonely grandeur
within much of the dystopian-utopian literature of today, would be
equally misguided.[34] Let us hope that someday it will be
worthwhile to put positive heroes—in a humanized setting—on the
stage again.

Translated by J. D. Steakley

Notes

1   Cf., for instance, Richard Herzinger, "Heiner Müller, Christa
    Wolf, Volker Braun—deutsche Zivilisationskritik und das
    neue Antiwestlertum," *Die Zeit*, June 4, 1993, p. 8.

2   Heiner Müller, *"Zur Lage der Nation." Interview mit Frank
    M. Raddatz* (Berlin, 1990), p. 11.

3   Cf. Jost Hermand, *Geschichte der Germanistik* (Reinbek,
    1994), p. 233.

4   Heiner Müller, "Der Lohndrücker," *Neue deutsche Literatur*
    5.5 (1957): 116-141.

5   The text of this play appeared in *Junge Kunst. Monatsschrift für Literatur, Kritik, Musik und Theater*, no. 1 (1957): 35-47. Müller later claimed that he had thrown away the manuscript of this play.

6   Ibid., p. 47.

7   "Gespräch mit Heiner Müller," *Sinn und Form* 18 (1966): 30-47.

8   Cf. my essay "Madison, Wisconsin, 1959-1973. Der Einfluß der deutschen Exilanten auf die Entstehung der Neuen Linken," *Exilforschung. Ein internationales Jahrbuch* 13 (1995): 52-67.

9   H. Gunnar Huettich published his Madison dissertation under the title *Theater in the Planned Society: Contemporary Drama in the German Democratic Republic in Its Historical, Political, and Cultural Context* (Chapel Hill, 1978). On Müller, see pp. 67-75 et passim.

10 Helen Fehervary, "Heiner Müllers Brigadenstücke," *Basis. Jahrbuch für deutsche Gegenwartsliteratur* 2 (1971): 103-140.

11 The translation of *Mauser* appeared in *New German Critique*, no. 8 (1976): 122-149.

12 Cf. "Geschichte und Drama. Ein Gespräch mit Heiner Müller," *Basis. Jahrbuch für deutsche Gegenwartsliteratur* 6 (1976): 48-64; reprinted under the title "Einen historischen Stoff sauber abschildern, das kann ich nicht," in Heiner Müller, *Gesammelte Irrtümer* (Frankfurt am Main, 1986), pp. 31-49.

13 Heiner Müller, *Stücke. Mit einem Nachwort von Rolf Rohmer* (Berlin, 1975).

14 On the Brecht stagings of the San Francisco Mime Troupe, cf. my article "Mit der 'Mother' auf Tournee," *Brecht-Jahrbuch* (1974): 138-142.

15 *Alternative*, no. 110/111 (1976): "DDR-Dramatik: Heiner Müllers 'Mauser.'" Hans Rosshoff wrote in this issue (p. 221) that *Mauser* ought really to be staged only in socialist countries.

16 See note 11.

17 Weber, *New German Critique*, no. 8 (1976): 150-156; Bathrick and Huyssen, ibid., pp. 110-121; Fehervary, ibid., pp. 80-109.

18 Cf. Jost Hermand, *Die Kultur der Bundesrepublik Deutschland 1965-1985* (Munich, 1988), pp. 471-506.

19 Cf. my essay "Zu Brechts Bearbeitungstechnik," in *Aktualisierung Brechts*, ed. Wolfgang Fritz Haug, Klaus Pierwoß, and Karen Ruoff (Berlin, 1980), pp. 122-142.

20 Cf. my essay "'Herr Puntila und sein Knecht Matti.' Brechts Volksstück," *Brecht heute--Brecht Today* (1971): 117-136.

21 *Brecht-Jahrbuch* (1978): 129-143.

22 Jost Hermand, *Sieben Arten an Deutschland zu leiden* (Königstein, 1979), pp. 127-142. I also deal with Heiner Müller in the essay "'Heines Wintermärchen.' Zum Topos der deutschen Misere," ibid., p. 50.

23 *New German Critique*, Supplement to no. 16 (Winter 1979): 7-64.

24 Heiner Müller, "Keuner +/- Fatzer," *Brecht-Jahrbuch* (1980): 21.

25 Helen Fehervary, "'Cement' in Berkeley," ibid., pp. 206-216.

26 Cf. also my essay "'Ihr zwingt mich ja, Weltliteratur zu schreiben.' Heiner Müller im Gespräch," in *Ich Wer ist das. Ein Heiner Müller Arbeitsbuch*, ed. Frank Hörnigk et al. (Berlin, 1996), pp. 00-00.

27 *Kultur im Wiederaufbau. Die Bundesrepublik Deutschland 1959-1965* (Munich, 1986) and *Kulturgeschichte der Bundesrepublik Deutschland 1965-1980* (Munich, 1988).

28 Cf., for example, Arlene Akiko Teraoko, *The Silence of Entropy or Universal Discourse: The Postmodernist Poetics of Heiner Müller* (New York, 1985).

29 Cf. the passage dealing with Müller in my essay "Fridericus rex. Das schwarze Preußen im Drama der DDR," in *Dramatik der DDR*, ed. Ulrich Profitlich (Frankfurt am Main, 1987), pp. 289-292.

30 Jost Hermand, "Regisseure unter sich. Ein Gespräch über den 'Lohndrücker,'" in *Heiner Müller Material*, ed. Frank Hörnigk

(Leipzig, 1989), pp. 236-250.

31 "Diskursive Widersprüche. Fragen an Heiner Müllers 'Autobiographie,'" *Argument*, no. 198 (1993): 255-268; also appeared as "Discursive Contradictions: Questions about Heiner Müller's 'Autobiographie,'" *Contemporary Theatre Review* 4.2 (1995): 37-48.

32 Cf. Richard Herzinger, *Masken der Lebensrevolution. Vitalistische Zivilisations- und Humanismuskritik in Texten Heiner Müllers* (Munich, 1992), p. 9.

33 Ibid., p. 10.

34 Shortly before his death, Müller himself summarized this outlook in these words: "I am no longer certain that communism is the destiny of humankind, but it remains a dream of humanity that one generation after the other will work toward fulfilling until the end of our world." *Was von den Träumen blieb. Eine Bilanz der sozialistischen Utopie*, ed. Thomas Grimm (Berlin, 1993), p. 8.

Helen Fehervary

Response

Among the vast numbers of people who paid public homage to Heiner Müller this past year was Mikhail Gorbachev, the former First Secretary of the Communist Party in the Soviet Union and the architect of Glasnost and Perestroika. The text of his eulogy is as unequivocal as Jost Hermand has been today in suggesting that Müller was not merely a great German writer, but one whose interest and import extended into the world, and who singularly probed the great questions of history and culture in our time: "I wish to express my deep sympathy at the death of the writer, playwright, and theatre director Heiner Müller. His death is an irretrievable loss not only for German culture, but for the culture of Europe, and the world. I have lost a person to whom I was bound for years in a sincere friendship. The memory of Heiner Müller will live in the hearts of human beings for a long time."

My mention of Gorbachev at the start of my response suggests no mean comparison, and perhaps an appropriate one, not only because it reminds us of an entire European generation whose adolescence coincided with the terror of fascism and the Second World War, and for whom, based on the immediacy of personal and collective experience, there remained only one alternative: socialism—or barbarism. That life-long conviction is as evident in Gorbachev's recently published memoir as it is in the paper Jost has read before us today. Virtually the same conviction underlies the writings, theatre work, political decisions, and social interactions that defined the life journey and historical legacy of this utterly political man, the writer Heiner Müller. This, I think, is the underlying argument of Jost's paper.

But we surely expected at least this much from Jost Hermand. There is in fact a much larger agenda in this workshop paper—the workshop is after all not about Heiner Müller, but about the GDR. And in this regard we can say without hesitation that for Jost the name Heiner Müller is by implication synonymous with the best in

GDR literature, indeed with the best in postwar German literature per se. Well, if the East German writer Heiner Müller was indeed the greatest German writer of the postwar era—a time span of at least forty years—then what might this say about the GDR, about its cultural policies and its literature, about the relationship between its writers and its readers? Can we separate the quality of a writer like Heiner Müller from the quality of the GDR "Literaturgesellschaft," however problematic and unfinished it was? Jost's paper implies that we cannot. Certainly I think this should be a main point in our discussion.

Another would be the question of the historical continuity of the antifascist tradition versus what Jost calls the ahistoricism of posthistoire and postmodernism. In this regard Jost suggests that Müller was not only the greatest virtuoso of the German language since Brecht; he also continued the Brechtian tradition of responding to the major political issues of his time. But Jost also complicates the issue of antifascism and the *Erbe*, and to do this he veers away from the strictures of this tradition, opting for what he calls a "biographical-autobiographical" approach. Surely this is no signal that he is about to jump ship and leap onto the dry land of the confessional bandwagon that has become so popular and so noisy in recent years. Instead I detect at least a hint of parody—Jost is after all no stranger to the literary text, nor to the theatre. But more importantly, he is no stranger to the experiences that led Müller in the first place to confront the alternative: socialism—or barbarism. I was particularly struck by his account of his intense discussions with Müller about *Die Schlacht* (The Battle), and to their shared experience in the Volksbühne of listening to the strains of Schubert's Unfinished Symphony, whose melody evoked the grotesque jingles of the Hitler Youth. In that section of Jost's paper the history of an entire generation's adolescent trauma, its coming of age after the war, its continued political and existential struggles over the next decades, came to life for me as never before.

This is hardly the antifascist attitude of a Brecht who after all was able to return home from exile to the country of his birth, however transformed it might have become. It is rather an antifascist attitude that grew out of a more fundamental experience of homelessness, an experience that continued long after the war. It is interesting to note how the encounters between Jost Hermand and Heiner Müller took place in virtual situations of exile—in Madison, to which Jost fled after his expulsion from the GDR and his inability to work in the Federal Republic, and where Müller withdrew more than once behind a "cloud of smoke"; in San Francisco where they both seem to have felt out of time and place; or in the territorial constructions of the postwar era known as West Berlin and East Berlin, which to both of them, if in different ways, appeared at once familiar and strange.

Whereas current discussions of Müller run primarily along East-West lines, Jost has taken the longer historical view, a view from where the geographic question is not determined by the division of 1949, but where that division becomes part of the problem; where the problem of antifascist exile is not resolved, but continued after 1945. I recall a seminar on antifascist exile led by Jost here in Madison more than twenty years ago, which he concluded by proposing that in the year 1945 the real problems of antifascist exile had only begun. And so the difficulties in communication described by Jost's paper hardly appear as having been based on personal differences with Müller, but as manifestations of the continuing divisions that characterize German history since 1933, or indeed, since 1918. If Jost's effort to rescue the last scene of *Der Lohndrücker* in 1988 was based on his perception of a political antifascist commonality with Müller in the postwar period, his paper today takes that commonality farther back to an existentially experienced antifascism in the last years of fascism itself. And in so doing he has been able to embrace even more of this "phenomenon" Heiner Müller who, in his words, was able to look "so closely and so fearlessly into the eyes of the angel of history."

Arguing that the debate surrounding the question of Müller's would-be postmodernism is a false issue, Jost ends his essay with a reference to Müller's "real enemies"—conservative critics like Richard Herzinger who understands that Müller's plays are intended to have a deconstructive effect in the West, but a constructive effect within socialism itself. And this distinction brings us back once again to the thirty volatile years in German history before 1949. That connection, Jost's paper suggests, is the challenge to Müller's critical reception today, and by implication, to the critical assessment, or as it were, reassessment, of the GDR.

Let me conclude by formulating two major points for discussion. The first, as I suggested earlier, would be the question: Can we separate the quality of a writer like Heiner Müller from the quality of the GDR "Literaturgesellschaft," however problematic and unfinished it was? Or to paraphrase what Martin Esslin once said about Brecht: was Müller a great writer despite the GDR? The second point would be the question of repositioning the critical discussion of Müller's work, shifting it away from the East/West, or as it were, socialist/postmodernist confrontation, relocating it within a larger discussion of German history, and thereby meeting the challenge of Müller's conservative critics. Here we might also consider the extent to which Müller's work, even at the height of his so-called postmodernism, was an effort toward political dialogue with the SED leadership within the context of socialist traditions, and with an eye toward the future.

Note

My translation of the German text kindly made available to me by Stephan Wetzel, Pressedramaturg at the Berliner Ensemble: "Zum Tode von Heiner Müller, dem Schriftsteller, Dramatiker und Regisseur, möchte ich mein tiefes Mitgefühl aussprechen. Sein Tod ist ein unersetzbarer Verlust nicht nur für die deutsche, sondern auch für die europäische, für die Weltkultur. Ich habe einen Menschen verloren, mit dem mich seit Jahren eine aufrichtige

Freundschaft verbunden hat. Die Erinnerung an Heiner Müller wird lange in den Herzen der Menschen leben." The original Russian text of Gorbachev's message to the Berliner Ensemble was not available to me.

David Bathrick

From UFA to DEFA:
Past as Present in Early GDR Films

The planning for film production in the Soviet Zone of Occupation was already underway a scant four months after total capitulation in May of 1945. The call for a gathering of those interested in working on such a project resulted in a famous meeting at the Hotel Adlon on November 22, 1945. Here Soviet occupation officers and political leaders of the KPD, together with German film and literary artists coming from Soviet exile, the so-called inner emigration and the Nazi film industry met for two days of discussion and long range preparation. The President of the newly formed Zentral-verwaltung für Volksbildung (Central Administration for People's Education), Paul Wandel, opened the proceedings with a call for renewal which was to be repeated in spirit, if not in letter, in the succeeding years: "Let us make films" he said, "which breathe a new spirit, films with humanist, antifascist, and democratic content, films that have nothing in common with UFA."[1]

Films that have nothing in common with UFA? That task, it turned out, would be far easier said than done. The two day meeting of the Central Administration, at one level devoted to laying the ideological and organizational groundwork for what would one year later emerge as the Deutsche Filmaktien Gesellschaft, known as DEFA, also quite literally prefigured in its very representation of personages assembled some of the confluences of old and new which were fated to make any renewal such a difficult and protracted affair.

Let us begin with ideology. Certainly the struggle against the "Ungeist der UFA-Traumwelt," as Wandel phrased it, was seen by all present and a considerable number of activist intellectuals of the time—regardless of their prior history—as the central cultural and political task for the rebuilding of mass forms of media communication which would potentially have an impact upon millions within a beleaguered population. "Everyone was united in their loathing of race hate and genocide, cult of the Führer and war mongering."[2] No more SA films with marching youth and hand salute; no more caricatures of the *Ostjuden* lying in wait for the good, upright German burgers, as were depicted by Ferdinand Marian and Werner Krauss in Veit Harlan's notorious *Jud Süss*; no more heroic *Durchhaltefilme* (hold out films) such as the one calling for German sacrifice to save the beleaguered 19th Century fortress of Kolberg from the ravages of Napoleon as a not so subtle allegory for contemporary Berlin; finally, no more triumph of the cinematic will as the implicit message of every form of news or documentary footage made during those twelve years.

Less clear, indeed, increasingly contested, already in the late 1940s with the growing cold war culture, were the meanings of the signifiers humanist, antifaschist, even democratic. If initially serving in the political policies of the Soviet Zone as the lowest common denominators for ideological reconciliation around a once imagined united front, they were gradually to transmogrify into the reifications of a binary reading process: the call for humanism—a term soon to generate its pejorative negation in the forms of "modernism," "avantgardism," "abstractionism," finally "degeneration;" antifascism—a legacy increasingly to be re-encoded within the discursive cultural encrustations of an emerging authoritarian Stalinist infrastructure; democratic—a once hoped for linguistic currency for shared notions of liberation, folded increasingly into the metanarrative of "dialectical materialism's" claim for a legitimizing power, and linked inexorably to the control of the means of production by the chosen iconographical representation of proletarian good will, the Socialist Unity Party of Germany.

These were the cultural and political frameworks within which all modes of political discourse were to find their expression— culture generally, literature more specifically—and to which we shall return in our discussion of individual filmmaking and its development into the 1950s. But what about the resources at hand—in this case the human material as well as capital equipment. A look once again at the 1945 conference, this time focusing on the immediate histories of the writers and filmmakers assembled, is revealing- in many respects. In addition to the literary figures Friedrich Wolf coming from Soviet exile and Günter Weisenborn, who was incarcerated by the Nazis in 1942, most of the assembled artists had been active participants in the Nazi Public Sphere. Of the nine filmmakers named in the program, seven had functioned in UFA and Tobis as leading artists. Most prominent among them were Wolfgang Staudte, Günter Lamprecht and Hans Deppe. Staudte, maker of the first German postwar film, *Die Mörder sind unter uns* (1946), had taken small roles in a number of films, including two of the most notorious Nazi feature films made during the period—Veit Harlan's *Jud Süß* and Arthur Rabenalt's *... reitet für Deutschland* (1941) before he directed one of the premiere comedies of the period entitled *Akrobat schö-ö-ö-n* (1943) Lamprecht and Deppe were both prolific directors of light entertainment films in the Third Reich who went on to make films for DEFA in the immediate postwar period. Lamprecht's *Irgendwo in Berlin* (1946) became the classic rubble youth film of the period. Deppe's *Kein Platz für die Liebe* (1947) and *Die Kuckucks* (1949) are considerably more forgettable, soon to be overshadowed by his now classical Heimat films *Schwarzwaldmädel* (1950) and *Wie Grün ist die Heide* (1951), which were made in the Federal Republic.

This high percentage of Third Reich filmmakers working and affiliated with DEFA was emblematic of an industry dependence as a whole, in all of the allied zones, one which was to remain such well into the 1950s. For example, one survey tells us that between 1949-1952 62% of all DEFA directors, 73% of their camera people and 60% of their producers had once worked for UFA or Terra.[3] Some critics have used these figures as de facto proof for a failure on the part of DEFA from the very outset to truly deal with the Nazi past. In moving towards an adjudication of the issue (I will be avoiding the word judgement), it seems to me important as a starting point to lay out the historical framework in which DEFA was forced to survive.

Already in their discussions in Moscow during Spring of 1944, the KPD cultural emigres and their Soviet colleagues were stressing the importance of film and the electronic media—the most "mass oriented of all the arts"—for postwar political rehabilitation, given that "still too many people would not be reading newspapers not to be speak of books, but would be going to the movies."[4] Certainly this emphasis upon the powers of "controlled policies" (gesteuerte Politik) carried over into decision to build a powerful centralized cinema industry, and as such marked clear differences already at this incipient stage between the Soviet and the other three zones. In contrast to the Soviets, the western zones, dominated by the United States, remained suspicious of the potentially manipulative, i.e. undemocratic powers of the cinema, embracing instead the print media as primary for political enlightenment and relegating cinema to the realm of entertainment. Thus, whereas western allies were initially concerned with breaking up the formation of German cinematic monopolies in order to prevent the development of politically dangerous or potentially competing larger enterprises, the east devoted itself from the very outset to building a concentration for large scale production and distribution in the areas of documentary and feature films.[5]

Such a project, of course, entailed an outlay of enormous material resources at every level of production, which in turn reminds us of the differences between reconstituting literary as opposed to cinematic public spheres during the initial postwar years. As is well known, the technical capacities of the once all powerful UFA concerns lay in ruins. The bombing attacks on Berlin in the last two war years and on Potsdam in August of 1945 had destroyed 90 per cent of the (then) largest film industry in Europe. The capital for rebuilding studios and individual cinemas, for producing technical equipment and film stock was challenging in and of itself, made even more so by reparation policies with the Soviet Union.

Even more staggering was the lack of experience and personnel in the form of artistic genius and technical know-how. Whereas a significant number of leading German literary writers from western and eastern exile had returned to the Soviet Zone to continue their careers (Johannes R. Becher, Bertolt Brecht, Friedrich Wolf, Anna Seghers, Bodo Uhse, etc.), the same could not be said for those emigres working in the cinema. Of the mass exodus of over one thousand top directors, actors, authors, producers, and technicians who had left Germany after 1932, mostly for western countries, because of race policies and political oppression shortly after 1933, only a minuscule number returned to Germany in 1945 and even fewer to the Soviet Zone. For instance, a filmmaker such as Fritz Lang, who had produced several antifascist films in the United States, did not feel it worth his while to return to Germany after the war. Moreover, leftwing film people from the Weimar period who had worked for companies affiliated with the SPD or KPD, such as Prometheus or Weltfilm, were also few in number and mostly unavailable. Slatan Dudow, the director of *Kuble Wampe*, and Erich Engel were exceptions and did go on to make DEFA films. Werner Hochbaum, who made political films for the SPD in the 1920s and became a well known "Frauenregisseur" of comedies for UFA, died in April of 1946 at the age of forty-seven.

The efforts by Soviet cultural authorities to meet viewing needs in a situation in which there was an initial dearth of indigenous filmmaking capacity resulted in two major policy developments which were to have far reaching impact upon the media public sphere in the Soviet Zone. The first was their attempt to provide cinema entertainment immediately, which in turn led them to release their own films for distribution. One month after the German capitulation, the Soviet Military Administration in Germany (SMAD) commissioned German technicians to refit a synchronization studio in Berlin for dubbing Soviet films for German audiences. Here the main emphasis was upon the "Soviet Classics," together with musicals and light entertainment, as a means for countering anti-Sovietism in the German populace and "making them acquainted with the achievements of Soviet art."[6] As a footnote, it should also be mentioned that for cultural and political reasons Soviet revolutionary avant-garde cinema of the 1920s—films by Eisenstein, Pudovkin, Vertov—were for the most part held back from distribution. Eisenstein's *Potemkin* was not screened until 1949, *Strike* and *October* were not shown at all during this period.[7]

A second source of immediate programming were UFA films from the 1930s and 1940s, for the most part "harmless light comedies and musicals" which had been inspected so as to determine whether they "contained subliminally (unterschwellig) traces of fascism, racism or militarism."[8] By 1948, the allies had cleared for distribution 454 of 1300 feature films and full length documentaries made in Germany between 1933 and 1945. Once again entertainment value was of prime importance, as we are reminded by Vladimer Gall, a cultural officer for the SMAD during this period: "For the most part these films were kitschig, sometimes even ridiculous (albern) and in no way did they contribute to the re-education of the German population...but they also weren't dangerous and they did provide people with diversion (Abwechslung)."[9] Finally, the Soviet Zone population were also permitted to view allied films from the US, Great Britain and France.

The second soviet commitment during this period was their complete support for the immediate production of German films and the building of a film industry: the first documentary shorts, cultural films and newsreels made by DEFA, beginning with Kurt Maetzig's newsreel series called *Der Augenzeuge*, appeared in the Spring of 1946 at the same time that initial shooting began for Wolfgang Staudte's *Die Mörder sind unter uns*, which in turn was followed by the official celebrated founding of DEFA on May 17th.

Much has been written about *Die Mörder sind unter uns* as a film which not only breaks with the political and cinematic past, but which does so in a way that takes direct issue with the war crimes of the Third Reich.[10] It has also been positioned as a work which is deeply concerned with a working through the past of the director himself. "I had to make that film," Staudte states, "caught in the horror of the final days of war it was an act of self understanding, my own spiritual settling of accounts (Abrechnung) with fascism and its ideology."[11]

The story of the returning soldier Dr. Hans Mertens, who hunts down and seeks to murder his former senior officer who once issued orders to kill a group of helpless Polish partisans which Mertens himself did not refuse to carry out is not, in a literal sense, Staudte's story. Yet like many of his cinematic colleagues, it served as a means for acting out and working through complicity and its aftermath—in this case, the desire for revenge as an act of repressing one's guilt. Staudte's threefold revision of the ending of the film itself represents a compulsive reenactment of the psychic\collective crime. In the original ending, the filmmaker has his wanton hero Mertens trap the helpless former officer Brückner, now successful capitalist and family man, and murder him on the spot. Told by a Russian cultural officer that "this kind of self-justice" would not be appropriate, given the potential mayhem which might be encouraged among the postwar German population, Staudte settles on a final ending which has Mertens simply attempt to assassinate him, only to be prevented from doing so by his good faithful woman, the concentration camp survivor Susanne Wallner, who throughout has stood by her suffering man as nurturing succorer, and who now quite literally enables his abrupt reversal to rehabilitation. Viewed from the perspective of postwar realities, the final words of this final version of the screenplay are indeed "politically correct:"

> Suzanne: Hans! we do not have the right to judge!
> Mertens: No Suzanne, but we do have the duty to bring an indictment, to demand atonement in the name of the millions of innocently murdered people."[12]

Yet as strategically wise as are these words politically, they also ultimately vitiate the need of the perpetrator\victim\surrogate Hans Mertens to activate himself as subject-doer, albeit after the fact, precisely by acting out and thereby forcing us, the postwar audience, to work through his initial failure of deed.

There is, it seems, no absolutely satisfactory ending to this film. To kill Brückner is to plunge Mertens into a vortex of hate, revenge and self-destroying denial, at the very moment he would finally and decisively take action. Not to kill him, as in the existing version's sutured deus ex machine of political redemption a la Hollywood closure, is denial twice over—the beginnings of a move toward socialist realism's illusory seamless resolution. That Staudte had to struggle and ultimately fail in attempting to fold it all together at the end is a credit to his own integrity and to his unruly film. For already here in this first post UFA feature, we find a number of the ingredients which will mark the fascinating interface of ruptures and continuities, pasts and presents, together with the extraordinary stylistic mixture of expressionist, UFA, Italian neo-realist and social realist aesthetics peculiar to early DEFA productions as a whole. For during this period we find individual filmmakers who project onto the screen their ongoing struggles to live through and subsequently reach resolution, replete with blockage, distortion and revelation; a potpourri of techniques, styles, personnel, variegated experiences; continued fascination with and confusion about the past which will haunt the present as a chosen means of producing the new through a re-enactment of the old.

In drawing on the terminology of trauma theory, I by no means wish to suggest an easy equation between the victims of political persecution at the hands of Nazi terror, on the one hand, and the experiences and activities of those who had "survived" Nazism in various forms of negotiated space within the interstices of everyday life in the Third Reich, and who then sought to deal with their complicity, failed active resistance or even guilt concerning survival through representations of what Staudte has called spiritual settling of accounts and acts of self-understanding. What I am referring to are not simply the projected intentions of individuals, but rather an aesthetics of representation which enable an acting out and\or working through precisely by means of the styles and stories employed at the level of cinematic production. The obvious recurrence and referencing of UFA films or the "UFA look" in so many of the immediate postwar films, often not even seen or noted as such at the time, is at once a problematic reeinvocation of the subliminal messages carried by the aesthetics of ecstacy and illusion from the halls of Babelsberg, while at the same time and within a vastly reorganized scriptural context, a potential link to and avenue out of the sublime and into cognition; a necessary prerequisite for a means by which to get through that earlier aesthetic lockage and its debilitating circularity.

Returning to the Staudte film, let us search now precisely between the cracks and in its pockets for the moments in which UFA is quoted, is either visually or aurally reinvoked. *Die Mörder sind unter uns* reveals its contradictions most egregiously in its bizarre mixtures of styles. It has often been mentioned that the mise-en-scene of the film represents a reenactment of German Expressionism.[13] The camera work of Friedel Behn-Grund is often portrayed as a reutilization of his pre-1930s work in its drawing upon differing dimensions of German silent film's suggestive "dramaturgy of shadow and light" as well as its extraordinary use of camera angle for distortion and highlighting: from Caligari, we get the painterly and architectural transformation of landscape, whether by demonizing ruins into haunting metaphors of a lost and moonscape world; or by the highlighting of physiognomy, particularly in the visages of the suffering Mertens, shot at low-angle and casting shadows for the haunting effects of a tortured soul. From Murnau's *The Last Laugh* comes the wildly distorted grimaces of the neighbors in the tenement house, replicated in a similar scene in Staudte's film by the viciousness of George Gross like caricatures gossiping about events around them. The effect is again one of distortion and exaggeration.[14]

Yet as much as Behn-Grund is quoting Weimar cinematic Expressionism, it is surely his use of light and dark contrasts emanating from a very different system that made him a premiere lighting designer for UFA and Tobis during the 1930s and 1940s.

For if we look more carefully at the camera work, particularly in relationship to its binary systems of shadow and light, then we see that the counter to the lurking, shadowy, melancholic Mertens is precisely that paradigm of goodness, virtue and above all patience, the character Susanne Wallner, played by Hildegard Knef. Not accidentally, Susanne's face is, from the very beginning and in every single take of it, whether close-up or long shot, bathed in bright light. In the words of a recent critic, Ralf Schenk, "Hildegard Knef hovers ever present as a figure of light (Lichtgestalt) throughout the film: with white make-up, her smooth even face highlighted mostly in bright hues as it rises up out of the darkness of its surroundings— she is indeed a principle of hope. 'UFA-Stil' we would say today, in a somewhat abbreviated and inexact way."[15] Schenk is not the only one to find in Behn-Grund's lighting techniques a return to the 1930s and 1940s. As we shall see in our discussion of *Ehe im Schatten*, Kurt Maetzig will characterize Behn-Grund's camera work not as expressionistic as all, but as the very essence of the idealization and anti-realism of the classical UFA aesthetic.

Yet important for our present discussion, finally, is not to demonize Behn-Grund or Staudte or the film itself, but to understand the function of the "UFA-look" within the dialectic of past, present and future as the coordinates for remembering and overcoming. Where expressionist lighting functions to depict depths of melancholia—the jagged scars, facially and spiritually, that escort the hero Mertens into a deep and desperate kind of repetition compulsion—it is the unrelentingly beatific visage and character of Susanne who provides our Blochian moment of utopian overcoming. Hans Blumenberg once said that pure light is an absolute metaphor, and surely that is one of its functions in regards to this figure. Susanne Wallner has been effaced of history, of character, certainly of a psyche—neither do we learn, nor does the tortured narcissist Hans Mertens have any interest in knowing about her past in a concentration camp, for here she is a vehicle for something else. It is the idealization of Susanne as pure signifier— seen close up and resembling similar blond and blue-eyed icons of

UFA, such as the incomparable Marianne Hoppe[16]—whose facial screen will, in its promise of identification and redemption via the familiar emotional cathect object of an UFA citation, facilitate forms of projection and seek to claim for itself a medium for overcoming, if not a moment of genuine mourning.

The next DEFA film to deal with memory and the Nazi past, one also involving a director exploring his own traumatic relationship to the Third Reich, was *Ehe im Schatten* (1947) by Kurt Maetzig. Where Staudte's *Die Mörder sind unter uns* focussed on the guilt of perpetrators among a military apparatus involved in clearly defined war crimes against foreigners outside the Reich, *Ehe im Schatten* tells about the persecution of Jews within and by the German population at home. In this film, the spotlight was on crimes of omission at the level of *Alltag*—everyday acts of cowardice, be they denunciations, a lack of civil courage, or simply a failure of will to do what one knew was right. Here everyone was implicated, even the victims.

Ehe Im Schatten was based on an unpublished "Filmnovelle" by former Third Reich director Hans Schweikert entitled "Es wird schon nicht so schlimm,"[17] which tells the story of the popular theater and film actor Joachim Gottschalk who, together with his Jewish wife and son, committed suicide in November of 1941 when it became clear that mother and son would be deported to Theresienstadt.[18] Gottschalk, who had repeatedly refused official commands to divorce his wife, precipitated the final crisis by appearing publicly with her at the premiere of his film "The Swedish Nightingale," leading to his *Berufsverbot* and an escalation of danger. These tragic events form the central turning point of Maetzig's cinematic diegesis, which begins in 1933 with the wife Elizabeth's expulsion from the theater, moves to the events of the Kristallnacht in November of 1938 and the couple's decision not to leave Germany, and finally, in an accelerating vortex of fear and persecution, to the suicide in 1943.

Although the filmmaker Maetzig did not know the Gottschalks personally, as a Jew and later Communist with an official

Berufsverbot preventing him from working in the film industry, their story paralleled his own. "Almost everything I portrayed in the film I experienced myself within my circle of friends and family," he writes, "it was reality: the deportations, the suicides. All of that was in me, in my memory, all of that was a part of my 'basic experiences'" (Grunderlebnisse).[19] Certainly as a story, Maetzig's reworking of the original screen novelle was to find extraordinary resonance among audiences in the east and the west. It premiered on October 3rd, 1947 and was the only postwar film to be shown in all four sectors of Berlin at the same time. Reviews and other documentary materials speak repeatedly of its enormous emotional impact on sold-out audiences. Seen by over twelve million people, which was an extraordinary number considering the decimation of the movie theaters at that time, it was the single greatest DEFA success of those years.[20]

Much has been written, and some of it quite critically, about the overly emotional, highly sentimental aspect of *Ehe im Schatten*. The film opens on a theater stage with the two main characters performing that melodramatic suicide scene par excellence from the end of Schiller's *Kabale und Liebe*—a clumsy foreshadowing of their own equally drawn out death scene at the end of the film—and the emotional indulgence never lets up. Although melodramatic excess was less of a concern in the initial reception of the film, Bertolt Brecht's response upon seeing it already in 1948 was one of surprise at "how one could have managed to take material such as that and portray it in such a sentimental way."[21] Looking back at his film in 1969, Maetzig himself had second thoughts about *Ehe im Schatten*, calling it artistically very out of date. "Back then I thought we had found the right tone for this tragedy. If I were to redo it today, it would be in a new and modern way."[22] Let us store for a moment Brecht's predictably rationalist remark about the film's lack of epic distance and focus instead on Maetzig's ongoing revisionist review of this early work as a way to reframe our earlier discussion concerning the aesthetics of trauma and their relation to reemerging aspects of the UFA style in postwar films.

In a recent article entitled "A New Train on the Old Tracks: Kurt Maetzig on the Founding of DEFA," the author writes that despite efforts for a new beginning and an antifascist cinema that would contribute to a democratizing of institutions, DEFA filmmakers as a group were often much more bound to the old UFA tradition than anyone was aware. "It was not just stylistically that my film debut *Ehe im Schatten* linked up, even if unconsciously, to UFA," Maetzig writes, "I also worked with film artists, technicians, and craftspeople who came out of the old companies. And where else would they come from?"[23]

The remnants from UFA in and around this film are legion, to say the least. The cameraperson was again Friedel Behn-Grund, whom Maetzig had credited with most of the success of his film in 1948,[24] but who now, forty-four years later, is held responsible ideologically for the importation of UFA "falsification" into the film, which in its "artistic artificiality" (kunstvoll Künstliches) stood in the way of a more realistic art form: "Those were the stylistic devices of aesthetic beautification (Schönmalerei), which sought to mirror 'an illusionary perfect world'."[25]

Certainly a similar argument could be made about the film's musical director Wolfgang Zeller, whose filmography resembles in many ways that of Behn-Grund's. He too had been involved artistically in approximately 150 films, first in the 1920s and then as a premier film composer in the Third Reich. While never a member of the Nazi Party, he did compose the music for a number of Veit Harlan films, including *Jud Süß* in 1940. Zeller has been described recently as a "paradigmatically non-political artist": having worked in Weimar theater with figures like Erwin Piscator, Max Reinhardt, and Heinz Hilpert, he remained under the Nazis "a late romantic German *Tonsetzer*, who in keeping with his political naivete and his simple craftsman's mentality—always capable of a well turned score, fluid sounding orchestra movements, brilliant, melodic ideas— subordinated himself to the cultural norms of the fascist regime and placed his considerable talent, with equal diligence, at the disposal of either "unpolitical" cultural creations or out and out Nazi propaganda films."[26]

Nor did the Nazis see him much differently. In a music interview for the leading journal *Film=Kurier* as part of the hype for the upcoming opening of *Jud Süß* in the Fall of 1940, Zeller is also described as someone who transcends politics, who is concerned only with the "higher" meaning and mission ("Sinn" and "Sendung") of the music: "He only composes a propaganda film (Auftragsfilm) if forced to do so, seeing that it really doesn't suit his most inner musicological being."[27]

And what then constitutes his most inner musicological being? I quote again the Nazi *Film=Kurier*: "In all of his musical work he searches the exciting moments, where music of necessity must make its entrance, where it can deepen and intensify the action, where it not only complements image and word, but dramatizes and even transfigures them."[28] Certainly these are precisely the strategies that Zeller employs in *Ehe im Schatten* in order to mark the vital turning points of action and identification and establish the emotional rhythms of the film as a whole.

As an illustration of UFA borrowings in this film, I would like to look at two of these turning points more carefully. In each case there is a coalescence of historical crisis and narrative urgency. In the first, Elizabeth comes to the full realization in 1933, following the Reichstag fire, that she must end her relationship with the Nazi cultural officer Blum, for it is clear that he is hopelessly locked into the system. Countering Blum's claim that the anti-Semitism of the new regime is limited to a few *Ostjuden*, Elisabeth dramatically asserts that all Jews are being systematically excluded, making impossible any liason between the two of them. The strains of a string ballad announced in the middle of their exchange represent what will become the major theme song of the film, one which Elizabeth will be playing on a piano as she and her husband move toward suicide at the conclusion of the film. In this passage, the music soon overwhelms the now redundant dialogue, building to a powerful crescendo of brass at the end of a shot-reverse-shot image sequence which cuts to Elizabeth's emotionally highlighted face to close out the scene and lend the decision its finality. Clearly there is musicological similarity here to any number of films by Veit Harlan, but more specifically, to the orchestrated turning points of *Jud Süß*.

A second narrative and historical turning point of *Ehe im Schatten* is also linked referentially to the UFA tradition, both by the distinct rhythms of Zeller's orchestration, as well as by direct graphic and characterological citation. The date is that of Kristallnacht, November 9, 1938, and shots of the rapidly accelerating violence against Jewish property are cross cut with those of Hans fighting to get through the crowded streets and to the side of his wife. His arrival home represents an apotheosis of sorts: man and wife pledging never to separate again, underscored by the musical crescendo and full lighted close up of Elizabeth's face.

In addition to the musicological and lighting effects, there are also direct references to Harlan's *Jud Süß* within this sequence. The close up of a Jewish shop with the name sign *Oppenheimer* leaves little doubt of its intended connection to the earlier film. Even more significant, the sequence itself begins with a brief seduction scene between Hans and an actress at the theater played by a noted vamp figure of Third Reich film, Hilde von Stolz, who also played the part of the wife of Duke Alexander in the earlier film, where she ends up having an affair with Süß himself. Here, as in the rest of the film, the choice of actors, music, lighting systems and tones of emotionality clearly serve to enhance through reference to familiar cinematic codes, regardless of their original narrative function or political context.

We have suggested ways that *Ehe im Schatten* is in dialogue with UFA, and more specifically, even with Harlan's anti-Semitic cinematic diatribe. Yet one could also argue for its compatibility with and even borrowing from Hollywood. And this, of course, is precisely the problem with the floating signifier UFA film, with which I started this essay. For what constitutes Zeller's "innermost musicological being," for instance, defined so appropriately in the *Film=Kurier*, is a notion of film music in terms of a neo-romantic illustration of action and word used for purposes of emotional enhancement and, yes, transfiguration. And this, like the camera work of Behn-Grund or the acting styles employed or the editing strategies were, in their stylistic, dramaturgical and, in part, ideological principles, undeniably compatible with those being employed in the major studios of Moscow, Tokyo, London or Hollywood during and after the war. Which forces us back to the question of how this aesthetic was to function in the new context as a part of the mourning process in the postwar period.

The supposed reappearance of what has become known as UFA-Style in some of the immediate postwar, antifascist DEFA films referred quite often to a set of aesthetic strategies, which might be reduced to the following components: Through structures of narration, characterization, framing, lighting, musical score, mise-en-scene and seamless editing: a) a tendency to idealize and transfigure characters and situations into a "heile Welt" at the expense of "epic," "realistic," "materialist," "distanciated," or even bourgeois critical modes of representation; b) the employment of an acting style or the emplotment of a narrative which consciously or unwittingly underscores the values of circularity, closure and individual transcendence in the name self-evident truth and ultimately a denial of "historical progress." c) an attempt to play to the emotions of an audience rather than to encourage critical and cognitive forms of coming to terms with social and political "realities."

That these techniques were employed in such abundance in films that ostensibly were devoted to an aesthetic as well as political break with the Nazi past was often criticized in retrospect, even by the artists involved, as a flight from the grim realities of a postwar status quo, a "papering over of contradiction," or a capitulation to the cultural politics of irrationalism or the Sublime which had led to the catastrophe' in the first place. Brecht spoke of a wallowing in sentimentality, and in so doing, invoked the principles of his own dialectical theater as the only legitimate antidote to the obfuscating dangers of cathartic release and its threat to critical thinking.

Wolfgang Staudte in his film *Rotation*,[29] Kurt Maetzig in *Die Buntkarierten*, Slatan Dudow in *Unser täglich Brot* (1949) all returned more consciously to proletarian and avantgarde traditions of the 1920s, moving thereby to what seemed to be a higher stage of realism and historicization, and clearly quoting and thereby linking up to segments of Weimar Film, which stylistically in some way privileged forms of distanciation, critical enlightenment and historical understanding.

What I would like to suggest is that antidotes to fascism or UFA at the level of collective aesthetic representations need not always be monolinear in their processes of unfolding or hinged inexorably to cognitive forms of "coming to consciousness." Indeed, in certain circumstances, they may even entail a revisiting of certain cites of trauma or forms of emotionally cathected, unsorted investments, *not* as an act of deflection onto an alternative, already pre-sublimated critical "understanding," but rather as the very practice of repetition compulsion. For as Freud has taught us in "Melancholia and Mourning," trauma produces the compulsion to repeat, which can only be ultimately overcome precisely in the process of "acting out." There is no working through without having indulged in the compulsion to repeat. The appearance of UFA's excess—its excessive look and its emotional surplus—in the antifascist films of DEFA after the war contained a very two-edged challenge. On one level, there is the danger in the name of nostalgia, and worse, of fixating on the return of the lost object to the exclusion of everything else. At the same time, we are offered the possibility of opening onto the emotional detritus of an unsorted past, strewn among the narratives and images of its overcoming, with the hope, but also the charge, to go beyond.

Notes

1   *Auf neuen Wegen* (Berlin: Filmverlag, 1951) 10. Quoted in Christiane Mückenberger and Günter Jordan, *"Sie sehen selbst, Sie hören selbst...": Die Defa von ihren Anfängen bis 1949* (Marburg: Hitzeroth, 1994) 25.

2   Mückenberger and Jordan 14.

3   Ralf Schenk, "Beiträge zur Film- und Fernsehwissenschaft," 28:3 (1987): 27, cited in Thomas Heimann, *Defa, Künstler und SED-Kulturpolitik: Zum Verhältnis von Kulturpolitik und Filmproduktion in der SBZ/DDR 1945 bis 1959* (Berlin: Vistas, 1994) 57.

4   Heimann 26

5   See Heide Fehrenbach, *Cinema in Democratizing Germany: Reconstructing National Identity after Hitler* (Chapel Hill & London: U of North Carolina P) 51-91 for a discussion of "American occupation and the politics of film, 1945-1949."

6   Heimann 64

7   Heimann 83

8   Heimann 63

9   Vladimir Gall, *Mein Weg nach Halle* (Berlin, 1988) 131

10 The main works of secondary literature which discuss the importance of *Die Mörder sind unter uns* as an antifascist film include: Mückenberger and Jordan 41-52; Horst Knietzsch, *Wolfgang Staudte* (Berlin: Henschelverlag, 1966) 10-14; Eric Rentschler, "Germany: The past that would not go away," in *World Cinema since 1945*, ed. William Luhr (New York: Ungar Publishing Company, 1987) 210-213; Wolf-Dietrich Schnurre, *Deutsche Filmrundschau* 11. November 1946; Peter Pleyer, *Deutscher Nachkriegsfilm 1946-1948* (Münster, 1965) 173-192; Egon Netenjakob, "Ein Leben gegen die Zeit: Versuch über WS," in *Staudte* (Berlin: Wissenschaftsverlag Volker Spiess, 1991) 22-28; Heinz Kersten, "Ankläger der Mörder und Untertanen," in *Wolfgang Staudte*, ed. Eva Orbanz (Berlin: Verlag Volker Spiess, 1977) 14-18; Die Mörder sind

unter uns/Ehe im Schatten/Die Buntkarierten/Rotation: *Vier Filmerzählungen nach den Bekannten Defa-Filmen*, ed. Ellen Blauert (Berlin, 1969) 9-73.

11 *Vier Filmerzählungen* 74.

12 For Staudte's own discussion of the endings see *Vier Filmerzählungen* 74.

13 Ralf Schenk, "Auferstanden aus Ruinen," in *Das Ufa-Buch: Kunst und Krisen, Stars und Regisseure, Wirtschaft und Politik* (Frankfurt am Main: Zweitausenundeins, 1992) makes the following qualification concerning the role of German Expressionism in Staudte's first film: "'It has been said a hundred times: in 1945 it was normal that German film would pick up again with Expressionism. That proves simply the sterilizing impact of the Hitler period and the fact that one had to start somewhere' wrote the French critic Chris Marker in 1954 in order to excuse postwar German film. Wolfgang Staudte's *Die Mörder sind unter uns* shows one important variation on this theme: with small, unimportant people, who are plagued by big problems, placed into real rubble settings, which appear to be constructed, Staudte gives a sketch of the spiritual condition of the German people. Real victims of the Hitler period are not to be found." (477)

14 Rentschler (211) mentions *Caligari* in relation to this film; Mückenberg and Jordan mention both *Caligari* and *The Last Laugh* (45-46).

15 Schenk, "Auferstanden aus Ruinen" 477.

16 It is interesting to note that one of Staudte's first films in the west, *Schicksal aus zweiter Hand* (1949), featuring Marianne Hoppe, suggested in its narrative as wall as facial lighting patterns something like a remake of Helmut Käutner's *Romanze in Moll* (1943), also starring Hoppe.

17 Hans Schweikert, *Es wird schon nicht so schlimm: Eine Filmnovelle*. This is an unpublished manuscript which has since disappeared.

18 See Ulrich Liebe, *Verehrt, Verfolgt, Vergessen: Schauspieler als Naziopfer* (Weinheim & Berlin: Quadriga, 1992) for an accounting of their life stories.

19 Kurt Maetzig, "Wir hätten auch Aurora heißen können," *Film und Fernsehen*, Berlin 2 (1974). Quoted in Mückenberger and Jordan 75.

20 These figures compare favorably with some of the the biggest successes of the Third Reich, where any film with more than 10 million viewers was considered to be a top box office hit.

21 Kurt Maetzig in conversation with Christiane Mückenberger. Mückenberger and Jordan 388.

22 *Filmerzählungen* 143.

23 Kurt Maetzig, "Neuer Zug auf alten Gleisen: Kurt Maetzig über die Gründung der DEFA," in *Das UFA-Buch* 472.

24 "An der Kamera Friedel Behn-Grund," *Neue Filmwelt* 2 (1948). Maetzig says here of Behn-Grund: "I am happy to be able to state emphatically and in public that a major part of the success of my film *Ehe im Schatten* is due to the work of Friedel Behn-Grund." (5)

25 Maetzig, "Neuer Zug" 471.

26 Wolfgang Thiel, "Kommentare und Analysen zur Musik in frühen DEFA Filmen (1946-1949)" (Berlin, 1986), Manuscript. Quoted in Mückenberger and Jordan 83-84.

27 Dr. Hermann Wanderscheck, "Wolfgang Zeller, der Komponist ernster Filme: Musikalische Vorbereitungen zum *Jud Süß*," *Film=Kurier* August 5, 1940.

28 Wanderscheck, "Wolfgang Zeller."

29 See the discussion of this film in Marc Silberman, *German Cinema: Texts in Context* (Detroit: Wayne State UP) 99-113.

Sabine Groß

Vergangenheitsbewältigung the gentle way?
A Response to David Bathrick

David Bathrick's topic is the ongoing revision of what was itself presented as a revision at the time, a new perspective on DEFA films that provided a new perspective on the recent German past in the postwar years. He reminds us that coming to terms with the past is a process that may well be interminable since it not only engenders its own variations and developmental dynamic as it unfolds, but also invites us into a continual layered series of re-analyses. In historiography as well as in aesthetic representation continuities, discontinuities, and breaks are always more complex than they appear at first or even second sight. David's paper moreover reasserts the fact that aesthetic-representational devices frame issues and affect those who use them in ways that may be not only unintended, but run counter to the professed or explicitly stated goals.

The revision that David records—and to which he contri-butes—brings to mind the case of Günter Eich's famous 1945 poem "Inventur" that was eagerly seized on and fashioned into the embodiment of a new postwar aesthetics, the *Kahlschlaglyrik* by—among others—Wolfgang Weyrauch, who asserted: "Die Kahlschlägler fangen in Sprache, Substanz und Konzeption von vorne an." (*Tausend Gramm*, 1949) "Inventur" was welcomed as representing an acknowledgment of defeat and guilt as well as an attempt to cleanse the German language from fascist contamination. This kind of thinking has a strong element of wishfulness in reaction to the perceived necessity or desirability of creating a new self-image. The need for a new beginning does not actually establish one. A comparison with what was being published at the time easily reveals Eich's poem to have been an exception; and in a move somewhat analogous to that performed by David and the critics he quotes, Klaus Gerth has pointed out recently that Eich's sparseness of language had predecessors both before and in Nazi poetry ("*Inventur* - das 'lyrische Paradepferd des *Kahlschlags*'?", Praxis Deutsch 22, May 1995: 52-58). But it has taken until the 1990s, it seems, for this kind of acknowledgment to become possible.

Did post-war artistic representation, then, claim or profess aesthetic breaks rather than carry them out? Contemporary critics emphatically praised the new look of "Mörder", and this view, or rather blindness, actually persists through 1992, with Wolfgang Gersch (in *Geschichte des deutschen Films* edited by Jacobsen, Kaes, and Prinzler; Metzler 1992: 323, 325) calling it an "ästhetischer Aufbruch" within the broader framework of a "radikale Realitätserweiterung" provided by the first post-war films. Upon the closer look possible half a century later, "Mörder" and "Ehe" provide strong evidence of a continuity that could have been neither consciously intended nor even acknowledged at the time, given the prevalent desire to establish a rupture.

In *Ehe im Schatten*, in particular, the presentation of the romance between Elisabeth and the Nazi Blohm hovers uneasily between citation and appropriation. The film blurs the lines between quoting and incorporating elements of fascist aesthetics in a couple of early scenes when it presents human beings moving in—and being dwarfed by—glorious landscapes. And to what extent do the haunting and magnificent ruins in "Mörder" preserve the same relation between human and surrounding, albeit in a post-defeat reversal of values? Along the same lines, Susanne Wallner's purity—established by virtue of how she is staged and through the similarity to UFA heroines—invokes a paradox that sums up the problematic of this aesthetic continuity: presenting Susanne as a blank slate—in hopes of overcoming the past—is what simultaneously turns her into a projection screen on which her UFA predecessors return to haunt us. (She is about as loaded with meaning as a sign can be, far from the "pure signifier"—a sign *lacking* its "signified" component?—David chooses to term her.)

Structurally, too, much has been kept in place. Both films provide an emotional plot; melodrama is punctuated, if not punctured, by more or less overt pronouncements, just as it might have been in a Nazi film—only the pronouncements have undergone a radical turn towards democracy and tolerance. The slots of good and evil characters—including those presented as possibly decent but finally lacking in morals or character—remain in place, but in filling them ideology has been reversed. And the role of the female protagonist as blank slate, healer, or the one sacrificing herself for a male partner (Elisabeth stays in Germany, because her husband implores her to, calling her his "Lebensinhalt") is woefully familiar. Perhaps Brecht's criticism—relegated by David to the cliché of Brecht as "predictably rationalist" advocate of distance—was directed specifically against the compromising of *Vergangenheitsbewältigung* through the very aesthetic terms that had helped shape the immediate German past?

As David has pointed out, the aesthetic continuity had pragmatic reasons, and it fulfilled emotional or psychological needs. To what extent did the resulting presentation of new wine in old jugs preclude or compromise attempts at working through and coming to terms with what had happened? If we concede that any division into form and content is highly problematic, and that aesthetic strategies inevitably shape the message and have an impact on recipients—then what message did this aesthetic continuity in the presentation of newfound postwar sensibility broadcast? What was the effect, moreover, of making available hundreds of supposedly ideologically innocuous entertainment films that the viewing public had watched during the 1930s and the Second World War, that had become associated with contemporaneous, blatantly propagandist films and with Nazi social politics in general, and that had been preceded by Wochenschauen when first screened?

Yet the very ease with which indictments of DEFA failure to sever its ties to UFA look and techniques can be—and have recently been—pronounced now should give us pause, for more than one reason, and David is to be commended for his intention to offer an "adjudication" rather than judgement. Revisionist denouncements of this kind are seductive because they afford us as critics a position of ideological superiority which is its own reward. They become even more problematic in view of the historical circumstances, namely, the fact that they are being offered with new vigor after reunification and the resulting fall of DEFA from grace (not only by critics, such as Ralf Schenk, but also by filmmaker Kurt Maetzig, who participated himself in continuing what he now denounces as UFA aesthetics). This form of smug revisionism respectively contrite recantation falls only too easily in line with other attempts to recast the GDR from antifascist hero to direct heir of Nazi totalitarianism. In this context, the term "UFA aesthetics" has taken on a life of its own and become monolithic before it has been properly interrogated. While David cautions us against an uncritically exclusive association of melodrama and *Einfühlungskino* with the cinema of the third Reich, he is not entirely without guilt in floating the "floating signifier" himself.

I would like to suggest that, having undone the repression of UFA influence on postwar films, we need to move beyond the simplistic and judgmental reversal that has given rise to exaggerated, if politically opportune, statements about how these films completely incorporated UFA narrative or aesthetic conventions, on to a more differentiating and dialectical assessment of the continuities and breaks. For instance, any assertion that DEFA seamlessly appropriated UFA style is complicated by the fact that the two films presented here as examples actually do not do a particularly good job. Both films follow plots that try hard to appear emotion-driven in order to mask their didacticism—but they fail to pull it off, which is all the more astonishing because "Ehe im Schatten" is based on real-life events. The plot and its emotional logic keep coming apart at the seams, distancing viewers through an inability to present a convincing and plausible fiction, and introducing a rather intriguing way in which both these films do subvert their own aesthetics and emotional dynamics.

David's intention is to advance a less one-sided view of the postwar use of UFA aesthetics. If we follow his logic, the presentation of new wine in old jugs might have been not just unavoidable, but also necessary in order to make the potion more palatable. His paper holds out the promise of a complex and dialectic approach which it, however, fails to deliver. His view of the role of aesthetics in mourning and coming to terms with the past, to the extent that it is formulated here, seems to be largely shaped by the idea of loss and carried by sympathy for the very nostalgia against which he cautions. His implicit critique of an absolute reliance on cognitive modes of "working through" is valid, but his model seems to offer little beyond a cathartic experience in the ancient Greek sense; a situational, unthinking purging of emotional excess, effected here through revisiting former sites—or, in this case, aesthetic modes—of cathexis.

It is illuminating that in this context, David chooses Freud's "Mourning and Melancholia" as ostensible authority for the claim that "trauma produces the compulsion to repeat, which can only be overcome precisely in the process of 'acting out'." "Mourning and Melancholia" is not about trauma—i.e. about shocks that leave the individual unable to respond and come to grips with what happened —but about loss and about productive (mourning) and less productive (melancholia) ways of coming to terms with it, about the alternatives of the work of mourning on the one hand, and the regression and loss of self-esteem associated with melancholia on the other. Interestingly, David presents the "compulsion to repeat" as something to "indulge in." But repetition compulsion has never been a way out. It remains unclear how the therapeutic effect of revisiting "the styles and stories employed at the level of cinematic production" can become an "avenue out of the sublime [subliminal?] and into cognition." David's examples suggest indulgence in a temporary catharsis and its soothing release rather than any working through. His assessment of the effect of stylistic continuities between UFA and DEFA comes dangerously close to an apologetic vindication of regressive aesthetics. To the extent David has presented it here, I find his position that nostalgic reliving and cathartic release can somehow take the place of working through one's attachment to positions that have become insupportable or politically unacceptable insufficiently analytical (and psycho-analytical) in its very optimism that analysis and critical distance can be dispensed with.

Frank Hörnigk

Reconstructing the GDR Canon of the 1960s and 1970s

1. Preliminary Remark(s):
"Contentious Memories" versus " simple truths", or a few comments about the merits of the distinction

There is no one definitive GDR canon of the 1960s and 1970s! I know—the topic is controversial; it belongs to the "contentious memories" on which one works a bit at a time, as we are doing today. In addition to their invitation to this colloquium, I also thank the hosts above all for the question into which they have integrated their topic. I come from a situation in which formulations of this type of question are not so often (or not yet again) worded as true theoretical disputes, for instance in dialogue with those whose own history is being shaped, as in the case of the GDR.

Of course there is no doubt that during the two decades that make up the historical middle of the GDR's existence, as was also earlier the case in the 1950s or later in the 1980s, one has to assume the reality of a state-sponsored canon that in this sense lays a claim to and exercises power, while serving as a formative pattern for literary production. At the same time, though, the attempt to reconstruct it (in reference to these years) leads to the telling of a story of failure, one which had its beginning exactly at this time and, until the end of the 1970s, marched on toward its final, in any case final ideational, failure. It is the crisis of a "dictatorial societal construction" from the perspective of one of its forms, observed at the stage of its beginning and advanced self-dissolution.

In observing the differences within the political system of the GDR, I am referring to current debates in the political and social sciences, which read somewhat as follows in their structural descriptions of political strategies in the GDR: "The noteworthy feature of the forty year history of the GDR is not that the Socialist Unity Party (SED) was successful in constructing a society according to a Marxist-Leninist blueprint. Instead, what is unusual is much more that this was attempted with a determination that has no historical precedent." [1] Simultaneously, necessary structural inefficiencies in state power, created by this very blueprint, logically led early on to the formation of a network of informal structures, which then led ever more strongly to a "specific constellation consisting of an ideologically based formation of society by the party dictatorship and the informal patterns related to it." These "informal interrelations did not just enter into the pre-existing structures and operate within them, but rather acted themselves as increasingly structure-formative." [2]

It is specifically this differentiation between the literary and the literary-political horizons during the 1960s and 1970s that the following text will address. That includes considering the historical self-deception of the majority of the active participants in this area, who only in exceptional cases (Uwe Johnson, for example) understood their own production as literary practice charged with an antagonistic quality (in the best sense of the word). They were farther still from perceiving, or wanting to recognize as such, the social criticism of the *Real-Sozialismus* in the GDR that was written into their texts in principle.

Provokation für mich (Provocation for My Own Sake), Volker Braun's first volume of poetry, from the beginning of the 1960s, was, in fact, a provocation of power inasmuch as the state rightly saw the essential conditions of this society being called into question rather than merely the provocation of an individual who wanted to "improve" this society without abolishing it.

This contradiction and the experience of its aesthetic resolution/radicalization in the later 1960s and 1970s should be considered, as should the accompanying and long-lasting experience of intellectual inconsistency in addressing the contradictory nature of the conditions. Here the discussion is above all about the attempts in literary history to describe this process.

Following from that, and in conclusion, the attempt should at least be undertaken to explain more exactly the paradigm "canon" as a concept and as a model of another understanding of literary historical thinking.

But that is enough for a preface—the actual talk follows, and it begins first with a digression which I find imperative, into the assessments made by literary historical research on the project "GDR-literature." The heading is:

2. The "spellbound" view: Between discovery and dismissal: "GDR literature" as an object of literary historiography or a digression on the interpretations of literary scholarship before and after 1989.

Of course we agree that writing literary histories is not easy. Not anywhere. But yet, or so it seems, this somewhat succinct assessment of a not exactly surprising universal dilemma in the study of literature can hardly be illuminated more distinctly by any other "case" in recent history than by the history of GDR literature. Bernhard Greiner pointed that out in a fundamental criticism as early as 1982. [3] The majority of the portrayals of this literature presented since then, especially the works appearing after 1990, have sharpened rather than taken the edge off of Greiners polemics. He argued that the answers provided by literary scholarship to the challenges of the literature itself proved to be answers to fundamental literary sociological questions that were not truly specific to the field of literary studies. I will come back to this later.

First allow me a short look at the pre-history. From the beginning—that is, since the time the literature of the GDR was understood at all as an autonomous field in literary historiography—the dominant view, lasting into the late 1960s, was that its literature should only be explained directly through the underlying conception at any given time of literature's relationship to society and state. It should be mentioned here in passing, that such beliefs in linear cause-effect relationships, even when diametrically opposed in their evaluative framework, dominated and shaped the discussion in the Federal Republic and interestingly in the GDR for a long time. Only since the 1970s has this view been replaced by more differentiating theoretical approaches, springing from the meanwhile growing insight into the reductionism of such an approach, the influence of contemporary international research, and the overall expansion and corresponding dispersion of the literary process itself.

Following this shift, "the origin and history of the literature of the GDR," (a more appropriate name for this newer approach had appeared by 1983) could not possibly be sufficiently explained by the claim of a "simple association with an ideological periodization."[4]　Rather, attention was drawn to a significant process of differentiation in research in the Federal Republic as in the GDR. This appeared in depictions that juxtaposed a centrally planned, hierarchical, functionalist culture and art practice with an increasing self-articulation and growing group loyalty among authors, caused by disillusionment and painful political learning processes.[5] Through this course of events arose the complementary dimension of the ambivalently evoked *Denkbild* of the (politically) mature reader (*mündiger Leser*)[6] which finally, in a logical extension, found its most radical and consistent form in a largely autonomous, self-articulating literary subculture in the GDR in the 1980s.[7] The prevailing findings in the study of GDR literature in those years could be summarized as sharing a basic tendency in literary history toward a "softening of a normative aesthetic."[8]

What was, however, critically observed again and again, not seldom with a touch of left-leaning melancholy and a gesture of reproach towards those directly involved, was that all of the onsets towards public ownership of social processes, though indeed quite revolutionary as originally proposed in the GDR and understood by the general public, were undermined by the bureaucracy and soon encumbered with substitute functions as "directed cultural revolutionary mass initiatives." However, to turn the argument on its head, even campaigns such as the "Bitterfeld Movement" would have offered the chance to bring about a societal discourse, "against the expectation of its initiators."[9]

At this point it seems appropriate to comment on a contradiction which I find extremely interesting. As suggested, in the 1970s and 1980s, in the East as in the West, the prevailing theoretical perspective on one hand endowed the literary process with its own autonomous precepts, yet on the other viewed societal conditions as essentially centrally structured. While it succeeded in negating the "simple truth" of a direct causal relationship between base and superstructure, this perspective could itself no longer sufficiently differentiate between the levels of state power and literary discourse. Instead, it had to debate them in the future increasingly in isolation from one another (or in fact leave them aside entirely) for the sake of their own fundamental argument (the often self-suggestively conjured up idea of autonomous literary conditions), as well as the possibility seen therein either for societal reform or political dissidence—depending on the expectations of the theory. In other words: Although literary texts and literary society could earlier be understood as a result of politico-cultural directives, with an ideologizing claim to be the true historical course of social changes and—if linearly—could be thought of together, the later, indisputably differentiated beginnings of a critique of such a concept of order lacked even a separate, theoretically convincing answer and perspective. From such a perspective, the highly complex arrangements between text and the conditions of literature, literature and the conditions of society as a whole, and historical and literary-historical movements could have been understood fundamentally differently (by which is meant not just politically differently).

The text and author centered interpretation method based in philology or intellectual history that dominates the international academic enterprise admittedly did not pose itself the question on this level for a long time. To the contrary: once the literature of the

GDR was admitted as a worthwhile object of interpretive endeavors in the area of contemporary German literature, it was principally coordinated and explained in connection with the different interpretative paradigms (structuralist, reception aesthetic, psychoanalytic, discourse analytic, etc.) (see K. R. Mandelkow 1976, J. Hoogeveen 1978, A.v. Bormann 1990). The "problem" was thereby subsumed under the concept of "context", without much consideration, and was taken care of with the introduction of a "GDR-index," the structure of which was left to the discretion of the particular mode of interpretation. "The new view" promised by the titles of so many series of literary interpretations seemed to apply not to the "literature of the GDR" but rather to some texts from the GDR, preferably those which best served as prominent examples for the process of analysis.

In exact opposite to these stood more extensive literary histories of modern German-language literature that were undertaken after the mid-1970s in East and West, which sought to extract from this "context" the literature itself as the object of study. The criticism from others in the field, admittedly, soon proved that the ambitious goal of this undertaking, inspired by the encouraging results of social-historical investigations in related fields, could not be reasonably achieved. The general inability in the field of literary scholarship to adopt corresponding theories in other areas was considered responsible for this apparent failure, as was the lack of reliable knowledge in the empirical sciences (contemporary and political history, empirical social sciences, etc.) In fact, the representations actually consisted of little more than individual studies, hardly connected to one another, whose internal coherence was the result more of genre theory and narrative structure than of an intention to be a social-historical representation, which would have found this approach quite problematic. The logical result was that all the following came to stand next to each other: literary historical narrative, trenchant interpretations of exemplary explained texts, rooted ideologies, the odd moment of biographical information, outlines of historical and social developments, reports of political "interventions," references to international movements in the aesthetic realm, and accounts of a cultural and educational policy either distilled from accessible semi-official documents or tacitly assembled. Such pieced together aggregates, though, served only as a reminder of the empirical breadth of phenomena to be integrated by a social history of literature, which was, however, not achieved. In the end, it remained unclear exactly what the object of these "social histories of literature" was: whether it was literary history in the traditional understanding, just with an expanded ("social") frame of reference, or whether it was the history of literature as a social institution. Regardless of such necessary—and soon pronounced—criticism, the object of study nonetheless manifested itself in a complexity that could no longer be overcome without a prior acceptance of theoretical reduction, that is, without reference to a systematic model.[10]

This conclusion should still be remembered and considered, even after 1989, "the end of the GDR." The thesis reads: the writing of literary history, since then and up to today (with some exceptions, one of whom is sitting here in the room and whose name is David Bathrick [11]) has still not sufficiently expanded the process of critiquing the overarching social conditions, and within those the specific conditions of literature, to include a self-criticism of the discipline. This includes criticism of its own earlier and also more recent judgments of the GDR-literature, in the sense not just of a changed political behavioral role, but also of a self-awareness that needs to be examined and theoretically grounded.

Two opposite tendencies in the discussion can be observed simultaneously. First, there is the trend towards completely rewriting the literary history of the GDR and subjecting it to what is, in principle, a reassessment. Secondly, there is the tendency to finally place it without qualification into the wider context of an "all-German" literature. Projects which organize literature from the GDR principally in reference to the relationship between "intellect and state power," and thereby judge it in a fundamentally new manner, correspond to the first tendency; examples include topoi such as "literature and the state", "literature and Stalinism" or "literature and *Staatssicherheit* ." The recently published, revised edition of W. Emmerich's *Kleine Literaturgeschichte der DDR. Erweiterte Neuausgabe* (1996) (A Short Literary History of the GDR. Expanded New Edition) could also actually be read in a new manner, against the backdrop of a paradigm shift in the author's understanding of literary conditions, perhaps politically motivated. There is also the dimension of a personal shift in experience, according to which Wolfgang Emmerich largely reformulates the first two versions of his literary history, both published in the 1980s.

Attempts at making the second call for integration have thus remained more or less pro forma,[12] since the classification of the literature from the GDR in an all-German literary history is more a pretense than an actuality, in that two as it were separately written volumes are broken down by chapter and then published in one volume. Since the internal comparison is still to come, the publishers have to maintain a separate department for "GDR literature" that exists alongside that for FRG literature, with its self-contained representation of itself. This is a dilemma inherent not only in representation.

It should be pointed out again here, that that which seemed virtually imperative for some culture and literary scholars in 1989, because of pressure from the changed historical conditions of their writing, proves today to still be an unsolved theoretical-methodological problem, particularly in the case of large-scale representations of literary history.[13]

A truly comparative approach, beyond simple rhetorical claims, seems to have been easier for foreign researchers, as I already indicated. However, at times when such comparisons were far from being called upon again, they themselves understood the two literatures in Germany only in terms of their transparent simultaneity. However, the attempts at a common German literary history that integrated GDR literature, which, incidentally, have since 1990 been undertaken in Germany only by West German literary specialists, presupposed research which had not been sufficiently undertaken since reunification even in the West. Not surprising, since the paradigm of the existence of two German literatures became invalid not because of scholarly investigation but as the result of political events and their ideological power of definition.

What is needed would be a theoretically critical self-assurance of the (in this sense) still unnamed object "German literature since 1945" that frees itself from the currently growing excess of ideological (pre)determination, using an expanded fund of literary texts and literary criticism, as well as new extra-literary sources, which would include those from the *Sicherungsbereich Literatur* of the *Stasi*. The question as to what aspects of all this made up the special quality of literature from and in the GDR, in my context here of the 1960s and 1970s, is part of this process of self-assurance. Conversely, the same question, albeit in a completely different system of coordinates, remains to be asked of the literature of the Federal Republic; it is still unanswered and remains, then as now, a contentious issue. Possible answers could come to light, given a willingness to at least seriously reconsider the reigning paradigm of an established, firmly-rooted canon, through which the horizons of the literary historical process are still viewed today.

On the basis of such an implied critique of the fundamentally problematic term "canon," problematic because of its inherited one-dimensionality, I would like to attempt to present you with a few possible alternative systematizations that result from this criticism, and discuss the implications for literary history that would follow. What concerns me both here in this specific context and more generally in the project out of which research this article emerged, is pursuing such questions as the changing practices of canonization, canon-building, canon preservation, canon reorganization, canon revision, etc. Keeping in mind the demand that literary historical research should not just silently exhaust itself in the establishment and continuation of canons, but rather also investigate their origin,[14] I will conclude by trying to illuminate the progress and crises in the establishment of an official canon, and the practice thereof in the 1960s and 1970s. As an example, I will use the topos "socialist realism," the most important system of standardization in contemporary GDR literature. But first:

3. A few reflections on the concept of the literary canon

This description of a new paradigm of literary history will in this context naturally just be a general sketch, taking on first the familiar, seemingly rather traditional connotation of a literary canon, with the intent of fundamentally expanding this so to speak "old" canon. This assumes an idea of "canon" in which texts and authors are not in the forefront, but rather literary-communicative behavior in particular patterns of social action. Understood as such, canon, standard, and canonization are therefore representative of developments and of stabilized, yet not immutable, structures that exist at any given moment. That is, the official canon (also that of the years being discussed here) will not be treated as a given quantity or elevated to the status of subject, but rather implies a debate about what should be canonized, what is already canonized, etc. and about the "canon principle" itself.

Following this line of argument, the critical revision of the concept "canon" in the literary didactic and literary scholarship debates since the end of the 1960s will also be examined in a theoretical discussion. This was a critique of the idea that "canon" as a structuring principle was grounded in itself or in an ideal hierarchy.

It goes without saying that an understanding of literature, founded on such a basis, cannot be determined solely by a body of texts, that, for example, marked with the stamp "GDR", make up an imaginary library. This understanding is thought of much more in reference to a framework, through which actions in societal conditions are organized. These include, but are not limited to, those which are considered "literary." The fundamental principles of this definition rest on the results of a dominant "empirical literary scholarship," as well as its furtherance through theoretical models of social systems such as those in the realm of radical constructivism, and their criticism. The social relationships in which literary actions occur thereby have a thoroughly systematic character attributed to them, although, at the same time—to remain with the example—one cannot speak of a "GDR literature system." Underlying this is the thought that for the topos "GDR literature" within GDR society, the process of a functional differentiation of specific social component systems, characteristic of western modernism, had to be withdrawn or at least modified, with the goal of constructing another societal totality that subsumed all component systems (including even the state political system) under the control of a hierarchical understanding of state power and public.

That raises the question, however, as to what extent in the case of GDR literature the prerequisites necessary to speak meaningfully of subsystems such as a literature system even existed: self-referential organization (differentiation), the formation of stable integration processes, etc. Consequently, one must also ask whether the issue of outside control vs. autonomy in the literature system of the GDR must not therefore be understood differently, namely as the argument as to whether there was a literature system in the GDR or if the GDR was instead simultaneously its own literature system (sarcastically, taking Johannes R. Becher literally: as a *Literaturgesellschaft*.)

It becomes obvious: a concept of literature founded on this *Denkbild* of literary communication means in every case a considerable increase in the complexity of the subject. At the same time, however, it should be equally clear that only when such complexity is accepted as a fundamental component of the literary profession itself can one observe those elements which otherwise would have to appear as irrelevant, as unnecessarily cobbled onto the actual literature: a host of mediations due to economic imperatives, foreign influences, external allocations of function, etc.

Considering the current literary political debates, a central achievement of such a perspective would be to force an expansion of the typical unidirectional question, "What influence did the GDR have on GDR literature?" Rather, the question would read, "What share did GDR literature (understood as a social process by which a meaning of a text is construed) have in the GDR?" Also here, therefore, it is a matter of scrutinizing the connections of the literary process to a phenomenon that is not the process itself but which contains it. That is, the above-mentioned quality of differentiation is not in a context that can be called into play or suppressed at will, on the margin of every investigation, but is instead crucial, and forms the central object of study! This conceptualization, although hard to carry out in practice, since it leads to nothing less than a representation of the entire GDR society under one single aspect, is nonetheless logically consistent and significant in its implications. It allows for the categorization of a phenomenon that we encounter in concrete cases in constantly new forms: a *mikado* of the most heterogeneous actions suddenly becomes part of an eminent literary historical issue and proves to be, to remain in the terminology of the model, a "literary" action or an "action related to literature," but this only in reference to the individual issue and without a prescribed function within the model.

Canonization can therefore be assigned a social character, in so far as the structuring of literary communication can be considered part of a more or less all-encompassing society. This can be observed in the way in which the canonizations form themselves through the interactions of individuals and groups participating in the literary process and through communication. One cannot, therefore, ask solely about the type of relatively unchanging selections and exclusions that are evident in the canon. Rather, what should be ascertained are the social spaces in which, through certain functions, these decisions are made (how they are suggested or dictated, win degrees of acceptance, accepted as established, subjected to criticism, suffer turmoil, undergo transformations or, lastly, even experience dismissal.) When considering the element of stability in the selection and exclusion, it is true that one can at times speak of "personal canons," but our interest should lie above all in the forms of societal canon-formation. To continue this point, a distinction should be drawn at the same time between the concept of community (*Gemeinschaft*) and society (*Gesellschaft*). Canon formations in the literary field develop as common ground among communities. They can be counted among the intellectual factors that, as trace elements in the consciousness, mentality and behavior, give rise to a community or the idea of a community. The effect of the self-articulation of the so-called "Saxon school of writers" of new literature (*Sächische Dichterschule*) in the 1960s can be understood in this manner.

From this perspective, canon formation can be regarded as a culture that develops out of comparison, differentiation and consensus building, or, in other words, as a social memory, formed through communication, that stands somewhere between remembering and forgetting. Accordingly, attention is directed towards the unique aspects of literary production and, in addition, necessarily towards the conditions of distribution and reception within a given society. One must consider, that is, those inter-relations that guarantee or further the continuity or discontinuity of literary appropriation and that produce or hinder parallel effects, etc. Each choice of historical texts and authors and every manifestation of the concepts of "classics," "heritage" or "tradition" always implies the element of a certain questionable claim to legitimacy by those who wish to be heir to this inheritance. It not seldom appears as a supposed redemption of desired traditions in current or future societal action.

The meaning that this correlation receives was inherent in all of those canonizations that were undertaken in the GDR by institutions of literature. They functioned even within other component systems and influenced those systems' roles in GDR society: for example, the literary policy (with the allocation of fame, promulgation of values and norms, bestowal of prizes, subventions and stipends, censorship or selling strategies); likewise, the political system and its repercussions on the other systems; in addition, the school system (with the choice of curriculum content); similarly, the book trade (with the advertisement and the determination of the number of titles and editions for sale); as well as the library system (with the choice of books kept on hand and their organization), and so on.

All of these factors had a decided effect on the whole of literary communication through their interpretive and opinion-building potential, and determined its structuring as much as those institutions working directly in the realm of literary communications,. These included publishing houses (with their choice of publications), literary criticism (with the *Feuilleton* and special literary journals as a place for information and for orientation for those involved in literary communication) and, finally, in the discourse within what is known in Germany as *Literaturwissenschaft* (at universities and academic institutions with their lectures, writings and literary histories, their selections and accentuations, documentations, and general understanding of what literature is).

A systematic investigation would also have to include canonization processes among the producers of literature—the authors themselves (for instance with their idea of a standard for literary creation, or notions of preferred subject matter), those who work with completed texts (such as in the choice of literature to be translated or adapted for film or the choice of theater productions), and finally segments of the general public or literary communities (for example, in the values incorporated in the bestseller lists). In the same vein, one could also examine the interrelation of ethnic, gender-related, social, political and philosophical orientations in canon formations (as they appeared in the GDR in the literature of the Sorbs, in literature written by women, in Socialist or Christian literature or in the literature of a "scene", etc., as vehicles of expression for the corresponding group's distinctive features and interests). In the literary discourse in the GDR there was generally little discussion of this group-specific quality of literature, and at times, in fact, the very possibility of its existence was heatedly dismissed. This had to do with the pressure of the official discourse and also with the illusions of the literary elite who maintained, although ever less tenably, a belief in the possibility of a community that could unite the entire population of the GDR. As a result, canonizations which attempt to build communities among overlapping groups or to span several particular societies became conspicuous (as with the canon formations in the GDR of national literature, of multi-national Soviet literature, of the literature of the socialist countries.)

Discussion of a society's canon, one that acts within the totality of societal relationships, must, in light of the variety of canonization processes, be subjected to special consideration. In any given society, there are different groups at work, possibly with different conceptions of a canon, related to each other in terms of subsumtion, opposition, subversion and indifference. Canons are afforded societal relevance to the extent that the political, judicial and economic power and the argumentative strength of particular groups can suggest them to or impose them upon other groups. Ultimately, one can speak of dominant, hegemonic canons in a society. If one speaks of canonization either as a function (of dependent variables) of society or if one speaks of the function (or utility) of canonization within society, these relationships must be considered. A method to empiricize them, however, is yet to be found. The tendency to establish these core areas in examining literature, as outlined above, and the exclusions that accompany them, are viewed as a fundamental structuring process in all dealings with literature. At the same time, it is assumed that this tendency is subject to historical and social differentiations and is an inherent element therein.

Considering the elements of canon formation particular to the GDR in the historical context of four decades, such differentiations can first be discerned in the periods immediately preceding and following the time period being examined. Specifically, I am assuming the period from 1945 until the end of the 1950s as a beginning and that from the end of the 1970s to the end of the 1980s as an end phase, both of which can be described here only in rough, generalized terms.

At the beginning we see the following: the establishment of a counter-canon (in opposition to German pasts and contemporary Western culture) and, simultaneously, the emergence of a canon that supported an *Aufstiegsliteratur* and the establishment of a soon dominant principle that embraced a specific understanding of an anti-fascist, anti-capitalistic, militantly humanistic and socialist canonization. In addition, a style of canonization was realized that through offensive, open propagation, and censorship sought to hinder societal spontaneity (the mechanisms of which were seen to be the market and ideological plurality or openness). At the same time it served to secure power attained with foreign help, in other words, the establishment of what were understood to be new societal relationships. Finally, a contradictory, often harsh discussion arose between the political elite and those members of the literary elite who had remained in the country about the correct handling of a principle and style which they largely agreed on, in which each hoped to gain something by employing simplifying dichotomies such as progress and reaction/decadence.

At the end quite different factors come to bear: first, a clear, by that point unstoppable, splitting apart of the contradictions within the framework of the canon along with increasing contrast between the "official" and variously differentiated counter-official canonizations, a development which marked a polarized literary landscape that was divided by deep fissures between the extremes. On the official side, there were attempts to construct a continuously overarching canon while still invoking the by then hollow precepts of "socialist realism." Among anti-official orientations, on the other hand, there was a suggestion and inclusion of new canon contents (or at least the acceptance of those previously marginalized into core areas and the admittance of those previously repressed into the margins)—a shift propelled by both the unfulfilled promises and the deficiencies in societal development. In addition, there emerged among other groups an indifference toward the official canon and a beginning acceptance of modernist and post-modernist canonizing tendencies. Finally, the period was marked by the influence of an official canonization style which oscillated between a forced tolerance and a confused, defensive, increasingly arbitrary censorship, the results of a varied and subversive circumvention of official canonization and censorship, and, lastly, the effects of open criticism of the dictated norms and censorship, and so on.

Situated between these extremes of the ascension of a canon and later its rapid fall at the end of the GDR, the actual moment of crisis for this official canon occurred during the two decades that ended the Ulbricht era and began the Honecker era and appears definable. It becomes concrete in the normative system of the term "socialist realism", the aesthetic dogma's most rigorous assertion and the dramatic loss in meaning it experienced soon thereafter. Now a few concluding thoughts on this subject. They will have to remain a sketch, however—the quantity of material related to the reconstruction of actual literary events of these years, in relation to that which was then discussed, dictated or understood under the term "socialist realism," is beyond the scope of this article. "Reconstruction" is here, in the end, actually rather understood as "construction"—the empirically authenticated construction of an interpretative possibility, contrasted with the custom of simply extrapolating reconstructed memories that continually orient themselves on each other.

Keeping that in mind, it is particularly interesting for me and for our context here to look at the major transformations that have occurred since the beginning of the 1960s in the use of the term "socialist realism," as well as in the way this term manifests itself, in contrast to the structure of definition and meaning of the dominant inherited frame of reference current until then. As already suggested, the term had once had *Kampfcharakter*, but in the 1950s, not least because of interests due to political alliances, it had to derive its justification and authority out of a comparison with critical realism. The year 1963 signaled an at first apparently minor change in the statutes of the German Writers' Union (*Deutscher Schriftstellerverband*) when "socialist realism" was officially made the sole and binding method of artistic creation for all the associations' members. The old formulation was deleted: "The associations' members see the socialist realist method of creation, which develops from the world view of Marxism-Leninism, as the best method to correctly understand reality." It is replaced and at the same time decidedly radicalized with the formula: "The association's members see in Socialist Realism, which develops from the world-view of Marxism-Leninism, their method to correctly understand reality. The new formulation amounts essentially to a completely, openly politicized disciplining and standardization of the entire literary production process. And this at a time in which the younger generation of authors, above all, were submitting texts that, in their increasing difference and their aesthetic obstinacy could hardly, or only with great difficulty, be interpreted as belonging to the pre-existing canon. There develops a formative impression of, on the one hand, a political debate that calls upon increasingly ideologically orthodox values and moral concepts and, on the other hand, poetic production that constantly calls into question the framework of aesthetic standardization. At the 11th Plenum of the Central Committee of the Socialist Unity Party (SED), the famous-infamous culture plenum at the end of 1965, the long awaited confrontation that had been looming on the horizon finally took place. From this point on, at the latest, there is a rift that divides all of literature and everyone and every institution involved with it. At the same time, the schizophrenia of the situation becomes clear, in that this condition is experienced for the first time as a contradiction, but at the level of authorship there is still a reluctance to perceive it quite so radically, so that in the end it cannot be formulated as an irrevocable conflict between intellect and power. The result: for a long time the discussion is still based on a superficial assumption of fundamental agreement that is no longer questionable (and is, in fact, increasingly, no longer questioned). The categories of True vs. False are elevated again to the level of criteria for determining the quality of literature and are accepted as such.   In this manner, then, the already long anachronistic question as to whether "social realism" is a world view or a method, how artistic mastery relates to a clarity of world view, etc., drags on through the years in the debates about the position of literature during the *Kämpfen der Zeit*.

The putative opening of the politico-cultural program after Honecker's takeover is, therefore, only feigned. Even when the SED leadership at the 6th Plenum in 1972 finally stood by the conclusion that art delivers an independent, original view of the world and not just one specific picture of it, the old understanding of "canon" does not change in any way, and the actual axiom remains untouched. It read: (famous in Honeckers formulation of the specific type of "mimetic reproduction of the world"): "Everything is possible and there are no taboos, as long as the world is understood from a socialist point of view." The phrase based on this, disseminated at that time, of the "breadth and variety of our literature" was always bound to the subordinate clause, "naturally on the basis of a shared ideology," and its continued existence was not called into question in any debate on art. The final breach, then, was tied to a rejection of a basic political question and not primarily to a debate about realism, about a true or false, socialist or not, "reflection of our reality."

In the blind decision to expatriate Biermann a few years later, this breach found its first, truly irreparable yet rather superficial, and rather spectacular expression; that it was used as a justification only reminds us once again of the misunderstandings in speaking about literature and in much too often overlooking the circumstances surrounding literature. Certainly here, at the latest, the actual work—the work on the material—begins, and, at the same time the attempt undertaken here to at least begin structuring this material ends.

Translated by Sara B. Young and Eric Jarosinski

Notes

1   Ralph Jessen, "Die Gesellschaft im Staatsozialismus. Probleme einer Sozialgeschichte der DDR," *Geschichte und Gesellschaft* 21 (1995), p. 100.

2   Ibid., p. 109.

3   Bernhard Greiner, "DDR-Literatur als Problem der Literaturwissenschaft," in *Jahrbuch zur Literatur in der DDR 3* (Bonn, 1983), pp. 233-254.

4   Hans-Jürgen Schmitt, ed., *Die Literatur der DDR, Hansers Sozialgeschichte der deutschen Literatur* (Munich, Vienna, 1983), p. 10.

5   According to Wolfgang Emmerich, particularly in the first two editions of his *Kleine Literaturgeschichte der DDR* (Frankfurt a. M. 1981, 1989).

6   In this context, the term refers to Dieter Schlenstedt, *Wirkungsästhetische Analysen. Poetologie und Prosa in der neueren DDR-Literatur* (Berlin, 1979).

7   See Antonia Grunenberg, *Aufbruch der inneren Mauer. Politik und Kultur in der DDR 1971-1990* (Bremen, 1990).

8   See Harald Hartung, "Die ästhetische und soziale Kritik der Lyrik," in *Hansers Sozialgeschichte*, vol. 11 (Munich, Vienna, 1983), pp. 261-303.

9   See Bernhard Greiner, "Im Zeichen des Aufbruchs: Die Literatur der fünfziger Jahre," in *Hansers Sozialgeschichte*, vol. 11 (Munich, Vienna, 1983), pp. 378 ff.

10 These and the following arguments regarding the concept of the literary canon, as well as the entire methodological structure of this presentation, is based on debates that are currently being held within the framework of a research project at the Humboldt University Institute for German Literature, which is funded by the Deutsche Forschungsgemeinschaft. The results of the project will be published in book form in 1998 under the title *Kanon und Norm. Zur*

literarischen/kulturellen Kommunikation in der SBZ/DDR (Canon and Norm. On literary and cultural communication in the Soviet zone of occupation / German Democratic Republic).

11 David Bathrick, *The Powers of Speech. The Politics of Culture in the GDR* (Lincoln, 1995).

12 See Wilfried Barner, ed. *Geschichte der deutschen Literatur von 1945 bis zur Gegenwart* (Munich, 1994); see also Ralf Schnell, *Geschichte der deutschsprachigen Literatur seit 1945* (Stuttgart, Weimar, 1993). Even reviewers whose opinions of these books are otherwise fundamentally opposed to each other agree in their criticism of the method used (e.g. H.G. Soldat, *Berliner Zeitung* (June 8, 1995) and H.H. Lehmann, *Neues Deutschland* (November 27, 1995)).

13 Klaus Briegleb and Sigrid Weigel, for example, thought it was self-evident that their history of "contemporary literature since 1968" would be the last that was "based on a division into two German literatures, that of the GDR and that of the Federal Republic." Klaus Briegleb and Sigrid Weigel, *Gegenwartsliteratur seit 1968* (1992), p. 9.

14 In particular according to Gottlieb Gaiser, *Literaturgeschichte und literarische Institution. Zu einer Pragmatik der Literatur* (Meitingen, 1993).

15 See Birgit Dahlke, Frank Hörnigk, Martina Langermann and Thomas Taterka, "Kanon und Norm. Zur literarischen/kulturellen Kommunikation in der SBZ/DDR, Projektvorstellung," *Zeitschrift für Germanistik* 5 (1995), pp. 74-81.

Hans Adler

Response

The most perplexing thing about Frank Hörnigk's contribution is that he does not realize the promise of its title. We simply do not find out what made up the GDR-canon of the 1960s and 1970s. How has it happened here that our expectations have been so flagrantly disappointed?

Frank Hörnigk's lecture is divided into three sections: the first consists of preliminary remarks, the second is a digression; and the third is made up of [preliminary] reflections on the concept "canon." This arrangement makes it clear how the topic has been interpreted: the most important point is neither the GDR, nor the 1960s and 1970s, but rather the reconstruction, more precisely, the problem of constructing a canon in general. The historically specific particulars are laid away in short enumerations. Therefore, we hear nothing regarding the propagation of a "socialist national culture as the realization of the humanistic culture of the German people" (Program of the SED 1963), nor anything about the "humanistic efficacy of the artist' in the socialist society (Resolution of the GDR Staatsrat of November 30, 1967), nothing concerning Walter Ulbricht's opening address in 1971 on the topic of "consultation with writers and artists concerning ideas," no discussion of the relationship between the party and the Union of German Writers, just to name a few things which constitute the parameters framing any discussion of the formation of the GDR-canon in the time period under discussion.

Frank Hörnigk is aware of all of this, of course. After all, he was once and is now again a professor at the Institute for German Literature at Humboldt University in Berlin. Moreover, he had been involved in the intellectual life of the GDR many times over, as he is now similarly involved in the new Germany. However, instead of immediately addressing the obvious in his project, Hörnigk takes a step back—an enormous step, to be sure—in order to allow history viewed from this new distance to become a problem of methodology. By doing so, he makes out of what had been a participant in the history of the GDR a committed (self- ?) observer, one who does not view the object "canon" as something given, but who rather concerns himself on a theoretical level with the conditions of its genesis. This leads to a deflation in importance of the particular which is marked not only by a distancing of oneself from experiences, but also by a methodologically applied sterility: "Canon," so Hörnigk, can in this view no longer be understood as a culturally and politically binding collection of texts and authors along with a set of prescriptions for artistic production. Instead, he maintains that "canon" is to be understood as "literary-communicative behavior in particular patterns of social action" (10). Not "canon" as *product*, as a tangible collection of documents, is meant, but rather canon*ization* as *process*. But even this, when applied to the GDR, is obviously for Hörnigk no easy task, for, on the one hand: "There is no one definitive GDR canon of the 1960s and 1970s!" (195). And, on the other hand: "Of course... one has to assume the reality of a state-sponsored canon" (195) that to be sure had failed in the realm of ideas by the end of the 70s—and with it the GDR. Hörnigk's magical solution to the dichotomy between ideal and actual existing reality is called "differentiation"—until reality degenerates into mere methodological problems or until the instrument of power called "canon" is dumbed down into a pocket-size concept of "personal canon" (others call this simply taste or preference).

As part of his methodological arsenal he resorts to empirical literary criticism and radical constructionism (S. J. Schmidt, Maturana, Varela), with the systems theory of Luhmann overlooking the whole affair as if in the role of godfather. The initial working thesis reads: the society of the GDR can be described as a functionally undifferentiated system, that is, a system which through central control reduced the process of fully-blown differentiation (*Ausdifferenzierung*). As a result of this, Hörnigk poses the question whether in such a system literature could even develop at all as a subsystem, or whether it wasn't the case that the

GDR "was instead simultaneously its own literature system" (11). Indeed, if literature and the state, system-theoretically considered, fall together, then the history of literature becomes the dialectical history of literature as conditioned factor on the one hand and as conditioning factor on the other. In other words, the history of literature of the GDR is reduced to the mere history of the GDR. However, does distancing allow for criticism? Or is it not rather the case that through this rather shallow variant of providing the system-theoretical foundations for his project the question of the functionality of discourses so dominates that no room is granted for criticism of the observed process itself?

Hörnigk calls the topic of his investigation "forms of societal canon-formation" (207) and returns to the difference between community (*Gemeinschaft*) and society (*Gesellschaft*). Communities, according to Hörnigk, work out and develop canons as the product of their understanding of themselves, canon formation is "a social memory, formed through communication, that stands somewhere between remembering and forgetting." (207). This, if you pardon me saying so, can be understood only as an attempt to defuse and render harmless the facts—and this first of all entirely independent of the GDR. Certainly, canons can be formed by means of consensus in groups or sub-cultures. But that should not permit us to forget what purpose canon formation serves: the formation of identity cannot be achieved without exclusion, no identity without alterity. Put in other words: be it arrived at via consensus, or decreed from above, canons are by their very nature able to define, that is, they draw boundaries and limits, they exercise power, possess hegemonical character. In this respect this not only is nothing new, it isn't even something specific to the GDR that Hörnigk wants to pursue with his research of canons as a critical questioning of the legitimation of a canon and its social powers. Only—I would be greatly hesitant to signify factors that condition the formation of canons as "referring to communities (*gemeinschaftsbezogen*)." Instead, one should stick to the task at hand—the institutionalized, social and state-sponsored mechanisms should be main focus of our attention. That is, unless (and this appears to me to be a GDR-specific proviso): one interprets now or interpreted the society of the GDR from the perspective of the "doers"—Hörnigk speaks of "elites"—as a "community" in which the influence of the elites is understood not as power, but rather as broadly consensual communication, as it was indeed understood in the GDR. This is erroneous only to those who ignore the systematic social and political integration of intellectuals, writers and artists in the GDR. One should not forget that the "elites" are elements of the state apparatus.

So, Frank Hörnigk's report constitutes *Prolegomena* to a future history of the GDR seen from a temporally and methodologically anaesthetized distance, expressed in part in piles of Byzantine syntax. That Frank Hörnigk never "gets to the point" results from the simple fact that he no longer sees the "point" as such, taking instead a series of measures designed to make it disappear entirely. By keeping in mind that the GDR is now history, one cannot develop a relationship to it by disengaging the role of participant and observer in such a manner that one's own experiences are methodologically rolled over and plowed under. It is my impression that by proceeding in this manner one never reaches one's destination, remaining instead permanently in flight, fleeing from a history which at one time one was able to support enthusiastically.

At the end of his report Frank Hörnigk concludes with the observation that *construction* rather than *re*-construction is actually his main concern. What roll do the facts of the past play in this? Or should the facts be subjected to the mercy of an effort of reconstruction to such a degree that they do not constitute history, but rather simply serve to verify a plausible *model* of history? In this case also I argue emphatically for the well-considered separation of events from the discourse of history in order to be able to keep the mutual relationship of each better in view, and because otherwise we would renounce the communicable dimension of criticism in scientific work. In addition, I find it difficult to imagine the construction of a bygone canon without this effort being bound to certain criteria of obligation. This obligation could, for example, consist in the intention to arrange the events in such a manner that later processes become plausible, or so adjusting the examination of the past that one can make an evaluative judgement of the past, and so on. Such a commitment seems to me to be the only way that one can differentiate between a modeling of the past and its mere manipulation. Frank Hörnigk positions himself in relation to this requirement of commitment such that the question whether he is modeling or manipulating is not even posed. Instead there exists an overpowering interest in "objective" presentation. This kind of being "scientific," this striving for purism appears to me to be the reason why the facts are missing, for: they do not exist until they have been subject to a discursive procedure. From scholars like Frank Hörnigk I would like instead a more dynamic stance, for time is quickly slipping by and together with scholars like Hörnigk facts will be irretrievably lost. A failed experiment as such is still no excuse to simply throw its paradigm onto the rubbish heap of history.

Translated by Gary M. Campbell

Frauke Meyer-Gosau

Outing to *Jurassic Park*:
"Germany" in Post-Wall Literature.
An Essay against Tiredness

"Whose problem is it, anyway?"

I want to start with what you might take as only a well-educated bow following the rules of classical rhetoric, according to which the *captatatio benevolentiae* is to appear at the opening of any elaborate speech. As will soon become clear, however, there is considerably more to it than formal politeness. Namely, at the beginning of this paper I should like to thank the students of my graduate seminar at Brown University—not only for the endurance and friendliness with which they followed the course of sometimes remarkably odd intellectual debates in Germany since 1989 but also for a very specific reason. One day after three hours of discussion about the so-called German dispute on literature ("deutscher Literaturstreit"), the students confronted me with a harmless question: "Whose problem is it, anyway?"

Being somewhat fundamental in itself and therefore, I admit, slightly shocking for the teacher, the question confused me. I started to muse about this and that before I eventually reached the conclusion that, well, we should perhaps come to this particular problem rather—next Tuesday... With a forgiving grin the students left. "Whose problem is it, anyway?" Theirs—although all three of them are Germans—it apparently was not. Sitting by myself in my office, it then occurred to me that with this seminar I must have taken them on something like an outing to *Jurassic Park* where they could observe the dinosaurs at work. At a peculiar kind of work, indeed, that dealt quite obsessively with literary and essayistic texts of the first and second generation of post-war Germans while the intensely engaged dinosaurs themselves seemed to take it for granted that this mountain of paper was of highest importance for almost everyone: marking the only way to master a troublesome present and, of course, to finally gain the future well-being of nothing less than the German nation itself. What I suddenly came to understand was: One of these dinosaurs was me.

Therefore, my following observations and remarks are dedicated to these students. It was only their question—"Whose problem is it, anyway?"—that made me aware again of the fact that in German affairs still nothing goes without saying, and that we do have to try to make ourselves understood to a generation that was not formed by the experience of immediate post-war Germany (something I had apparently completely forgotten in the meantime). What we could possibly gain ourselves from such an attempt is to overcome our own tiredness with some of the notorious German questions and answers, such as these, for example: What has become of Germany after the unification, and what does current German literature have to tell about the changes of the countries' inner landscape?

Looking at these questions under the perspective my students had opened up, my paper is thus also meant as an "Essay against Tiredness". Maybe it eventually even leads the immovable dinosaur out of his homely zoo of *Jurassic Park*.

"That peculiarly German obsession with identity"

"It should be said that in the fifty years since the German field marshal Wilhelm Keitel laid down his staff and his hat on a Berlin table, and the war in Europe ended, Germans have been trying to talk their way out of an unutterable past and back into what they like to call history. They have been talking mainly to one another. (...) By history, Germans mean German history. They call it a *Wissenschaft*—a science—though it is arguably more alchemy than science, since it has always had to do with turning the myths, memories, and language of 'Germanness' into a kind of collective destiny known as the German nation. It may be history's revenge that today, fifty years after the surrender, Germans are still arguing about what to do with the destiny that they invented."[1]

What the journalist Jane Kramer observed in and about Germany in August 1995 is obviously summarized here in an extremely pointed (and thus in some aspects incorrect) remark on Germany's difficulty in coming to terms with its own past—the past of Nazi Germany, that is to say. Forty years of *Vergangenheits-bewältigung*—which means nothing more than the effort of critical examination that had been going on in West Germany for decades (with most different symptoms and effects, as we know, including the students' movement of 1968 on the one hand and the Historians' Debate almost twenty years later on the other)—and also forty years of declared *Antifaschismus* on the other side of the wall that in its self-definition finally managed to have the people of the GDR counted among the moral victors of the Second World War. The complex of guilt and expiation was thereby left to the capitalist FRG, where fascism was allegedly still alive and active, as was indicated, for example, by the GDR's official description of the wall as "antifaschistischer Schutzwall" (antifascist wall of protection). Both approaches—characterized by Kramer as the attempt of the two Germanies "to talk their way out of an unutterable past and back into what they like to call history"—had led by 1989 on both sides to a remarkable difference between the respective ruling politicians, their views on and images of the Nazi past, and a majority of intellectuals and writers of the older generation who would still maintain that neither Helmut Kohl's "Gnade der späten Geburt" (the grace of belated birth) nor Erich Honecker's claim of antifascist socialism could free Germany from its historical burden. Which meant that for Germans after the Holocaust there was no way to 'normality' at all, as much as politicians in both countries tried to deny any lasting traces which could possibly disturb the reputable appearances of their—as they saw it—mature states. Being a subject mainly of political lip service, politically motivated payments, and history classes at school, Germany's fascist past, with its structures of long-lasting duration (as Foucault would have put it), had become a 'theoretical' issue.

Welcome to *Jurassic Park* then! You might ask yourself now whose problem this is, was, and has been, anyway. As for Germany in its two parts up to 1989 the answer seems to be simple: After Helmut Kohl became Bundeskanzler in 1982, there were certain indications that his efforts to "normalize" the image of the Nazi past were supported by a number of historians, art historians and even by the formerly socialist writer Martin Walser in his notorious speech "Talking about Germany" ("Über Deutschland reden") in Munich in November 1988. But apart from them, hardly anyone was all too thrilled by the state's attempts to polish German honor, and the Historian's Debate already seemed history itself. Instead, it was the concept of *posthistoire* which was discussed widely among West German intellectuals, together with matters of post-modernism, whereas in East Germany the young artists of the "Prenzlauer Berg" scene were obviously interested in anything but politics (except the random agent of the Stasi here and there) or even German history. The older writers such as Christa Wolf, Volker Braun, Christoph Hein or Heiner Müller just continued their almost ritualized struggle with the cultural bureaucrats of their country while occasionally donating a reading from their works at gatherings of the peace movement and civil rights groups in churches of Leipzig or Berlin.

Wondering whose problem "Germany" and its relationship with its most recent past at that particular time was, the answer is: almost nobody's—most people could not have cared less. This fact of, so to speak, life beyond history which concerned East and West Germans equally in the late eighties, would, however, turn out to be crucial very soon: Without a past that has been integrated consciously and deliberately into the concept of the present as something alive and lasting, "future", in a meaningful sense of the word, cannot develop. As we have come to see in both parts of Germany, there is mainly a helpless and hysterical (at times timid, at times aggressive) perpetuation of the mere present. In this respect, dealing with the past (and not: burying and preserving it in all sorts of memorials) is fundamental to everybody's life and thus everybody's problem.

The difficulty in making people aware of this very fact, however—as was so alarmingly indicated in my students' question—lies not only in the process of communication itself but, as far as I see, primarily in the perspective we choose on the highly contaminated material. Neither the moralistic approach which would only cause a vague guilt-complex—and therefore provoke, sooner or later and most understandably so, dismissive reactions—nor the purely scientific way of presenting figures, statistics, photos etc. seems appropriate to gain what I should like to call emotional awareness. This state of mind is, to my belief, only to be created if questions are opened up and kept open for more questions instead of closing them by moralistic determination, detached knowledge or pure shame—all of them attempts to do away with the past by putting it out of reach. If anything, we can study the consequences of this common German practice in the phenomenon of the "Black Holes" around which the literary imagination of quite a few of the literary works in Germany's recent period of transition are centered. What we get to see here is the paralyzing effect of a Nazi past that, in so many ways, has been made untouchable.

Literature as well as the public discourse of the intellectuals in a given society both function as a stage and a mirror. Fundamentally, they provide a sphere where thoughts, concepts, visions and ideas can be developed, tried, examined and proved—a "test bed" for what German language quite poetically calls *Möglichkeitssinn* (sense and sensitivity for the possible). The genuine quality literature adds to these general elements of discourses in the field of culture now is: emotion. It is the form of literature itself that offers the possibility to put every scenery, character, relation or idea envisaged at existential risk—a capacity which eventually implies no less than the opportunity to try out the humanity of concepts and visions the author has his or her piece of art based on.

So, if Germans start anew after 1989 to—as Jane Kramer puts

it—"reinvent Germany for themselves"[2], and assuming that the "peculiarly German obsession with identity" [3] will inevitably lead to "readings and misreadings of 'Germanness'"[4], literature is the field where contradictions and inconsistencies of thought as well as characteristic formations of hope and fear, anger, shame, innocence and (self-)deception will emerge. Once again a tradition of form and feeling will become visible here—emanations of history altogether in the formally rather strictly determined world of literary imagination.

"Whose problem is it, anyway?" Seen from a historical point of view, the German literature of transition in general offered a medium for a shattered mentality to find out what it still or already was able to think and formulate about itself under the condition of disturbing change. Literature served in that respect as a means of self-exploration and self-expression—no question whose problem this was in Germany after 1989 (and no matter whether anybody except the author him- or herself would make any use of this offer).

Worth a question, indeed, seems again the perspective the individual author adopts on his or her chosen historical material. What I mentioned above about the peculiar ways Germans developed to rid themselves of the dark epoch of the Holocaust, applies equally to the epoch of "German Socialism" that had become history almost overnight. Would it be possible here to open a broad field of questions concerning the immediate past whose traces affected so visibly the present of the now formally united Germany? Would both parts of it eventually come under scrutiny? Would the same mechanisms be reproduced which for forty years had made sure in both countries that the unthinkable and untouchable—Auschwitz—dominated the landscape of thought and imagination just as the permeable concrete coffin of Chernobyl towers over the contaminated area? Would memory finally become a driving force for social and mental change or would "memory", again, as simply another version or specific formation of repression, block the way for "rethinking Germany" within the complex of its pre- and post-war history and identity?

As for literature and its ability to free memory from its habitual ideological patterns and boundaries (as Uwe Johnson's novel of 2000 pages, *Jahrestage*, Christa Wolf's voluminous memoir *Kindheitsmuster*, or Ingeborg Bachmann's novel *Malina* and the fragmentary part of the cycle *Todesarten, Der Fall Franza*, at least partly succeeded in doing), the perspective taken on the material as well as on the aim of writing itself is crucial. The perspective of the writer here depends basically on the definition he or she ascribes to. Post-war literature in West Germany, especially that by authors of prose like Heinrich Böll and Günter Grass, had upheld role models of the artist as a critic of society and mainly of its concept of "progress". During the Seventies, however, the politically relevant position of the author as *Gewissen der Nation* (conscience of the nation) faded. This was a consequence of political change as well as an indication of the generation gap after the generation of 1968 gained decisive influence on the cultural discourse in West Germany (which, on its very last leg, showed up once again in the "German dispute on literature" and since then has widely disappeared from the cultural scene). In West German literature, at the latest from the early eighties on, the author as a figure of representative qualities who is destined to admonish and exhort the mighty in the name of the voiceless had eventually lost its social and political capacity. Consequently, serious West German writers of the younger generation strictly abstained from political interventions as from something alien to their work.

As for the specific situation in the GDR, the image of the author as guardian of the utopian 'truth' who, under the condition of censorship, maintained his version of socialism in contradiction to the official interpretation of "Socialism as it exists in reality", was predominant until the end of the state—at least for the older generations. To western observers the model itself appeared as historically delayed as the paternalistic authoritarian system as a whole (which by no means denies that quite a number of readers in the West still longed for explanations of reality that were secured by literary authority and thus found in Christa Wolf's novels, for example, telling images for the suffering of the individual).

When the wall came down, the two antagonistic concepts of the author's role in society collided fiercely. As soon as Christa Wolf published her novel *Was bleibt* in 1990, West German literary critics took the opportunity to attack most aggressively the self-image of the "Staatsdichterin" (state poet)—it was here that the first phase of the "German dispute on literature" originated. Indeed, this dispute as a whole was very much a debate on the past, centered around "La trahison des clercs" (the betrayal of the intellectuals). On the surface the leading writers of the GDR were accused of collaboration with the socialist dictators and of participation in the power game of the state which allegedly led them to betray the ordinary people about the true character of the system. An ulterior motive for non- or post-sixty-eighters among the West German journalists was obviously the intention to discredit the last shreds of respectability for socialist thought in Helmut Kohl's extended Federal Republic. The course of the debate itself, however, brought about what psychoanalysts would call "Deckerinnerung" (substitute memory), the creation of a second past, so to speak, that from a western point of view could easily be handled with severe criticism and thorough analysis without hurting the self-definition of the own tribe. In this respect the different debates on literature (and later those on the matter of the Staatssicherheitsdienst) presented themselves not only as "Wiedergutmachung", namely as a compensation for the fact that the intellectual and literary history of the Third Reich had not gained nearly as much attention as now was the case for the literary careers of GDR authors and their involvement in evil state politics. They also appeared, moreover, as a tool to finally cover the 'first past' under a thick layer whose material was provided by the second German dictatorship. Thereafter, manoeuvres like a second "Historikerstreit", for instance, would only seem irrelevant.

To touch once again upon the initial question, it is not hard to recognize that the West German intellectuals mainly got themselves into shape for a united Germany through their ongoing debates (and as excitement and agitation were everything in those days, highly provocative contributions such as Botho Strauß' *Anschwellender Bocksgesang* and Hans Magnus Enzensberger's essay on Civil War ("Ansichten über den Bürgerkrieg") served mainly as a means to draw the line against an intellectual "New Right" instead of discussing these essays as a material of specific importance with regard to the new Germany's relationship with the Nazi past).

The turmoil within the West German intellectual scene after 1989 was thus, in the first place, a matter of and for the intellectuals: the swansong of the first generation after World War II and their generally undisputed position as opinion-leaders up to then. As all this, however, affected and influenced the so-called "gebildete Öffentlichkeit" (the educated public) it indicated at least the possibility of a drastic change in German mentality: the beginning of posthistoire in respect to the Nazi past.

"What was this? What have we done?
Why aren't we happy any more?"

That's what *Jurassic Park* is all about: digging. Shoveling background to a material which in itself seems comfortably obvious and in no need of further explanation. Wasn't it then simply logical and in a way just human nature that West German intellectuals and writers tried to close their East German brothers and sisters off from what they regarded as their own realm of interpretation? That they were prepared to do almost anything that could guarantee their "Diskurshoheit" (sovereignty over the discourse)? The true dinosaur, of course, can only be bored by such a view. His interest is focused on the zones of silence, on the calm eye of the storm and much less on its fast-moving edges—and I can feel your compassion now with the poor individuals who had to endure the relentlessly rummaging fossil. "Whose problem is it, anyway?" Put into the historical context of a repressed past, and seen on the horizon of changes in mentality in West Germany during the 1980s and, moreover, taking into account the different models of the author in Western and Eastern society, the literature of transition gives an impressive account of the return of the repressed—in the form of a Black Hole.

"What was this? What did we do? Why aren't we happy any more?" ("Was war das? Was haben wir gemacht? Warum sind wir nicht mehr froh?") In 1993 the playwright Botho Strauß published a play under the title *Das Gleichgewicht* (The Equilibrium)[5]. Here he demonstrated that to the avantgarde of West German authors the irritation with the German unification as such was already over —basic issues regarding the idea of "Germany" seemed no longer to be important, at least as far as their literary work was concerned. "Was war das? Was haben wir gemacht? Warum sind wir nicht mehr froh?" These questions in Strauß' play of 1993 refer exclusively to its West German characters as they reflect on their past as members of the students' movement of 1968. The reply comes from one "Gregor Neuhaus"; it is clear-cut and, by the way, reasonably characteristic for an ex-68er in West Berlin who has turned modestly hedonistic in the meantime: "Come on, serve us something", Gregor answers—and that is about it. What Strauß shows not only in the dialogue between Marianne and Gregor but throughout the whole play is a split that no longer separates the East German from the Westerner in principal, as it had been the case in one of the final scenes of Strauß' play *Schlußchor* (Final chorale)[6] of 1991. The split two years later marks a deep conflict within every single character. It is an inner ambiguity, not just an ambivalence, which makes it almost impossible to maintain the equilibrium: "Zwie, zwie, zwie" is consequently the repetitive code word of his main figure, Lilly. The play as a whole gives a social panorama of the "scene" in West Berlin and their desperate pursuit of happiness. Only one person is left here from the process of unification, situated literally on the fringe of this advanced part of society. Strauß has given him no name (whereas all the others have one) but presents him as "der Mann vom Grünstreifen" (the man from the grass verge). On that spot the former party bureaucrat lives in a tent, joyfully prepared for the imminent "big trek from the East". "I have already been here", he shouts proudly, "I am settled, me, your dismayed servant, my dear state!" ("Ich war schon da, bin eingerichtet, ich, dein bestürzter Diener, mein lieber Staat!")[7]. Neither the "dear state", however, nor the author himself seem particularly interested in their "servant" who is condemned to play a minor role and then disappears.

Most surprisingly, a similar phenomenon can be observed in Martin Walser's latest novel, which appeared likewise in 1993 and whose title alone sounds like an ironic statement toward the process of unification: "Ohne einander" (Without one another)[8]. Here the only character from the former GDR is again a minor figure who now works at a publishing house in West Germany where it is his responsibility to supervise the correct use of the German subjunctive in the company's publications. He himself, although he would love to and, as the author suggests, would also do very well at it, is not allowed to write a single word. In the novel as a whole, which deals with the peculiar worries of the rich and beautiful in West Germany and their hopeless love affairs, the funny character Wolf Koltzsch is as much a curious footnote as the man from the grass verge is for Strauß' *Equilibrium*.

It is interesting to note that both authors had published literary works two years earlier which had been regarded at that time as genuine contributions to the process of unification. In 1991 Martin Walser brought out *Die Verteidigung der Kindheit* (The defense of childhood)[9], a novel that caught widespread attention and was widely acclaimed as an account of the desperate but hopeless longing of Germans to reunite the two parts of the country in order to regain command of their own history which the author here sees falling apart and dissolving in an 'unhistorical' present without any fruitful contact to either the past or the future. The novel shares with Botho Strauß' *Schlußchor* the view that the loss of history in the individual himself leads to symptoms of madness and despair. Those who—if always in a frantic way—do care for the memory of a disturbing German past, inevitably become outsiders with no hope of integration into the fractionalized and strife-torn society of the present.

Whereas Walser shows his hysterical but loveable main character Alfred Dorn in a bizarre effort to get hold of any material object of his childhood—first in Nazi—and then in socialist Dresden—for his private "Alfred-Dorn-Museum" in West Germany, Strauß creates in *Schlußchor* two characters who are also stricken with neurotic outbursts of memory. The first one, called "Der Rufer" (the shouter), is characterized as a person who is incessantly rushing around. He likes to get on the nerves of high-class party-guests and the members of the happy few in a posh restaurant by flinging doors open and shouting "Deutschland!" before he disappears again. Finally, he grabs a couple of GDR-citizens at night in the streets of West Berlin after the wall has been opened for the very first time and presents these "people in their grey blousons" ("die Blousonmenschen"), as Strauß calls them sardonically, to the guests in the restaurant: "That's what people look like", he announces to them, "who for forty years wouldn't believe that Monte Carlo really exists!" ("So sehen Menschen aus, die vierzig Jahre nicht glauben konnten, daß es Monte Carlo wirklich gibt!")[10] While der Rufer dashes back to the street ("This is history, mind you, Valmy, mind you, Goethe! And this time w e were there!"[11] "Das ist Geschichte, sag ich, Valmy, sag ich, Goethe! Und diesmal sind wir dabeigewesen!"), an odd conversation unfolds in the bistro. Everybody else has left, eager to experience "history in the making", when a historian whose special field is the German resistance against Hitler gets involved in a dispute with the daughter of a Nazi general. Obviously, he claims, the general was shot dead as a notorious womanizer by the jealous husband of one of his lovers. But the daughter pretends to know better: According to the biography she wrote on him, her father was killed as a member of the group of July 20th. Trying to convey the difference between historical truth and wishful thinking to her—whose name, Anita von Schastorf, reminds us more of a soap opera than of a German heroic tale—, the historian displays all the likeable qualities of a man of enlightenment. To no avail, however—the voice of reason fails to reach the mind of the obsessed, enlightenment and the fantasy of historical heroism have no basis in common. In the final scene in a zoo, Anita first lures an eagle out of his cage; then she murders him since he is no longer the symbol of strength and power to her but imbodies only repulsive weakness...

It seems appropriate here to recall these scenes and characters at some length in order to give an impression of the ironic approach both authors have chosen toward their 'German' topic which thoroughly characterizes their literary images of the German relationship with the past. The outbreaks of hysteria, mania and delusion, nevertheless, that drive Alfred as well as the Rufer and Anita von Schastorf to insane behavior, will sooner or later direct the reader's attention to the serious matter behind the amusing facade—to the sad fact, namely, that in this picture of enlightenment and intellectual clarity the realm of emotion at its core has still remained unaffected. Other characters in Strauß' play show similar difficulties in finding a socially adequate and understandable translation for their overwhelming feelings, but it is only in reference to German history that deviant behavior is linked with pathological madness. In Walser's novel there are also a number of figures who display serious distortions of personality but, again, Alfred is the only one whose obsession with the past (which, by the way, is symbolically and symptomatically linked with the wish to possess his mother...) makes him a maniac.

It seems important to note that the effect of both literary works is based on the distance the authors keep from their material —distance is in both cases the core mechanism of the narration. Walser and Strauß offer a view on reality which exposes the characters, their striving for respect and attention as well as their weird visions, as something fundamentally alien to their social environment. They then appear equally alienating to the readers and the audience. "Very wryly, talkatively and without a hint of grief he handed the heap of rubble down to us " ("ganz trocken, mitteilsam und ohne alle Trauer hat er uns den Trümmer-haufen überliefert"),

Walser once remarks in his novel about the painter Canaletto who saw and painted Dresden after the 3rd Silesian War. Walser and Strauß take up the same position toward the "heap of rubble" of German history in this century—a position that allows them to point at hidden, insulated zones within the individual himself that hold unsocialized, 'uncultivated' emotions, untouched by reason, knowledge and rational explanation, and in danger of exploding at any time. Needless to say, this literary conception of distance and exposure contains no solution (not even in the subtext). There is no culprit or authority in these works to be held responsible by the contemporaries they show. And there is no "realism" in the narration at all which would evoke tangible solutions for real problems. Finally, Marianne's anxious questions: "Was war das? Was haben wir gemacht? Warum sind wir nicht mehr froh?" remain without answer. Strauß and Walser prefer to leave it to the reader or spectator to create a translation to their personal concerns—if they can think of any transfer at all.

Mission accomplished

When these authors had already proceeded to topics that had left the unification of Germany behind them, the so-called "Wendeliteratur" was just scoring a boom: the number of fiction and poetry works concerned with "Germany" as a first divided, then reunited country reached its peak in 1993 and 1994. What had started very reluctantly and modestly with the small novel *Wendewut* (*Rage of change*), published in 1990 by the journalist and former permanent representative of West Germany in East Berlin, Günter Gaus, was followed over the next two years by only three works of well-known writers such as Friedrich Christian Delius, Monika Maron and Kurt Drawert. It was not before 1993 that books by Günter Grass, Rainer Kunze, Ulrich Woelk, Helga Königsdorf, Wolfgang Hilbig, Bodo Morshäuser and many more eventually appeared, and in 1994 Sarah Kirsch, Adolf Endler, Brigitte Burmeister, Fritz

Rudolf Fries and Angela Krauß added their share. Four years after the wall came down, authors from both parts of the country finally let it be known that "Germany" was again an issue for literature.

Three ways of dealing with this most complex subject had become apparent by then: Firstly, Strauß' and Walser's literary imaginations of a German state of mind that is shattered by the unsolved relationship with the past and increasingly in danger of losing touch with reality opened the stream of genuinely literary approaches—a group of works which neither intend to influence the course of politics, nor restrict themselves to accounts of personal experience with one Germany or the other, nor take the complicated situation as a cause for unrestrained fun and laughter. This branch of 'literature-literature,' however, is by far the smallest in comparison with the amount of works based on autobiography or, on the other hand, the stream of what I would call 'message-literature' or the literature of ideological projection. A range of purely comic works are the latest phenomenon in this line of publications and form, at least for the time being, the smallest group. Their authors are the youngest, and this might finally point to the possibility that German seriousness and rigidity in regard to the "German question" could be coming to an end with the first post-war generation.

The beginning of the literature of transition was, as I mentioned, slow, and it illustrated once again that ideological patterns can make it considerably easier to create and handle literary images of the troubled present. Günter Gaus[12] and Friedrich Christian Delius[13], West German authors with a reputation in the SPD-Ostpolitik and in the students' movement respectively, chose, interestingly enough, everyday life in the GDR as their topic, and both of them had a message to convey. Adjustment and adaptability—a behavior connected explicitly here with the fact that people in the GDR had put up with the conditions set by the ruling party and hardly ever opposed the system since 1953 (and at the same time a central accusation in the debate on Christa Wolf)—, adjustment and adaptability were the qualities Gaus' and Delius' main characters were endowed with. They presented ordinary people who were able to lead their normal lives only because they patiently took the political situation as it was. While Gaus praises those who have the ability to be satisfied with strange and annoying living conditions, Delius in *Die Birnen von Ribbek* (*The Pears of Ribbek*) laments over the basic rule of German history according to which the little man was forced to develop this quality. Both authors then conclude that the historical change from two countries with contradictory political orientations to a united Germany under the rule of capitalism again imposes the same necessity on the average citizen—again alienation, not freedom will result from the historical process.

The perspective Gaus and Delius take is interesting in many ways. Firstly, they adopt the role of advocates acting in the name of those who cannot speak up in public—a position known from littérature engagée that usually opposed authoritarian regimes or systems and one which had just come under attack in the second phase of the dispute on literature as being outmoded in general and being particularly out of touch with the political reality in present-day Germany. Secondly, both authors suggest that the political change from one system to another was not exactly what the ordinary citizen wanted—a claim that again hinted at non-democratic conditions during the period of transition. Thirdly, if we put these literary texts into the context of the cultural discourse of the time, it turns out that Gaus and Delius twice take a defensive stance here: first, they oppose the general applause for the defeat of socialism in West Germany, and second, more importantly, they take a position in the current debates on the concept of literature. Writing on behalf of the supposedly oppressed part of the population, Gaus and Delius maintain the role of the author as a representative and understand literature as a means of politics. The "German dispute on literature" at the same time, however, is eager to do away with the idea that literature had to serve anything but an aesthetic purpose.

Although both *Wendewut* and *Die Birnen von Ribbek* are

undoubtedly minor works as far as their literary importance is concerned, they gain a certain significance as they indicate altered conditions in new German literature. The common view that the former political border between the two Germanys meant a demarcation line to literature as well is increasingly losing ground. From the early 1990s on, German literature will no longer be divided by the respective place of residence of the author but primarily by the concepts writers base their work on. Gaus and Delius were the first to prove new alliances; from 1993 on Günter Grass, Helga Königsdorf, Marion Titze, Fritz Rudolf Fries and many more would follow. Books as different from each other as Günter Grass' sonnets *Novemberland*[14], Helga Königsdorf's novel *Das Ende des Regenbogens* (*The end of the rainbow*)[15] or Marion Titze's novel *Unbekannter Verlust* (*Unknown loss*)[16], for example, are joined beyond form and content through their authors' adherence to an ideological framework or perspective which interprets reality as something generally regular and well-ordered according to given rules. The literary picture that results from these preconceived patterns is consequently determined by narrow boundaries: the narration is designed to prove what the author already knew beforehand. The above-mentioned ability of literature to experiment with ideas and visions of human life in creations of fantasy and imagination cannot be challenged by definition if there is no "experiment" as the outcome was settled before the beginning. Literature here has to execute and illustrate an opinion.

Of course, there is no question that these books also are (or at least can be) works of art. Their basic condition, however, which could be summarized in the maxim "Imagination follows analysis," essentially subordinates them—in their capacity as literarized political commentaries—to the intellectual discourse of the time. The works mentioned play a role there as manifestations of the author as a critical intellectual who finds himself in a defensive position against the prevailing view that literature and politics are to be regarded as strictly separated spheres.

Nevertheless, up to 1994/1995, both parts of Germany had

indeed come under severe criticism. As far as literature itself is concerned, the imaginative re-considerations hit the West German lifestyle and ideas significantly harsher whereas the debates on the feature pages launched their fierce attacks preferably against the former GDR and its culture. The latter is certainly due to the fact that the intellectual discourse was almost exclusively led by West German authors and journalists who intended to make way for new ideological and cultural patterns that were to lead eventually to a newly politicized conception of 'culture' in the press. The literary image of the period of transition, on the other hand, has been equally shaped by both East and West German authors. Furthermore, those West Germans who dedicated their work to the topic of transition not only sympathized very often with the former GDR citizens who were treated so badly in the papers and magazines and thus decided to counter these stereotypes by more differentiated pictures. More often than not their writings were also motivated by a fundamental mistrust of the West German version of capitalism and the ruling Christian Democrat government in particular—a political position which had gained increasing influence among intellectuals during the sixties and then became one of the inspiring sources for the movement of 1968. Finally, the more diversified picture of the GDR and FRG in literary texts after the unification resulted from the diverse forms and approaches literature itself has to offer. To the works of "literature-literature" Wolfgang Hilbig added his fictional account of Stasi-mentality with his novel *Ich* (*Me*)[17] in 1993, the young author Ulrich Woelk published the novel *Rückspiel* (*Replay*)[18] (an attempt to reflect the Nazi past together with the aims of 1968 in the light of the fundamental changes of 1989...); and these were followed in 1994 by Brigitte Burmeister [19] and Fritz Rudolf Fries[20] with novels on East-Western dissolution and incomparability.

Besides these texts and the already mentioned accounts of the "literature of admonition," the majority of texts concerned with the new Germany consisted of autobiographical works. They came either in the form of slightly fictionalized novels and stories [21] or in memoirs that referred back to the post-war era and reflected personal experiences with East-West history from 1945 on[22]. In addition, numerous diaries gave an impression of the turbulent phase between 1989 and 1992, while another author recalled his life as an artist in the Prenzlauer Berg scene during the Eighties[23].

At first sight one might be taken by surprise that these autobiographical works were written not only mainly by authors who come from the former GDR but predominantly by those who had either been forced to leave the country—like Sarah Kirsch or Reiner Kunze—or had kept their distance from the state and its policies, like Adolf Endler, Angela Krauß, Kurt Drawert and Peter Wawerzinek. Looking closer, however, this peculiarity will appear only too understandable. Obviously, coming to terms with fiction that recalled a country which did not exist any more was considerably easier for those who either had not been involved at all (as was the case for West Germans) or had maintained widely respected positions as modest reformers (which applies to the majority of leading GDR-authors). For those, however, whose stance toward the GDR had been unstable, ambiguous or indifferent for a long time, it was evidently more difficult to develop a view which could appear as accurate and legitimate to themselves. Stepping back to authentic material—to personal recollections of real people, events and places, to the writer's diary or even to Stasi-files—was certainly a solution of inner consistency and respectability in this situation.

Altogether, these literary as well as the more or less literarized texts up to 1995 achieved a colorful and controversial image of the *Mirror-Country* as Kurt Drawert had called it. Lamento, accusation, cool and wry reflections on the past, there was nothing lacking —apart from jubilation, which is greatly to be appreciated. A vision of the "future", however, was equally absent here, which remains somewhat puzzling.

The literature of transition thus resembled a thoroughly empirical field study listing and describing almost every rare plant and specimen of any endangered species. It traced their roots and origins back to the two countries which they stemmed from. But there the research ended and led no further: The present is the present is the present is the present...

The last laugh

At this point the dinosaur must finally return to his workplace. Does the appearance of rather hilarious novels by two East German writers in 1995—the most applauded work of male potency, *Helden wie wir* (*Heroes like us*) by the young author Thomas Brussig [24] and the not quite as funny but considerably shorter book *Der Zimmer-springbrunnen* (*The living room fountain*) by Jens Sparschuh[25]—do these ostentatiously relaxed books possibly establish a new rule? The extremely enthusiastic reviews for Brussigs "Helden" could at least inspire the idea that it is generally most welcome now simply to laugh off the burden of five years of unification—and then to leave it at that: after the tragedy the satire that closes up a chapter of bitter experience in a good mood.

Or has this part of worrisome history once and for all come to an end through Günter Grass' voluminous novel *Ein weites Feld* (*Far afield*) [26]? The damning reviews made almost unanimously clear that the critics never wanted to hear anything again about borrowed characters such as "Fonty" and "Hoftaller" in gloomy East German circumstances whose literary picture seemed to drip with political resentment—a far step back equally into history and literary history that fortunately does away with the literature of transition, and at its grave, in deep concern, stands the writer himself who displayed for the very last time the gesture of the representative author of the Sixties?

It is all too obvious that the literary scene does not expect much anymore from this stream of German literature—at least for the time being. Over the years, one definitely has become overfed with endless replays that only vary the same story of evidence. This impression, of course, is deeply unfair to the authors and their carefully written works. It first of all seems to be due to the fact that after six years everybody is tired now of the process of unification itself. But, nevertheless, the judgment as such is correct: Indeed, the literature of transition did not have much to tell about the changes of the inner landscape which were brought about by the political landslide of 1989. As a whole, it did not open up new questions from perspectives that were hardly ever seen before, and it usually restricted the possibilities of self-exploration to a very limited period of time: anything after 1945. Memory as a driving force to (re-)gain emotional awareness of this country in its recent history of boundless violence and calculated mass murder, or fantastic explorations of the sleeping giant, which the country poses as now—nothing of all this has as yet come to life.

The literary debates and the literary works concerned with "Germany" after 1989 both finally produced the same disconcerting configuration: Only very briefly and most rarely did they touch upon the Third Reich, but this contact produced a cipher mainly for rhetorical means designed to pursue political goals which were almost exclusively oriented toward the present.

A vivid and cruel context of history which had for once become visible in flashes of madness in Strauß' *Schlußchor* and was reconstructed in detail as an incomprehensible and unbearable confusion from the perspective of the neurotic hero Alfred Dorn in *Verteidigung der Kindheit*—a context of this kind has never again been evoked in the process of rewriting "Germany" (not by Strauß and Walser either).

It seems absurd, however, to blame the authors who so anxiously cling to secured concepts of literature and long over-used approaches. It seems absurd to complain, as it may be supposed that there is a cogent reason for this phenomenon that concerns more or less all of them. Obviously, the writers' fantasy is blocked here by something they cannot face (and actually it does not matter whether they do not want to or just do not know how they possibly could). The German "politics of memory" on both sides of the wall has quite successfully buried the guilt-ridden past of this century. That this act was a 'project' that unconsciously unified both Germanies after 1945 can now be recognized in the first accounts of the reunited German literature—and it might not be by mere coincidence that of all the writers in question, two whimsical born-again conservatives like Strauß and Walser who themselves have a history in left-wing theory turn out to be those with the widest literary scope—driven by a vague and evidently problematic feeling of loss, they were able to disregard the taboo and thus left the rules of political correct-ness behind them (which is not at all a guarantee for a work of art but presumably one of its main prerequisites).

In any case the experience with the latest German literature on "Germany" proves that the more conventional the chosen form and the more traditional the perspective of the writer, the more reduced the reach of the text itself will be. Consequently, conventionality in any sense has so far been the mark of the literature of transition. Its particular achievement, however, lies in the deep-reaching deficit it has made obvious: the hidden past as the turning point and boundary of the narration.

It should go without saying that this symptom is not to be mistaken for the notorious "normalization" Helmut Kohl and his companions have been trying so hard to establish over the last fifteen years—a conclusion that applies at least to the older generation of writers in both parts of the country. As for the younger authors, however, the outcome once again might be different. And it is here that the still curious dinosaur finally gives every sign of being animated: Could the younger generation's thoroughly light-hearted and even amused view on "this peculiarly German obsession with identity" (Jane Kramer) possibly point to a major future change—to the fact, namely, that among them there is no "obsession" any more, no oppressive question of "identity" and thus no problem any longer? Or did the repression of the past simply take a different shape in the meantime?

Either way, it eventually comes down again to the question that had been asked by my students: "Who is having a problem here, after all?" The answer in this case, I assume, may no longer be found within the limited area of *Jurassic Park* alone. And I can already see my students' compassionate smiles...

Notes

1   Jane Kramer, The Politics of Memory (August 1995). In Jane Kramer, *The Politics of Memory* (New York, 1996), p. 256.

2   Kramer, *Politics*, p. XVIII.

3   Kramer, *Politics*, p. XV.

4   Kramer, *Politics*, p. XVIII.

5   Botho Strauß, *Das Gleichgewicht* (München, Wien, 1993); all translations of titles and quotations here and in the following by myself, F. M.-G..

6   Botho Strauß, *Schlußchor* (München, Wien, 1991).

7   Strauß, *Gleichgewicht*, p. 18.

8   Martin Walser, *Ohne einander* (Frankfurt a.M., 1993).

9   Martin Walser, *Die Verteidigung der Kindheit* (Frankfurt a.M., 1991).

10 Strauß, *Schlußchor*, p. 87.

11 Strauß, *Schlußchor*, p. 86.

12 Günter Gaus, *Wendewut* (Reinbek b. Hamburg, 1990).

13 Friedrich Christian Delius, *Die Birnen von Ribbek* (Reinbek b. Hamburg, 1991).

14 Günter Grass, *Novemberland. 13 Sonette* (Göttingen, 1993).

15 Helga Königsdorf, *Das Ende des Regenbogens* (Berlin, 1993).

16 Marion Titze, *Unbekannter Verlust* (Berlin, 1994).

17 Wolfgang Hilbig, *Ich* (Frankfurt a.M., 1993).

18 Ulrich Woelk, *Rückspiel* (Frankfurt a.M., 1993).

19 Brigitte Burmeister, *Unter dem Namen Norma* (Stuttgart, 1994).

20 Fritz Rudolf Fries, (München, Zürich, 1994).

21 Kurt Drawert, *Spiegelland* (Frankfurt a.M., 1992); see also Drawerts collection of prose concerned with the period of transition, *Haus ohne Menschen* (Frankfurt a.M., 1993); as well Bodo Morshäuser, *Der weiße Wannsee* (Frankfurt a.M.,

1993), and Angela Krauß, *Die Überfliegerin* (Frankfurt a.M., 1994).

22 Ruth Rehmann, *Unterwegs in fremden Träumen* (München, Wien, 1993); Hans Pleschinski, *Ostsucht. Eine Jugend im deutsch-deutschen Grenzland* (München, 1993); Peter Wawerzinek, *Das Kind das ich war* (Berlin, 1994).

23 Martin Gross, *Das letzte Jahr. Begegnungen* (Berlin, 1992); Reiner Kunze, *Am Sonnenhang. Tagebuch eines Jahres* (Frankfurt a.M., 1993); Adolf Endler, *Tarzan am Prenzlauer Berg. Sudelblätter 1981-1983* (Leipzig, 1994); Sarah Kirsch, *Das simple Leben* (Stuttgart, 1994); Peter Rühmkorf, *Tabu I. Tagebücher 1989-1991* (Reinbek b. Hamburg, 1995); Fritz Rudolf Fries, *Im Jahr des Hahns* (München, Zürich, 1996).

24 Thomas Brussig, *Helden wie wir* (Berlin, 1995).

25 Jens Sparschuh, *Der Zimmerspringbrunnen* (Berlin, 1995).

26 Günter Grass, *Ein weites Feld* (Göttingen, 1995).

Carol Poore

Comments

My comments begin with a specific question and then proceed to several more general points. In dealing with the German literature of transition, Frauke Meyer-Gosau has chosen to concentrate in the most detail on West German authors such as Walser, Strauß, Gaus, and Delius, and she maintains that Walser and Strauß have achieved the most literary depth in their works through their sensitivity to unsocialized, irrational zones within the psyches of the individual characters they portray. I would have been interested in hearing more about the works by GDR authors mentioned here, especially those included in the category of "literature-literature" (Wolfgang Hilbig, Brigitte Burmeister, Fritz Rudolf Fries). How do they depict the entanglements of individual characters in society? What memories of "Germany" are presented in what forms in these texts? What are the similarities and differences between these authors and the West German writers discussed here?

But after hearing such a wide-ranging paper, one based as much around questions as around answers, the main response I would like to give is to indicate some of the directions for further investigation which this presentation pointed me towards. I began to think with a certain degree of identification about the metaphors of dinosaurs and tiredness, and especially about the phenomenon of black holes, and was led along a trail where I was finally struck by two more absences in the literature under discussion—absences which seem to me to be of central importance to the questions of identity being raised here. While I would be the last to deny the need to preserve awareness of long-lasting fascist structures in any discussion of "German identity," it seems to me that something "tired," something repetitious, has often crept into even these memories, in a play such as Strauß' *Schlußchor*, for example. In thinking about the question one of his characters asks in the play *Das Gleichgewicht*, "Why aren't we happy any more?" I would add that these works should also be read with a view towards whether or how they—as Frauke Meyer-Gosau says—"open a broad field of questions concerning the immediate past," that is, the "epoch of German socialism that had become history almost overnight." For after all, most of the older GDR writers mentioned here had once identified deeply with a project of breaking down social barriers, of overcoming painful, restricting divisions of labor. And the generation of the 1968ers in the West had also wanted, in our best moments, to overcome intellectual insularity.

If this paper has shown that the absence of the Third Reich and pre-1945 German history is a "black hole" in most of these works, then I would also say that the absence of what was earlier called the "social question" is another apparent and gaping "black hole" in them, too, and hardly enters any longer into their portrayals of "German identity." On the one hand, many writers of the older generation who may have identified strongly with the socialist project of the early years in the GDR (Endler, for example), or as West Germans, with more anti-authoritarian efforts to connect intellectual activity, artistic expression, and "life," seem to have worked through these parts of their biographies in many ways, put them to rest with sadness, resignation, or relief, and moved on. On the other hand, it appears that a much younger writer such as Thomas Brussig depicts reminders of the social question as nothing but oppressive or ridiculous injunctions (issued by threatening, moralizing mother-figures who constantly remind his narrator of the sacrifices and pathos of the "Aufbau" period and enjoin him not to be such a rabid consumer). It is striking, then, that in these works the existence, and more than that, the intensification, of socio-economic class differences in our world today hardly appears as literary material any more. Such a statement, however, should not be taken as an accusation against these writers, but rather as an observation about a present condition or state of mind whose causes certainly range far beyond and outside the purely literary realm. In the few instances I know of where these writers actually do reflect perceptively on their distance from the worlds of those with little or no access to money or power, the emotions expressed range from anger to grief over loss. The novel *Unter dem Namen Norma* (1994), for example, by Brigitte Burmeister, contains a key passage where the narrator observes two workers in a bar whose GDR clientele is being rapidly displaced by "Wessis." [1] In an effort to imagine how the "transition" is affecting them, the narrator tries to draw on her memories from her "year in the factory" long ago in the GDR, between school and university study. However, she finds that such a bridge to the workers' world in the past was much too tenuous to enable her to read their faces or imagine their thoughts in the present. Another depiction of such broken connections appears in the brief prose text by Volker Braun entitled "Die Leute von Hoywoy II" (1992) [2]. "Hoywoy" is Hoyerswerda, the paradigmatic site of socialist construction in the 1950s and early 1960s, the site of the journeys of many GDR writers into this world of work (such as Inge and Heiner Müller, Brigitte Reimann, and Volker Braun himself), and most recently, the site of racist attacks against asylum seekers in 1993. In Braun's text, the narrator is watching these attacks unfold on his television screen and reflecting on his distance from these "people of Hoywoy" who had once been his workmates. In this text, the narrator can only assert his perceptions of these people as victims themselves who are reacting with classic scapegoating mentality, and he can conclude only by asserting defiantly that in spite of everything, "I still belonged to them." While this is an admirable moral declaration of solidarity, it does not become the material for a literary text grounded in the search for emotional connection any longer—or for the moment, at least, since of course the project of giving literary form to such efforts to break down the barriers of social class will resurface again in the future.

As Frauke Meyer-Gosau demonstrated, after writing works immediately after the reunification which concerned themselves centrally with history and with German "identity," both Strauß and Walser went on to treat this theme in their next works as if it had been wrapped up. Consequently, these works focus again on an upper-class milieu in West Germany, the milieu Strauß and Walser are most familiar with. East Germans figure only as peripheral figures here, and memory of the GDR has now evaporated. But just as striking to me is another absence: that of the many "non-Germans" in Germany, in these works which all deal in one way or another with national identity. I think that this is also a source of tiredness (and tiredness in my response to many of these works), and I would like to illustrate what I mean with a brief example. In 1992, as attacks against foreigners in Germany were on the rise, *Die Zeit* invited Emine Özdamar (what to call her? A Turkish writer living in Germany and writing in German? A writer of migrants' literature?) to comment on the state of relations between Germans and foreigners at that point in time.[3] Rather than responding with a factual or overtly political statement, Özdamar elected to tell a story. The first part of *this* contribution to the "literature of transition" was a retelling of her story "Blackeye in Germany" which appeared in her book entitled *Mother Tongue (Mutterzunge)* in 1990, and the second part related her experiences with staging this text as a play, working together with actors who were German, Turkish, and of several other nationalities. That is, in response to a question about national identity and about the relations between Germans and "non-Germans," Özdamar responded first by telling a story about a Turkish foreign worker, a story with fairy-tale-like elements, in which Germans and Germany hardly appeared at all, and second, by recounting a situation in which, while Germans appeared, they were by no means in a central position. Such a parable gives a fresh perspective on "German identity." It would be a significant further project to read the "German literature of transition" by "non-German writers" with a view toward how these questions of self-understanding and national identity are presented in their works.

Notes

1   Brigitte Burmeister, *Unter dem Namen Norma* (Stuttgart, 1994), p. 81ff.

2   Volker Braun, "Die Leute von Hoywoy (2)," in: Braun, *Die Zickzackbrücke. Ein Abrißkalender* (Halle, 1993), p. 63-64.

3   Emine Özdamar, "Interview," In: *Turkish Culture in German Society Today* David Horrocks and Eva Kolinsky, eds., (Providence, 1996), p. 123ff.

German Life and Civilization

German Life and Civilization provides contributions to a critical understanding of Central European cultural history from medieval times to the present. Culture is here defined in the broadest sense, comprising expressions of high culture in such areas as literature, music, pictorial arts, and intellectual trends as well as political and socio-historical developments and the texture of everyday life. Both the cultural mainstream and oppositional or minority viewpoints lie within the purview of the series. While it is based on specialized investigations of particular topics, the series aims to foster progressive scholarship that aspires to a synthetic view of culture by crossing traditional disciplinary boundaries.

Interested colleagues are encouraged to send a brief summary of their work to the general editor of the series:

Jost Hermand
Department of German
University of Wisconsin
Madison, Wisconsin 53706